The Best of the Worst News

The Best of the Worst News

Tales of Inspiration from Around the World
and My Life with ALS

Norman MacIsaac

INSOMNIAC PRESS

Library and Archives Canada Cataloguing in Publication

Title: The best of the worst news : tales from around the world and my life with ALS / Norman MacIsaac.
Names: MacIsaac, Norman, 1963- author.
Identifiers: Canadiana (print) 20190187883 | Canadiana (ebook) 20190187891 | ISBN 9781554832392 (softcover) | ISBN 9781554832439 (PDF)
Subjects: LCSH: MacIsaac, Norman, 1963-—Health. | LCSH: MacIsaac, Norman, 1963-—Travel. | LCSH: Amyotrophic lateral sclerosis—Patients—Biography. | LCSH: Terminally ill—Patients—Biography. | LCSH: Community development personnel—Biography. | LCSH: Death—Psychological aspects. | LCSH: Life. | LCGFT: Autobiographies.
Classification: LCC RC406.A24 M33 2019 | DDC 362.1968/390092—dc23

The publisher gratefully acknowledges the support of the Canada Council for the Arts and the Ontario Arts Council.

Printed and bound in Canada

Insomniac Press
520 Princess Avenue, London, Ontario, Canada, N6B 2B8
www.insomniacpress.com

Acknowledgements

I've been fortunate to live a full life. I've spent the lion's share of my time surrounded by interesting, compassionate people, learning more and more about the world around me. Everywhere I've lived and travelled, I met people with different backgrounds who shared their world and culture with me. In return, I tried their patience as I learned—and often massacred—their beautiful language. This book won't make up for those unfair exchanges, but it's my acknowledgement of how fortunate I have been, even in my misfortune—even after my diagnosis with the worst disease imaginable.

I wrote this book over a period of more than four years, and I would like to thank my readers, who commented on what I wrote and gave me so much positive feedback. I'm lucky to have friends who support me and appreciate me for what I am. A special thank you goes out to my friend Benj Gallander, who encouraged me to publish this book and put me in touch with Insomniac Press.

Most of all, I thank my life partner. Christine is my soul mate, my muse, my caregiver, my harshest critic, and my biggest fan. She also gave me three children, Samuel, Émilie, and Alexandre, who make me laugh and make me proud. They also read and commented on my writing and, most impressively, have survived decades of my dad jokes with only modest psychological scarring.

Contents

Preface

I was alone on that icy cold day in December 2014 when I received my worst news. Sure, I'd checked my symptoms on some Internet sites, and they all pointed to amyotrophic lateral sclerosis (ALS), or Lou Gehrig's disease, but I dismissed everything outright. I tucked it away with all the other unpleasant memories and untoward ideas that cluttered my brain. However, despite it all, I went alone for that definitive test, an electromyogram (EMG), and I wasn't the least bit prepared to be diagnosed with an incurable disease that would lead to gradual paralysis and death. I didn't know what to do with a prognosis of just a few years to live, of growing more and more disabled until I could no longer move, swallow, or, ultimately, breathe.

Later, I looked for a book that would guide me through this process. I wondered what to expect and how to share this news with colleagues, kith, and kin. Would I get angry? Sad? Depressed? How long would I remain in denial?

I never did find that book. Instead, I began writing.

This book grew organically from my own emotional and physical journey. I knew about the Kübler-Ross model, which is better known as the five stages of grief, and I guessed that I could apply it to a degenerative disease that involves mourning incremental losses. My book would have been limited to five clearly defined chapters if grieving were as simple as five clean-cut stages. Instead, it reflects a more complex process.

The challenges I've faced in my youth and throughout my international career have shaped my perspective. Following a childhood marred by domestic violence, I spent my life working on social justice issues while living in Asia, Africa, and Latin America. I managed projects and supported local organizations in the fight against poverty. A friend who worked with me in Nepal recently introduced me as someone who's "helped countless people." I can't say how true that is because I feel these people helped themselves, but I know for sure that I've learned a lot from them. Now, as I face my greatest challenge, I draw on my international experience and reflect on all it has taught me.

This is not a self-help book. It's just one man's journey. Yet it's also a journey to share with others so that they can reflect on their own challenges. Our lives are full of unexpected snags, seemingly insurmountable obstacles, and outright misfortune. This book proposes to not just make the best of it but to also boldly delve into and savour the best of the worst news. It's about how such challenges allow us to focus on what's really important. It's about daring to explore the best experiences that remain to be lived—and living them.

When I left the hospital alone after the diagnosis, I struggled to stay vertical as I made my way along the icy sidewalk to my car, which was parked just a block and a half away. I was still physically shaken by the results of the EMG, compounded by the shock of the nightmarish diagnosis that had just decimated my previous plans of retiring, volunteering overseas, and growing old with my wife, Christine. My mind was racing. I pondered whether I should just leave the car and call Christine to pick me up. But I was mostly wondering how I was going to tell her my earth-shattering news.

As I waited at the traffic light that separated me from my car, my sight was drawn to a police officer who was controlling the traffic. He was properly attired for another brutal Canadian winter, with thick gloves and a wool scarf covering his face just below his eyes. Yet he wasn't grumbling and whinging; instead, he was bouncing up and down to keep the blood flowing to his extremities. He turned and smiled at me with sparkling eyes. It was the look of his inner child greeting an exciting new season. He seemed happy to be a cop and determined to make it through the winter smiling. Looking back, it's as if his resilience and joyful expression were encouraging me to greet my own impending winter with a smile on my face.

Travel with me in search of perspective, wisdom, and strength. Conveyed through imagery and stories that will take you around the world, *The Best of the Worst News* is an ode to positivity and a life worth living.

Chapter 1

Denial and Acceptance
Tales of Boots and Blogs

Nepal 1997

The snowfall had come quickly and unexpectedly. It fell at a forty-five-degree angle as I treaded along the rocky path, wearing flip-flops over bare feet. As I rounded the bend, where the majestic snow-crowned mountain range that separated me from Tibet should have reappeared, I could see only a white veil of snowflakes blowing in the wind.

My feet were bleeding—not a lot but just enough that the cold was actually a relief below my ankles. I had also lost sight of Sita, Bishnu, and the porters. I wasn't worried they would leave me behind though, nor did I mind walking this section on my own.

I crossed paths with an old man. He was hunched over as he walked, probably from a life of bearing heavy loads for the likes of me. As we approached each other on this narrow pathway, he looked me over from head to toe. I read his expression as one of disbelief over this barefoot *bideshi* who walked alone in a blizzard in Nepal's most isolated district. *Crazy foreigners.*

I had spent *weeks* to get here. Not hours or days. Weeks. In September, I spent day after day going back and forth from the most decrepit hotel in Nepalgunj to the airport. *That* airport. An airport of corruption and incompetence, where getting to Humla District was an exercise in political lobbying. Why was it so difficult? The official reason was the weather. The real reason was probably more about somebody having to earn baksheesh on every flight.

A friend who worked with aviation authorities in Nepal at the time told me that in the late nineties a surprisingly large number of staff at Tribhuvan International Airport in Kathmandu hadn't collected a paycheque in months. The reason? It wasn't worth their time. Their *real* source of income was from bribes and kickbacks. And we could see signs of it everywhere in Nepal. Duty-free wine was sold out in the open at our local grocery store, Bhat-Bhateni. It was stamped "Duty-Free: Not for Sale." Next to the ominous stamp was a price tag in Nepalese rupees. I imagined the same sort of corruption was preventing me from getting from the airport in Nepalgunj to Simikot, Humla.

We waited for nearly two weeks in early September before I eventually gave up. I had the choice of waiting for the next opportunity or returning to my family in Kathmandu. My daughter's birthday was just a few days away, so I hopped on a flight back to the capital with nothing to show for my absence but bedbug bites.

I tried again the first week of November and succeeded. This time, it took only a few days to get a flight on a cargo plane. I flew to Humla on a jumper seat with a sack of cauliflower on my lap.

A plane lands at Simikot Airport in Humla
Photo by Norman MacIsaac

The landing was spectacular. We flew due north from the southern lowlands of Nepal toward the Himalayas, over the foothills and between the mountains, until we veered west and then north again to the grass landing strip at Simikot at an altitude of 2,945 metres. Just to the west of the runway was a small airport graveyard. I noticed the wreckage as we headed toward the short, upward-sloping landing strip. It was like a warning, a wake-up call, to all concerned. Many had tried to land here, but not everyone had succeeded.

Yet we made it. We then proceeded to a small, simple one-room building with a dirt floor. This was the field office of Unitarian Service Committee (USC), a Canadian NGO. Sita, the local USC fieldworker, greeted us, invited us to have tea, and mobilized porters to carry our large backpacks. I left my bag there on the dirt floor. It was a typical fieldworker's rucksack. I had tied my running shoes together and hung them from the bag.

My colleague Bishnu and I headed out on our five-hour trek. I was looking forward to visiting and interviewing leaders of the savings and credit cooperative in this most remote district within eyeshot of the border with Tibet. Sporting my brand new hiking boots, I set out on this adventure with excitement and enthusiasm.

The first hour went well. We chatted along the way, and I revelled in the scenery as we made our way toward our destination. Humla's beauty resides in its harshness. It doesn't invite as much as it dares you to discover its unique splendour. As I walked, I didn't just feel the altitude in my lungs; I saw it in the steep slopes above and below. After each mountain I hugged and each hill I crested, a new perspective revealed itself to me. Between the summits of the Himalayas above and the glacial waters flowing through the deep valley below, I felt like a speck on these golden-brown slopes—a fleck at the mercy of the powers of nature, on my way to meet with people who'd learned to harness her potential for livelihood in what looked to me, the outsider, like a resolutely inhospitable region. It was otherworldly.

The second hour, however, was challenging. I hadn't yet broken in my hiking boots, and I started to pay the price. Hurrying over the rough terrain, it took me half an hour to finally catch up to the porters.

In Nepali, I asked them for my shoes.

They smiled. "But you are wearing your shoes."

Indeed I was, but these were my *hiking boots*—my *new* hiking boots—and it was time to change back into my trusty old running shoes. They were worn in and would allow me to walk the rest of the way without any problem. I planned to wear my new hiking boots for a little more time each day on the way back until they were more comfortable.

"But you are *wearing* your shoes. Everybody has their shoes."

Obviously, something wasn't getting through. Something was lost in translation.

I explained that these were new hiking shoes just for special trips but that I still had to break them in. No worries, though, as I had brought another pair of shoes to change into.

The porters looked at each other, then they looked at me again.

But you are wearing your shoes. This time, Sita, the USC fieldworker, said it with her eyes only. "We saw a pair of shoes at the office," she explained, "but we didn't understand where they came from. Everybody was wearing their shoes."

Indeed they were, and now I could no longer wear mine. They had given me blisters. Now my blisters had burst, and the raw skin was rubbing up against the rigid leather of these new boots.

But it was useless to argue. My shoes were back at the office, like the unsolved mystery of the curious fellow with two feet but four shoes. Two pairs, in fact: one worn in, and one new pair.

Ke garne? This Nepali expression said it all. It means "What can you do?" However, in the Nepalese context, it's all about accepting the things you can't change, and there seemed to be a lot of those in Nepal.

I dug into my rucksack and found my flip-flops. I took off my boots and put on my convertible footwear. The porters continued on their way, and I continued on mine, but I was now sporting cheap rubber sandals and a cane I had bought more than a decade earlier in Somalia. I would walk the rest of the trip to the village Thehe, over the rocks and through snow squalls, in footwear that the Nepalese call *chappal*.

Fast-forward more than seventeen years to the first few weeks after my diagnosis of ALS. This ailment is clearly not in the same category as blisters, but like the trek to Thehe, the journey continues despite my challenges. This time, though, it was more complicated than changing footwear.

I first told my wife, Christine; then our eldest son, Samuel; followed by our youngest son, Alex. We then had to wait until we travelled to China to tell our daughter, Émilie, before we could share the news with others. In other words, we had to keep it to ourselves. There was also a healthy dose of denial involved at the outset, so it remained our secret. The more we tried to keep it in check, however, the more invasive the notion became.

ALS—those letters appeared everywhere. It didn't help that ALS societies everywhere had just completed the best fundraising and awareness campaign of all time—the Ice Bucket Challenge—and Hollywood kept churning out films about ALS, including *The Theory of Everything*, for which Eddie Redmayne won an Academy Award for Best Actor, and *You're Not You*, starring Hilary Swank. We could go on, including Stephen Hawking's guest appearances on *The Big Bang Theory* and *Last Week Tonight with John Oliver*. But it wasn't just because of Hollywood or television that Christine and I couldn't block out that annoying, invasive abbreviation.

"The last couple of days, I have awoken to a large neon sign with the letters *A–L–S*," Christine said to me at 6:30 a.m. on a weekday in December as we shared our morning coffee.

Ominous but not subtle, I thought. I didn't know whether she was overwhelmed or if her subconscious were trying to knock her out of denial or if she wanted to shake *me* out of denial.

As I slowly rose from bed, my legs were stiff as they usually were those days. It felt like someone had strung a hundred elastics to the back of my thighs. I strained to straighten them and re-establish the normalcy of my gait, the movement of my body as I walked.

Gait—I don't think I'd ever used that word before I searched my symptoms online. With each passing month, I felt my gait become more and more...well, gimpy. That I could handle. What worried me was that each stage was a marker closer to no more walking *at all*. Most of the time, I succeeded in living in the here and now, but every once in a while I was jolted back to reality, like Christine's flashing neon sign reminding us that my ALS was progressing.

No matter whether the disease progressed slowly or the degeneration was fast, I felt the symptoms evolving, and

I couldn't forget those twitches and cramps. ALS isn't easy to forget, and during the first weeks and months after my diagnosis, ALS was everywhere.

Shortly after the diagnosis, I went ahead with the mission I had planned in the Philippines. I met with partner organizations, the Canadian embassy, and the families and children in the projects supported by the foundation I managed, but I must admit I was almost constantly chasing away thoughts of ALS.

I kept on planning for the future. As we talked about five-year funding, I chased away the notion that I might not be there for the end of the project. The "average life expectancy of two to five years" invaded my thoughts like a tune—a brainworm—that I just couldn't get out of my head. I shooed it away like a pesky fly. I convinced myself I have never been average. My ALS will progress relatively slowly. I will beat the odds.

But I was still thinking of ALS, and it kept reappearing. Even in our discussion of programs, that annoying abbreviation would reappear somehow. In a discussion about street kids and education, we referred to the Philippines' Alternative Learning System, but all I saw was ALS.

At the end of the day, I entered the sanctity of my hotel room, determined to relax. *Think about something other than ALS*, I told myself. Anything so I could forget those three letters. As I sat on the edge of the bed after a long day of project visits and meetings, I turned on the television and tuned into the first show I saw. It was a crime drama with familiar American actors. The main character, a badass FBI agent with an attitude, was confronting the all-powerful evil main character. Then the scene switched, and he was taking a stroll with his brother.

"Do you ever think what things would be like if Mom hadn't died?" asked the badass agent.

"All the time," said the soft-spoken younger brother.

"Then why don't you use that pharmaceutical company of yours to find a cure for ALS?"

They lost me at "ALS."

Let's go back to Nepal in 1997.

I finally caught up with Bishnu and the porters. We reached Thehe and conducted our interviews with the members of the local savings and credit groups.

The next morning was unforgettable. Snow covered the entire village, and I could see children on flat rooftops, throwing their first snowballs of the season. All around me were hills and mountains. To the north, up in the snow-capped mountains, I could see what appeared to be a monastery on those peaks that marked the border along the Tibet Autonomous Region.

There was no respite from the cold, and my feet ached from the blisters. I had reached the edge of the earth, but despite my discomfort, I experienced one of my most memorable field visits ever.

Norman posing with denizens of Thehe, Humla (1997)
Photo by Bishnu Shrestha

As I readied my backpack for the trek back to Simikot, I placed my footwear options in front of me and turned to Bishnu for advice. Bishnu was a proud Nepalese man with dense black hair and an ample moustache that would put to shame even the likes of the late Burt Reynolds.

"My blisters are still raw, and we have to walk mostly downhill for hours. What would you wear, *chappal* or hiking boots?"

"In Nepal, in such cases," Bishnu responded confidently, "we put shoes on tight and do not remove them until we have arrived."

So I followed his advice, suffering for the first half hour or so, until I could go on without thinking about my feet. In doing so, I was able to descend at a good pace without the risk of slipping or tripping on my flip-flops—and without falling behind.

❖

I applied the same logic to ALS. In the metaphorical equivalent of tightly lacing my boots for the walk back to Simikot, I started to write.

I registered a domain name and set up a website. I would write down my thoughts, hopes, and fears. Putting aside my insecurities and worries that my thoughts were disjointed or that I might be overly optimistic or naïve, I would let my feelings pour out onto my computer screen to be uploaded to the Internet for all to see. Unsheathed and exposed. I would let my sores bleed so I could continue my trek. I would let everything out rather than keep it inside me. In any case, I'd concluded, it would otherwise surreptitiously seep out, tainting my reality and hijacking the here and now.

I began to write my blog as a cathartic experience. It was indeed liberating, just as writing a diary would have been, but there was one aspect I hadn't taken into account: a blog isn't a one-way street. I was writing for me, but I was also writing for others. As others read my blog, they were with me, rounding that rocky path through the snow on the path to Thehe or struggling to focus on my work in the Philippines in the weeks following my diagnosis. I set up my website so they could share comments or contact me about what I'd written.

Those who read my blog would gain insights into my evolving thoughts as I went through denial, acceptance, and everything in between. That way, I told myself, if we ever met in person, I could skip the long explanation of my challenges and focus on sharing the present moment.

I fell behind on that trek in Humla because my blistered feet and inadequate footwear slowed my pace. Then, more than seventeen years later, my pace had slackened anew, and I once again walked with a cane. I could enjoy the solitary, pensive moments of this journey, however, because I *owned* this challenge. I shared my hopes and fears, and I wasn't alone.

I wrote about my experiences, drawing on my life and travels, starting with my first piece, which I shared with friends and family less than five months after my diagnosis. It related how I discovered I had Lou Gehrig's disease and the process of grieving the capacities I'd lost and would continue to lose.

Chapter 2

Sharing the Worst News
A River I Could Skate Away On

I had a confession to make: I was afraid to go skating.

Here's the thing though. I love skating. I love the sound of my skates cutting into the ice as I glide gracefully around the rink. I love to skate forward, spin around, skate backward, and spin around again to face forward without missing a beat. I love to play hockey. I love stickhandling and to spend hours just shooting the puck. I particularly used to enjoy skating and playing hockey with my three kids on our outdoor skating rink in our backyard.

To skate outside is pure joy. The air is crisp, and the ice is harder than at an artificial rink. The surface is seldom even, so there's always an element of challenge in it all, but that's what I really enjoyed.

When I worked in Ottawa, I used to love skating the entire length of the Rideau Canal Skateway on my lunch break on cold weekday afternoons in February. I would skate down the canal all the way to Dow's Lake and be back at Confederation Square within less than an hour. That would make the day at the office feel like playing hooky.

On the Rideau Canal —
the "world's largest skating
rink" 7.8 kilometres of pure
joy in Ottawa, Canada
(2008)
Photo by Marie-Christine Tremblay

Skating takes me back to those early morning skates on Victoria Pond in Kitchener, Ontario, with my childhood friend Graham. We were on the ice before anyone else and had the pond to ourselves. It was *our* pond.

When I was a boy, I would fantasize that the water on the streets would freeze overnight, converting the entire neighbourhood into a giant skating rink. I dreamed of skating everywhere. Like that song by Joni Mitchell, I dreamed I would find a river I could skate away on.

As I said, I love skating. On one of my first dates with the love of my life, Christine, I took her skating. I impressed her at the time, and now I was afraid I wouldn't impress her anymore.

My fears were not unfounded. I could have been frightened by the cramps I got in my left foot and then my left leg in March 2013, but I attributed them to the medication I was taking to lower my cholesterol. Online there were numerous accounts of Lipitor, or atorvastatin, causing muscle cramps, so I simply stopped taking it.

By the way, these were not your normal everyday cramps. These were crippling cramps that twisted my foot and ankle, and they ached for days, even weeks, following each incident. So, after trying everything from multivitamins to stopping training altogether, I finally consulted my doctor.

I have a great family doctor. He's a regular twenty-first-century Marcus Welby, M.D. He listens, he cares, and it's as if he always has as much time for me as I need or want. So he listened to me before asking to take a look at those pesky muscles of mine.

He found something strange about my reflexes. They were hypersensitive on one side and almost non-reactive on the other.

"Have you ever noticed that about your reflexes before?"

No.

"Have you had any accidents?"

One spill on my bike came to mind. But it was nothing major, I thought.

So he sent me for an MRI. "Let's check that out. And I'm going to refer you to a neurologist to check out those reflexes."

I wasn't afraid.

The MRI showed a couple of herniated discs. *Aha!* We found the culprit, I concluded. I then went about my life as usual until I finally got that appointment with the neurologist in the spring.

It was the neurological examination that really got me worried. You see, a neurological exam is up close and personal. The neurologist asked me to move my hands and legs and to walk, sometimes while talking or counting backward. Throughout the process, I was realizing all the things I couldn't do as well on my left side, such as repeatedly touch my left index finger and thumb at the same speed as I could with my right hand, or tap my left foot.

What was happening to me?

The answer was more tests—the process of elimination.

Back at home, I shared this information with my wife. As you might recall, she's the love of my life whom I'd impressed with my skating skills more than a quarter of a century earlier. She reassured me that it was probably nothing. Not to jump to conclusions. Not to worry. It must be those blasted herniated discs, I thought.

Still, I couldn't help but Google my symptoms. I found medical sites where you enter your symptoms and they generate all the possible ailments. The one that kept reappearing was so frightening that I told Christine. There's no limit to the good, the bad, and the ugly that you can find on the World Wide Web. Despite it all, the voice of reason told me not to worry. I knew she was right. The worst thing you can do is search for your symptoms on the Internet. I mean, you find a mole, and now you're dying of cancer? I mean, come on!

The doctor had ordered another MRI, so I waited for the results. But the symptoms I noticed were worsening, and it irked me. My daughter joked about my uneven reflexes and my slow movements with my left hand. She wasn't joking in a mean way; it actually made me laugh at myself and worry a bit less.

A year after the cramps had started, I started noticing other symptoms. I began feeling less confident going down stairs, and without thinking, I began placing my hands on the wall as I descended. There were times when my left leg just seemed to not respond. I was often tripping and breaking things. I'd broken so many cups and plates that we had to buy a new set of dishes. Okay, I knew I was clumsy—but not *that* clumsy!

By August, I was getting impatient, so I went back to see my family doctor. He reassured me that the second MRI confirmed that my brain was free of tumours and lesions. The herniated discs were actually shrinking. So, despite the symptoms, I began feeling positive, and I was confident that my body would heal from those nasty herniated discs.

I finally went to my follow-up appointment with the neurologist. However, he was not as reassuring as I'd hoped he'd be. He confirmed that the symptoms had progressed. He therefore called for an electromyogram (EMG) as soon as possible.

At that point, I should have been more worried than ever. Strangely enough, though, I wasn't. I had grown accustomed to the tests. I was going through the motions. This was just another test, just one more box to tick off in the medical process of elimination.

It wasn't that I was blind to the symptoms. I was just so damn healthy! I could bike up Mount Royal like I owned that mountain, and, at the age of fifty, I had a slim yet muscular frame—and abs! I might have sounded a bit like Alfred E. Neuman from *Mad* magazine: "What, me worry?" But I was at the top of my game. *What, me sick?*

Less than two weeks later, I would find myself in the neurology department at Montreal's Hôpital Notre-Dame, being poked and prodded until the repeated shocks sent my leg muscles into uncontrollable spasms. Following the technician's examination, the neurologist redid the tests. It wasn't pleasant.

This was the first time I met this particular neurologist, and before arriving that day, I wasn't even aware that she, not the neurologist who examined me before, would be doing the test.

"Do you know what the problem is?" I asked her.

Instead of answering my question, she asked, "Did your doctor say what we were looking for today?"

"No," I answered. "I have a lot of questions and no answers."

She took a deep breath and began by introducing her area of specialization. Her introduction was a lead-up to a diagnosis I didn't want to hear and the reason I'm afraid to get back on the ice: "I'm a specialist in motor neuron disease."

Shit. I knew what that meant. Remember how I told you I'd searched my symptoms online and repeatedly came up with the same top result for a diagnosis? The result was so horrible that I determined that self-diagnosis itself was an ailment in its own right. Self-diagnosis was the problem, not the solution, I had told myself. That diagnosis was too horrible. I had classified it in my mind as my own personal worst-case scenario, and I'd buried it deep in the recesses of my brain, where I store my nastiest fears.

Nevertheless, the Internet had taught me about motor neuron disease (MND). It's another term for amyotrophic lateral sclerosis (ALS), or Lou Gehrig's disease. I'd also read more about it because of the world-famous Ice Bucket Challenge, the enormously successful campaign to raise awareness of and funds for the disease. ALS is a brutal degenerative condition that leads to total paralysis and death, usually within a few years. It's terminal and incurable.

So that was it. I had ALS. Months later, it still seemed unreal despite the confirmation of the diagnosis and the continuing advancement of the symptoms.

The winter was particularly difficult because I had developed hypersensitivity to cold. My left leg simply wouldn't react at times, especially on the coldest days. On top of that, February 2015 was the coldest on record in Montreal. So imagine my fear of skating. I really wished I had a river I could skate away on. However, finding such a river—or canal—would now be far easier than skating down it.

It was actually more than fear; it was mourning the loss of something that had been a part of my life for as long as I could remember. It was, in my mind, the first loss I would grieve, the first of many to come. The challenge for me, a product of our goal-oriented society, was to find the strength and wisdom to simply let go.

Chapter 3

Nepal and the Art of Letting Go

The MacIsaac family at Swayambhunath in Nepal (1997)
Photo by Martha McGinn

Meanwhile, the first country where we lived abroad as a family, Nepal, was experiencing its own worst news. While I struggled with my own earth-shattering news regarding ALS in the spring of 2015, a quake with a magnitude of 7.8 rocked this tiny landlocked country, resulting in massive destruction, nine thousand deaths, and tens of thousands injured. The disaster prompted all sorts of emotions, and I reflected back on this Himalayan land that was a kingdom and that was my home for four wonderful years.

On our first evening together on October 1, 1985, in another "kingdom"—a region affectionately referred to as the "Kingdom of Saguenay," five hours northeast of Montreal—I had shown my future wife photographs from my first overseas experience in Somalia. I later told her I would show her the world. And I did.

Nepal was the country that taught us about letting go. We left for Nepal with three young children, the youngest still in diapers. At our destination, we had to deal with them while our fifteen checked bags spewed out onto the conveyer at Tribhuvan International Airport. To say it was chaotic would be unfair. Let's say it had a logic of its own. After all, it was Kathmandu. Christine took charge of the children, and I swung into action to gather the luggage as Nepalese baggage handlers eagerly offered to help.

"How many bags, *daju*?"

"Fifteen."

"Fifty?"

"No, fifteen...*pandra*." I had learned a little Nepali before leaving home.

"*Pandra! Baaprebaph! Panch, hoina ta?* Five bags?"

"No, fifteen."

He called a posse.

I imagined this would be a tale they would tell to their friends over chai or raksi (Nepalese rice wine): the guy with the most suitcases ever! I was, however, just a man who left my paying job for a volunteer posting that inspired me. I wasn't a jetsetter with a diplomatic posting or some cushy UN posting with a six-figure salary and a shipping container full of my belongings to follow. I didn't bring along a year's supply of diapers for my pampered First World baby or my favourite tissues for my pampered First World nose. Rather, my wife and I had three kids in tow, five pieces of carry-on, and twelve pieces of luggage, minus our television, computer, and other items that would soon end up "stuck" at the airport and would take months to extricate from the corrupt and disorderly customs department.

Christine stayed with the children while I dived into the chaos of the luggage carrousel. I disentangled the first piece, and as I turned around to show it to her, a fellow Canadian greeted me with a broad smile and firm handshake. "Welcome to Nepal!"

As a luggage handler pulled at my suitcase, eager for the opportunity to earn a few rupees from the newly arrived family of foreigners, my Canadian host turned to him and rattled off something in Nepali. Now that's where I want to be in a year's time, I thought, and it must have showed.

François smiled at me. "You'll be speaking better than I do in no time. You'll see."

Never had chaos generated such elation in me before. My adrenaline was pumping. My fatherly instincts were actively watching over my family while I absorbed the whole scene. I was jetlagged and exhausted from nearly twenty hours of travel, yet I didn't remember the last time I had felt this alive.

We filled out some forms to acknowledge the missing or delayed television—nobody could really tell us anything about its whereabouts—then headed toward customs with our luggage. Other arriving foreigners lined up dutifully for luggage x-raying, but François took charge, ushered us past the line, swayed his head, said a few more words in Nepali, and directed us toward the exit. I double-checked the status of my gaggle and our possessions as we headed toward the sunlight and the pandemonium of voracious taxi drivers vying for our business.

Upon departure from Canada, I remember feeling that we had reduced from so much stuff to this modest existence. *Everything in fifteen suitcases and five carry-ons.* Yet, now, as I arrived in a country where most had only one pair of shoes and the poorest wore only rudimentary sandals or went barefoot, I suddenly felt overburdened with an embarrassing amount of stuff. I felt like lying: "Oh, no, this? No, this isn't all our stuff. No, no, no. We're bringing a lot of gifts for friends, clothing for the orphanage in Lazimpat, and books for the literacy centre in Lamjung." But there was no denying it. What seemed like "roughing it" to my fellow Canadians still looked like opulence to my Nepalese counterparts.

I watched my family's reaction as we headed off in a Toyota Land Cruiser, following another vehicle transporting all of our worldly possessions. My wife was soaking up the atmosphere, but my kids quickly relapsed into more typical childhood concerns. My youngest was thirsty, my eldest was telling me how Nepal was going to be different from Canada (repeating almost textually what I had told him before we left), and my daughter, Émilie, was sucking on her fingers. I was worried about the germs. Somehow, despite already having lived overseas on my own and having been to Nepal many times before for work, I still managed to worry about the dangers of hepatitis and a host of other nasty tropical diseases. I pulled Émilie's fingers out of her mouth and feigned a smile, but she just put them back in without even thinking about it.

Despite the jetlag, my family and I would sleep more in that first month in Nepal than we ever had in our lives. I assumed it was just system overload. We were constantly taking in new information: smells, sights, feelings, words, expressions, challenges…you name it! This was my new life, and I embraced it.

Alchi Lagyo

It was a spiritual experience. There is no other way to describe it. And I'm not talking about some born-again, speaking-in-tongues, seeing-the-light kind of spirituality. I'm talking about waking up, going up onto the roof early in the morning, and just soaking up my new environment.

There I was, smelling the air. I could smell the smoke from the stall on the corner where the small old man made morning tea, the diesel exhaust of a passing Tata truck, and the incense burning at the temple just down the narrow path travelled by pedestrians, cyclists, motorcyclists, and cows. I wanted to (and finally had the time to) feel my environment, to see the snow-tipped mountains on sunny days. I felt like a child again: not quite knowing how the seasons worked. When would the clouds break? When would the colder season begin and end? And was it really cold, or was it just cold for a tropical country? Sure, I had been to Nepal several times before but never with family and never for long enough to really get to know the country.

Next, I listened. The neighbour was coughing. I could hear pots clanging in kitchens as people prepared their morning tea. I then saw the tiny puffs of incense rising above a stone statue of one of thousands of Hindu gods at the temple nearby. It was more of a cubbyhole or a pit stop than the temples that tourists typically visit. This was a neighbourhood religious site. It struck me as a walk-through, drive-through temple, frequented by a wide array of passers-by.

An auto rickshaw, a motorized three-wheeled taxi, scurried by. It buzzed by like a tiny motorcycle and was followed by a cycle rickshaw that rattled as it careened over potholes. These were some of the early-morning sounds of a residential neighbourhood in Kathmandu. I would soon familiarize myself with the evolution of these sights and sounds as the day progressed. I would learn, for example, that soon after morning teatime, vegetable vendors would hit the streets, chanting a melody that advertised their items for sale: "*Cauli, aloo, gholbera!*" *Cauliflower, potatoes, tomatoes!* I would learn when all the children would head off to school, mostly in three-wheeled taxis with a frame on the back that seated about a dozen of them. Some walked to school with a family member or "*didi*" (a big sister or female domestic worker). Others joined their father on a motorcycle. It wasn't unusual to see an entire family of five on a 100 cc Honda motorbike.

So many new sights, smells, and sounds. Everything was different. I felt more alive than I had felt in a long time—perhaps since those days of my youth when I really knew how to let go. I thought about that offbeat teen angst movie *Pump Up the Volume*. It's about a teenager, played by Christian Slater, who sets up an FM pirate radio station. He rants about warnings from parents and authorities, declaring that he doesn't care about the consequences. "So be it," he intones. "So be it." It had been a long time since I recited such a statement of indifference in the face of warnings, since I had thrown caution to the wind.

In coming here to this Himalayan country, I was shirking the path that society typically sets out for an adult with three kids. So standing on that roof in Kathmandu in the early morning, with the contents of fifteen suitcases and five pieces of hand luggage constituting my household belongings, I realized I had somehow succeeded in rekindling that desire to live fully. I had managed to trump societal norms and expectations, and I found myself contemplating my new life on the rooftop of the world.

I imagined those I'd left behind back home. They counted the days of the week. They winced at traffic reports on the radio or squeezed onto public transportation. They fought the subtle stress of line-ups for morning coffee or getting through a busy intersection on their way to work. They planned how to drop the car off at the garage and still get to work on time or how to finish work early to grab the dry cleaning before picking up the kids at school. They seldom had the time to listen to their environment or to smell the air or to marvel at the buzz of life around them.

In Kathmandu, the familiarity was gone; it was replaced with surprises and challenges. Getting to work was suddenly new. Those around me spoke a different language, which I was learning. They lived their lives differently and had different expectations. I associated breakfast with cereal and toast, but they saw breakfast as early morning tea followed by mid-morning rice. In the West, we ask people how they feel, if they are well, if they are happy. In rural Nepal, they ask if you have eaten rice.

In Nepal, there's plenty of time—time to do nothing at all. Back home, we would refer to this as "wasted time." This is the time between activities, the time we desperately try to minimize so we use our time efficiently. In Nepal, they use this time to sit, to enjoy watching people smile, to breathe slowly and to listen.

I will never forget what my brother-in-law asked me when he came to visit us in Nepal: "What are people doing? I mean, people everywhere are just sitting and doing nothing." Indeed. Nothing but living. But what else is there to do?

In one of our first lessons in Nepali in Bhaktapur, we learned to express basic feelings and to respond to greetings and simple questions about our well-being. The expression that surprised me most was *alchi lagyo*, which means "I am feeling lazy." My wife and I looked at each other. "Is this really a useful expression?"

Yet, soon, as we adapted and grew in Nepal, we realized this honest expression of having had enough stress, and wanting to slow things down, would soon become part of our vocabulary. And it was part of our lexicon because our thinking had changed. We had grown to appreciate the downtime. Whenever we arrived on time and others weren't there yet, we would take the time to interact with those around us, those on the periphery whom we never met when we were in the hustle and bustle of North America.

Another aspect of *alchi lagyo* is the syntax. Basically,

in the Nepali language, you don't say, "I am hungry," or, "I am lazy." Rather, you say, "Hunger has attached itself to me," or, "Laziness has occurred to me." Instead of saying, "I did this work," you should say, "This work was done through me." *I* is no longer at the centre of my language. I gradually grew accustomed to saying that laziness had attached itself to me: "*Malai alchi lagyo.*"

My perception of time also changed. In Nepali, "it's raining" is expressed as "water has fallen." The immediate present is expressed as the past. If I can say it's raining, it means that water has fallen. So, in a way, I'm expressing myself in a simpler way that eliminates personal interpretation. I don't determine that it's raining; rather, I simply affirm that water has fallen.

Likewise, there is no future tense in Nepali. I can't say I'll be at the office at 9 a.m. After all, who am I to foresee the future? Rather, I might express that my coming to the office may be around 9 a.m. *hola*—a notion similar to the Spanish *ojalá* ("hopefully"), which, incidentally, isn't too far from its Arabic equivalent, *insha'Allah* ("God willing").

As I learned the language, I realized the audacity and arrogance in our day-to-day affirmations of what will happen, what is happening, and our role in making things happen. I wasn't just learning new words; I was learning a new way of thinking and of seeing my own place in the world.

Here's a final example, and this was a tough one to assimilate at first: There is no word for just "no" in Nepali. You can say, "It is not," or, "There are none," but you can't say just "no." The longer you live in Nepal, the more you come to understand that this is because nobody ever says no. For instance, if someone asks if your colleague is about to arrive, who are you to say yes or no? First, there is no future tense, so you can't say it. You could, however, say that he is, hopefully, on the way. You could also say that he called to inform you he's not on the way or is ill or is stuck in traffic. But you can't tell the future, and you definitely can't deny a future possibility, even about your own actions, since—unlike the Western perspective—you aren't the centre of the universe.

Now, all of this mushy cultural openness doesn't mean that life was suddenly effortless. Au contraire! As our routine disappeared, so did our familiar sources of support and reliability. However, we developed a new routine over time, as one would anywhere.

In recent decades, we have built up an environment of reliability in the developed world, especially in the urban centres. The world is increasingly anglicized and franchised. For example, I can get a latte and a date square at Starbucks at the major airports in Beijing, Winnipeg, or Surabaya. But at the end of the twentieth century, there was still no McDonald's anywhere in Kathmandu. The major fast-food chains hadn't invaded it yet. Many years later, as I write these lines, that has started to change.

Having left behind a world of standardized reliability and trademarked consistency, I entered a world where I had no references. I was halfway around the world from home, and I felt vibrant and new.

Namaste
Nearly two decades later, I was once again greeted with "namaste," this time at the YMCA in my corner of Montreal known as Monkland Village. I rolled out my yoga

mat, removed my shoes, and assumed the meditation position. I imagined myself back on that roof in Nepal, listening to new sounds, discovering the smells of the different times of day and each new season. Rather than breaking my concentration, the honking of horns soothed me. I imagined myself in Kathmandu in 1997 and thought of everything I had let go of. I had let go of the daily mail and the 9-to-5 hustle and everything associated with it.

"Breathe in four to five seconds, then breathe out more slowly to practice the art of letting go."

I deliberately breathed in and then out. I let go.

We then switched into downward-facing dog, then the plank, then cobra. I hadn't practiced yoga before returning to Montreal. I started about a year before my diagnosis when I'd occasionally join my wife. I then started going regularly after I was diagnosed.

Unlike on the rooftop, though, I felt alone here in the yoga room at the Y. In Kathmandu, there was a feeling of communion, of oneness with the environment, of assimilating my new world. Here at the Y, I was blocking out the world.

"Leave your to-do list behind and let yourself go," the yoga instructor coached us.

She would repeat these same lines every class. For me, it was a source of inspiration and calm, very much the way devoted believers recite scripture at Sunday Mass. I looked forward to hearing her tell us for the umpteenth time to "Think kind thoughts" and "Be gentle to your body."

I smiled. I tried to forget that I was doing yoga as part of a strategy to slow down the degeneration that ALS causes. I told myself that the changes in my body, while not the least bit welcome, were something to learn and assimilate, like my first days and months in Nepal. It's my journey, and the key to making the best of any situation—good or bad—is the art of letting go. I let go of skating, for instance, and the dream of one more trek in Nepal. Could I accept I would have to let go of more? Would I have the strength to go on despite the loss of control of my muscles? Would I succeed in letting go and in accepting reality in order to be there for my family and friends?

I recalled what my youngest son, Alex, asked me when I told him I had ALS: "Will you still be yourself? I mean, in your mind?" Yes, I answered. Yes, indeed. A fully functioning mind in a body of melting muscles. But to better capture the real challenge, I should have answered like so: "Yes, I'll be there, if I can just manage to let go."

So I remembered Nepal, where I lived in the here and now, without a future tense, and where I wasn't the centre of existence. On those spring days of 2015, my heart was filled with a deep sense of mourning for all that Nepal had lost in the earthquake. The photo of the collapsed Swayambhu temple brought back fond memories of my children at that special place, marvelling at the majestic stupa, the prayer flags fluttering in the wind, and the monkeys dancing around mischievously. I smiled as I recalled the time a monkey grabbed a candy bar out of the hand of my eldest son, Samuel, and recalled the countless visitors I accompanied to share the beauty and serenity that Nepal has to offer. Nepal gave me so much—more than I could ever give back.

When I finished writing my second blog post, I let go of my troubles and focused instead on helping with the relief effort. I wouldn't be able to go physically but would contribute as best I could from where I was. Once again, Nepal challenged me and encouraged me to practice the art of letting go.

Dhanyabad, Nepal. Thank you.

Chapter 4

Anger, Apathy, Incompetence, Indifference...and the Most Beautiful Little Flower

It can be difficult to remain positive and mindful, especially when incompetence and thoughtlessness abound. By the spring of 2015, I walked with a cane, struggled to make my way downstairs, and had a couple of nasty falls. But life didn't stand still so I could deal with my personal crisis. Flowers still bloomed and life was still fraught with challenges. It reminded me that, with or without an incurable condition, the best one could aspire to is to face the latter while stopping to smell the former.

One day, a driver at the pharmacy on Monkland Avenue took up not one but two handicapped parking spaces. She wasn't handicapped—not physically handicapped anyway. When I asked her if she knew that she was taking up two handicapped spaces, she criticized me for my tone. Beside her was a man who sat silently in the passenger seat. He looked like an abused puppy. I assumed he was used to this and knew better than to get involved. I was shocked and annoyed by her reaction but full of empathy for her prisoner in the front seat.

At the Hôtel-Dieu de Montréal, one of myriad hospitals on the island of Montreal, the woman at the wicket called my number. "*Prochain*. Next."

I quickly and obediently proceeded to the wicket with my ticket in hand, bearing the winning number. Bingo, I thought.

I couldn't move as quickly as I used to, but I wasn't dawdling. I sat in front of her and offered her the ticket. She avoided eye contact and ignored the ticket in my outstretched hand. She instead turned to her colleague and proceeded to talk about her breakfast. It was burnt toast, which apparently she did not appreciate. She griped about her boyfriend, whom she appreciated even less than burnt toast, and segued into a diatribe against a woman named Jeanne, who, apparently, "just doesn't get it." I took out my iPhone and opened the camera in selfie mode, just to see myself. Nope, I wasn't invisible.

At yet another hospital, the largest in Montreal, I went in person to find out what was holding up my appointment. A clerk there had called and committed to getting back to me by the end of the week, but nothing had happened.

After a long wait, I finally made my way to the counter, which consisted of a small shelf over the bottom half of the door. The upper half of the door was open, and a clerk was sitting at the opposite end of the room, several metres away. When she finished her phone call, she put away a file and removed another from a desk drawer. Without getting up from her chair, she looked up at me.

"Can I help you?"

I explained about the calls and my hope to one day get an appointment.

"What's your name again?"

I told her once again, carefully spelling my last name.

"I don't have a file for you."

I explained that I was referred and that she had called me.

She didn't have a file for me, she repeated. "When was this?"

I had the dates in my iPhone, so I gave them to her. Finally, a light bulb ignited above her head.

"We *do* have a file for you." She explained that she had given the file to the doctor before going on leave.

Oh, I get it, I thought. It's someone else's fault.

So, once again, as she had done previously over the phone, she committed to getting me that appointment. But it clearly hadn't worked out before. She had given me the wrong date when she called, a date when the hospital was apparently closed. (I didn't even know that hospitals closed!) On that day, I spent over an hour wandering the empty corridors of that ginormous hospital, only getting more and more exasperated as each hospital employee sent me in a separate direction. I didn't get treated; I got frustrated. An hour later, I found myself in a parking lot on a cold winter day, alone in my car, screaming at the top of my lungs.

Did I mention that the appointment was supposed to be with a psychologist?

Then I began doubting myself.

When the clerk had called, I immediately entered the date in my agenda and repeated it back to her, just to be certain. Maybe I misunderstood her. Maybe it was my fault.

So, what was it? I knew I wasn't invisible, and I knew that the person at the wicket should have acknowledged my presence with the typical Montreal greeting: "*Bonjour*. Hi." I knew that she should have served the patients first and kept her story about burnt toast and her awful boyfriend for her coffee break. That I knew.

But maybe my tone was too aggressive, and maybe I had entered the wrong dates. It wouldn't have been the first time.

Or maybe not.

Let's face it. No tone of voice would have ever been good enough for the self-important halfwit who took up two handicapped parking spaces.

And that appointment? Well, it turns out the clerk had left a message on our answering machine, and it was indeed the date she'd given me.

So, there you have it, like the three dark horsemen of modern life: apathy, incompetence, and an overdeveloped sense of entitlement with a generous helping of "I couldn't give a shit."

Expressing my anger didn't seem to help though. It just

made *me* the bad guy, the guy whose tone wasn't quite gentle enough. I remembered my wise mother giving me a lot of good motherly advice, but I didn't recall her telling me to speak especially politely to douchebags. But she might have told me it wasn't worth the effort to talk to such people.

I'm told I'm supposed to be angry. Not always but at some point. It's one of the stages of grief that you're supposed to experience when you're told you have a terminal illness.

I guess the classic formula would be to clench my fist—not my left fist because that would give me cramps—and raise it toward the sky, where apparently the guy with the long grey beard lives in the clouds, and ask, "Why me?" as if somehow it would be more sensible for someone else to have ALS instead of me. Maybe the able-bodied person who took two handicapped spaces and then had the nerve to ball me out for my tone? It was just a suggestion, God.

Let's be clear: I don't believe in an angry God with anger management issues, and I don't believe in a God whose plan includes giving me ALS. I mean, really, that would be one twisted Supreme Being.

So where did all of this leave me? I was supposed to be angry, but getting angry just made me more frustrated with myself. I didn't like "angry me" any more than I liked the Old Testament God backed by a prophet who looks like Charlton Heston during a protracted Gillette strike, with a penchant for rage and who's always packing heat or, worse, thunderbolts and flash floods.

So what was I to do with my frustration? I committed to trying another approach. Next time, I told myself, I'd think it over and use the power of words to respond. That sounded like sage motherly advice.

The opportunity came in the mail. It was a letter I had been expecting for months. It was from a local rehabilitation centre that could offer me all the services I so badly needed to adapt to my degenerative condition. *Finally*, I thought, as I opened the letter. I would be able to get the support I needed for all of those daily tasks that were growing more challenging by the day, from clipping my fingernails to buttoning my shirt. This was the place that was going to prolong my autonomy and my quality of life. When I opened the letter, however, I discovered that I was now on a waiting list with an estimated wait time of seven to nine months.

The letter threw me off kilter. I felt defeated. *Au revoir*, positive momentum. I was on my own. I decided to take twenty-four hours before responding. I was both surprised and dismayed by the wait time, so I breathed deeply and tried to get a good night's sleep.

I then began to respond to the letter.

It started off with the "in your face" approach: "You put a man with a terminal illness on a waiting list." This would call for what my kids call a "mic drop." If you don't understand what that means, ask someone under twenty-five years old to explain it to you.

But this approach somehow seemed disingenuous, as I had chosen not to live my life with a "terminal illness" sign hanging over my head. I mean, let's face it. Life is always a terminal, sexually transmitted condition. We're all going to die, and I had set my sights on being the exception, on being more than ALS. I didn't want to be the one labelling myself as a dying man. I was a living man.

Then I got to wondering if they had any idea what illness I had. I would encourage them to visit the ALS Society's website. Did they know that most of those afflicted live less than three years after diagnosis? It took me nearly two years to get diagnosed, then several months after that to get referred to a rehabilitation centre. Now I'm on a waiting list for seven to nine months?

So how much time would the average "person with ALS" (PALS) have left? For those who are part of the unlucky fifty percent: not much. But if one had to wait for more than a year in total, from what, may I ask, would a PALS be rehabilitating?

Again, though, I felt somewhat duplicitous talking about the unlucky fifty percent when I was focused on my ALS progressing more gradually. I decided to focus on what their letter meant to me. I'm a constructive, optimistic guy. I should have been able to remain active for some time, especially if I got support early. I was doing absolutely everything I could to prolong my quality of life and the time I had on this earth to be there for my family, friends, and others who might continue to benefit from what I had to offer. So here's what I concluded:

What does a seven to nine month wait time mean to me?

First off, it means I'm not doing everything I can to prolong my quality of life. It means accepting more rapid degeneration in the face of this merciless ailment.

Second, it means I spend more time doing the

little things that frustrate me, like buttoning my shirt; less time doing meaningful things, like enjoying time with family; and even less time doing the physical activities that are crucial to my psychological and physical well-being. I was hoping to continue doing what I love and feeling alive. I hoped to continue making it on my own to work, and I hoped to continue cycling for one last season. Never mind that I can't go nearly as far or fast as I used to or that I have to avoid inclines and any sort of challenge. For me, keeping on cycling is plenty challenging at this point.

Finally, it means I'm no longer moving forward. Do you know what that feels like? It feels like the incurable, terminal illness started winning again as soon as I opened that letter. I'm on a waiting list. Waiting for what? That's a rhetorical question, so don't answer it.

I will maintain forward motion, and if a rehabilitation centre can't adapt to that, I will find my own way with whatever I can find. I will fashion a splint for my left arm with sticks and duct tape if that's what it takes.

But it would be so much better with your help. You have the training, the expertise, and the mission to help me through this time when I need help more than ever. And this isn't easy for me because I'm used to being the one who helps others and solves the most challenging problems. I'm not used to asking for help.

So if you can help me, I thank you in advance.

If your centre is committed to making rehabilitation the discovery of new possibilities for its clients, I thank you for all the possibilities you make available to me.

I copied the letter to the client review committee at the centre in addition to the Montreal Neurological Institute and Hospital (aka "the Neuro") and the ALS Society of Quebec. Within twenty-four hours, the centre got back to me, and I had an appointment—not after seven to nine months but within a few short days. That's the power of the written word. It's also the power of channelling your anger. Mom would have been damn proud, I thought.

I wondered if those words, even the first two paragraphs that were a tad over the top, contributed to shaking someone out of their insensitive, automated, one-size-fits-all approach in addition to perhaps helping me personally. Perhaps I was just writing for my own benefit, as well as a cathartic experience, as an alternative to bottling all that aggravation inside me.

I also accepted that maybe I'm just not good at being angry. Sure, I've gotten plenty frustrated, and sometimes I've lost my cool. However, when I returned home one day after experiencing frustration, I found my brother-in-law together with my nephew working hard on building me a new handrail for the stairs in my house, and it looked amazing! I would have to wait for the rehabilitation centre, and I would most certainly continue to face frustration with hospital bureaucracy, but so many others—health professionals, the ALS Society, friends, family, and colleagues—were there to support me.

I put aside my frustrations over the apathy, the incompetence, and those with an overdeveloped sense of entitlement with a generous helping of "I couldn't give a shit." When I saw them working on the stairs, I was filled with admiration for my brother-in-law's craftsmanship and was grateful for his act of kindness. That handrail was going to make it so much easier for me to make it up and down our winding staircase.

But it was more than just a handrail.

This all reminded me of a classic Buddhist fable. It's the story of a monk who is chased by thieves to the edge of a cliff. To save himself from their long, sharp blades, he jumps off the edge and miraculously manages to grab onto the branch of a lone tree growing from the cliff face. On a ledge below him are four hungry tigers. Their piercing eyes are focused on the monk. Their open jaws reveal razor-sharp teeth. He's stuck between the ferocious carnivores below and the murderous thugs above. The branch is on the verge of snapping. He then looks at the tree and sees a bright purple blossom. What a beautiful flower, he thinks. So beautiful.

Chapter 5

Our Loved Ones:

Sunshine and Shadows on Route 66

A catastrophic diagnosis such as ALS propels you toward the most important things in life. For me, that's my family and my relationships with my children, and that's what I address in the next three chapters.

In my first summer living with ALS, I undertook the classic American road trip with my eldest, Samuel, and I was confronted with the challenges and rewards of dealing with the impact of my worst news on family and friends.

Samuel (left) and Norman (leaning on a cane)
at the Grand Canyon (2015)

ALS is a team disease. Studies show that ALS patients live longer and maintain better quality of life when they receive strong support from family and friends. I was fully aware of this fact. I just wished I could maintain that delicate balance between ensuring I had the me time I needed while also giving ample attention to my loved ones. Either way, I wouldn't always know what my friends and family expected of me.

While I was with friends on vacation that summer, there were many days when we didn't discuss my condition at all. There were long evenings of reminiscing about old times, sharing stories, and just enjoying each other's company. Then there were times when we talked about the elephant in the room. And I never really knew for sure if I got it right. Maybe it was better not to talk about it so much— or maybe I didn't share enough. I knew that some people liked to address the issue head on; some needed more time; and others preferred to focus on our time together rather than delve into what they saw as my private issue.

I figured I had thought this through. So how did I manage to underestimate the importance of my disease for Samuel? How did I fail to adequately prioritize communication between us? I guess it's like the desert. You know it's more than just sand and rocks, but it's easy to misjudge this ostensibly straightforward ecosystem. Hiding away from the sizzling sun is more life than you might imagine, and it's definitely more than you'll ever see over the hood of a car barrelling down an asphalt highway.

Duel
Heading east from Los Angeles on a two-lane interstate

across the Mojave Desert, David Mann masks insecurity and anxiety behind yellow tinted glasses. Traversing this inhospitable land on an isolated stretch of dusty highway in a red Plymouth Valiant, he is terrorized by a semi-trailer truck that tries to run him off the road.

Anyone who knows anything about North American vehicles of the seventies knows that the Valiant was designed for neither performance nor reliability. So it should come as no surprise that this middle-aged salesman didn't have the horsepower to outrun a souped-up truck driven by an unseen maniacal driver who's hell-bent on duelling Mann to the death. More important, when this non-confrontational urbanite faces off against his road rival under the blazing sun, he must cast aside the assumptions and rules of his middle-class existence and summon his primal survival instincts.

David Mann is no acquaintance of mine. Rather, he's a character written into public consciousness by author and screenwriter Richard Matheson in a 1971 made-for-television movie directed by twenty-five-year-old Steven Spielberg. Although few had heard of Spielberg back then, this story, entitled *Duel*, had left a lasting impression on my young mind. Mann, played by actor Dennis Weaver, was a nervous driver who reminded me of my uncle André. And his boxy Plymouth was eerily similar to my dad's 1970 Plymouth Duster, a sportier derivative of the Valiant.

As an eight-year-old watching this drama on television, I had this barren and isolated landscape etched into my mind as a portrait of the desert as a formidable foe and a place where you'd better be ready to face adversity because it's merciless. Under the oppressive sun, there's not a soul to call upon and nowhere to hide.

Nearly forty-four years later, I found myself in this same desert. Fortunately for me, I wasn't driving a Plymouth with a faulty radiator hose, nor was I alone en route to a sales meeting and pressed for time to make it back home for a family dinner in the big city. I had a cell phone, hundreds of miles of open road, lots of time, a glove compartment full of road maps for four states, and enough muscle under the hood to outrun just about any demonic truck on the road. My eldest son and I were here for a father and son bonding experience, a classic road trip, and an encounter with a two-billion-year-old landmark sculpted by the Colorado River.

Driving a sleek silver Ford Mustang convertible along this route was nothing short of bucket list material. We picked up the rental car and, with the top down, headed directly from McCarran International Airport over parched land to the Hoover Dam. There was no way we were going to put the roof up and crank the AC despite the 45°C weather, scorched lips, and sunrays that went right through SPF 50 sunscreen as if the blazing sun enjoyed the challenge.

Over the years, my expectations from this desert road had been moulded by films such as *Duel*, *Easy Rider*, and *The Good, the Bad and the Ugly*.[1] Yet I wasn't riding a horse, riding a motorcycle, or driving a giant tin can masquerading as an automobile. I was cruising over this scorched landscape in a classic American muscle car,

---

[1] Sergio Leone's epic spaghetti western *The Good, the Bad and the Ugly* was actually filmed in Spain, not the US. It nonetheless informed the author's and others' perceptions of the rugged American/Mexican desert terrain.

soaking up rays like an iguana warming up after a cool desert night.

I can't say I enjoyed the wind blowing in my hair, but I particularly enjoyed the expression of pure joy on Samuel's face as he steered with his left hand and relaxed his right hand on the gearshift. I thought of the hours I'd spent with him at the wheel as I taught him to drive nine years earlier. It was like a flash—as if every moment like this one were melded together into one. I enjoyed watching him steer his way through life, learning to do everything from walk to graduate from university. Observing this against a backdrop of a deep blue sky and a rugged landscape, I swelled with pride and joy.

He turned twenty-five the day before we flew into Las Vegas, reaching a significant milestone: the right to drive this rented convertible across this country where the automobile is the undeclared national religion.

This was supposed to be an epic road trip, but it was more than that.

Simpler Times

A quarter century earlier, our relationship was so utterly straightforward. Swaddled in hospital linens with only his tiny face exposed to the strange world around him, Samuel looked directly at me with dark, piercing eyes. I knew there was no afterthought, only his young eyes soaking up his new environment and the face of his young father basking in the joy of the moment.

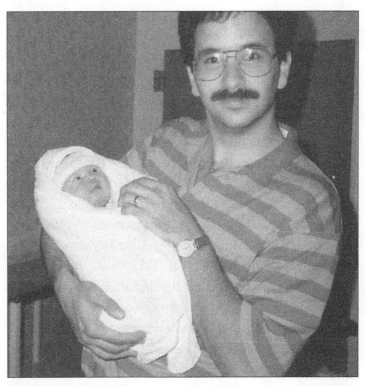

Norman and his newborn son at Ottawa Civic Hospital
(June 1990)

The photo does capture some of the young father's delight but not the fullest extent of my elation. We don't have a picture of me overeagerly rushing in, just after he was born, to hold him in my arms. Just after they weighed him, I turned to the nurse, ready to take him into my arms. I didn't even think that she would place him directly into his mother's. Christine had held him in her for nine months, and I longed for that same feeling of proximity and intimacy. The nurse nearly scoffed at me for approaching ever so momentarily and partially raising my arms to take my son.

I was euphoric at the birth of my son, but I managed to swallow my pride and realize how selfish my brief gesture had been. But in that *glorious* moment, the first of only three instances in my life that ever warranted that adjective, I immediately switched back to the look of pure joy on Christine's face as she revelled in that unparalleled sensation of finally holding her firstborn in her arms.

Later, though, after Samuel was well fed and Christine was fast asleep, I found him awake in the nursery, took him in my arms, and walked with him to the empty waiting room. The June sunrays shone through the windows, generating soothing warmth. Perfect for a newborn.

He looked up at me with those big, beautiful eyes.

Life Gets Complicated

Nearly twenty-five years later, Samuel still looked at me with those same piercing, honest eyes. In front of a warm fireplace in our Montreal home in December 2014, Christine and I waited for his visit that weekend, less than two weeks after my diagnosis. He was our eldest, and we would tell him first.

I spoke to Samuel as I always had: openly and honestly. I started with the original symptoms, explained the long process of tests, and led him to a description of ALS and the prognosis, a vague one at best, with a likely scenario, a worst-case scenario, and an optimistic scenario.

Those dark eyes dampened. We talked more. We shared our feelings, our shock, our disbelief, our acceptance, our determination, and our caring. When we had drained our energy and time, we hugged before going to bed. He went downstairs to the TV room, and I went up to my bedroom with the weight of his sorrow on my heart.

We spent the rest of that weekend talking. I brought out the old albums to look at baby photos of him that I hadn't looked at in years. It was a bittersweet melancholy. Maybe this is what the Portuguese call *saudade* but in the context of grieving what was to be lost. The funny thing is, it was one of the best weekends I have ever spent with Samuel, or with anyone for that matter. It filled me up with love.

Following that weekend, though, we lacked the time to touch base on our evolving feelings. I felt overwhelmed by my responsibilities as a father, a leader, and a friend. Three months after my diagnosis, it dawned on me that I was spending the lion's share of my time managing how others dealt with my diagnosis and very little delving into how *I* felt about my new reality.

In the spring of 2015, a friend asked how I felt about it all. I went into my usual spiel about medical issues and managing symptoms. Yet as I was talking and my own voice echoed in my head, I realized I didn't really know how I felt. I'd spent most of my time managing others' re-actions, juggling appointments, and making adaptations to my daily life but almost no time reflecting on how I was actually feeling inside. So, in April, I started a blog and "came out of the closet," announcing my diagnosis to all on Facebook.

Although the blog was immensely helpful to me in an-alyzing my feelings and coming to terms with them, to Samuel, my blog meant that my own flesh and blood was getting the news along with everyone else. For him, it was like a slap in the face. He wanted to speak with me personally and discuss this with me, but the blog had depersonalized that. I didn't know this until we were in Arizona. And like most dangers in the desert, I didn't notice it until it had already bitten me.

Mojave Desert en Route to the Grand Canyon, June 2015

As we began our road trip, the rugged landscape bore few signs of life under the blazing Nevada sun. With temperatures that can reach 58°C, any life remained safely under the surface. The cacti and other plants also hid their secret to livelihood, with their deep roots or with moisture tucked away inside, protected by thorns. Large rocks perched upon smaller rocks made the landscape seem unreal, like a set for a movie. In fact, this area had been the set for countless westerns and even the cartoon duo of my childhood, Wile E. Coyote and the Road Runner.

Yet we know the desert comes alive each night with countless creatures, including snakes, spiders, scorpions, and coyotes. This contrast reminded me of human emotions, often so well hidden away, safe from the elements and potential predators. Six months after my diagnosis, it was as if our respective feelings were buried, and Samuel and I were in the desert both physically and metaphorically.

From the red cliffs of Sedona to Prescott National Forest, the Grand Canyon, and a Navajo reservation marked by grandiose monuments like statues watching over the landscape, this was a road trip spanning four states. We had an idea of the main sights we wanted to see, but I had neither the time nor inclination to elaborately plan each stop along the way. Instead, with only our plane tickets and car rental reserved in advance, we improvised our tour as we went along. We travelled old school, shirking GPS technology in favour of the maps I'd ordered from CAA just two weeks before our departure.

The choice of the Grand Canyon seemed like a suitable destination. Apart from being the ideal destination for an unforgettable road trip, the Grand Canyon is supposed to be so grand that it invokes profound reflection and introspection. This ancient, massive, and majestic structure is touted as the place where one sits, gazes in marvel at such unparalleled beauty, and then questions one's own modest place in the continuum of human existence. It's considered an ideal venue to reposition oneself in the vastness of creation.

Without a doubt, the dramatic entrance amplifies the impact of seeing the Grand Canyon for the first time. You reach the canyon through the trees, leaving the breathtaking discovery of this awe-inspiring natural wonder until the very last possible moment. You don't look at the canyon from afar before witnessing its beauty up close. Rather, you are confronted with it all rather suddenly. Your first glimpse at the Grand Canyon is guaranteed to be memorable.

Of course, the canyon was everything it was purported to be. It proved to me, as it has for millions of others, that it deserves to be called grand. It was so grand, in fact, that we kept going back to visit it from various perspectives: from the road, on foot, from the South Rim, from the North Rim, and even from the air, hovering godlike over this natural spectacle in a helicopter. We delighted in each new perspective and each new encounter.

I would like to say that all of this made the first day of our visit to the Grand Canyon just perfect. But it didn't.

In those six months since I first shared the news of my diagnosis with Samuel, a gap had widened between us—a gap so daunting it appeared to me as insurmountable as the Grand Canyon itself.

Rather than simply sit together to contemplate the beauty and significance of this sight, Samuel and I continued an argument that had commenced in the car hours earlier and would drag on into the next day. On the surface, our argument was about different things, and few of them were important. Yet, under the surface, it was about the gap between us in how we were each dealing with ALS.

The truth be told, I don't think we really settled anything per se. We just managed to empty ourselves of all the pain and frustration so we could move on. We shared our respective views on how ALS affected us, and we came to terms with ALS as a shared challenge. We talked about our fears and our limitations. We concluded that since I—no, we—had limited time and were both affected by my condition, we needed to keep open the lines of communication.

Once we'd gotten over that hurdle, we spent the rest of the week just driving, visiting, and communicating. There was no epiphany against a backdrop of a sunset that transmuted sublime geology into a colourful, awe-inspiring canvas. In fact, it was the antithesis of eloquence. If there were a conclusion to be drawn from our desert road trip, it was simply that ALS affects *everyone* around me. Blogging wasn't enough; there had to be more direct communication. The more significant the people in my life, the more ALS affected them and the more I needed to listen to how ALS affected my loved ones.

In movies about terminal illnesses, they tend to skip the tough part. They usually go from the diagnosis to a scene where life goes on around the central character as she quietly hides her pills or takes one last toke of medical marijuana before visitors arrive. She puts on a brave face and sits quietly as the world buzzes around her. She doesn't tell them about the phase-four cancer, the unbearable pain, and the depression.

In real life, or at least in my life, things are more complicated than that. Maybe it's my hot-blooded French-Italian nature, but we don't bottle things up. We talk. We sometimes scream and shout. Either way, we don't remain quiet for long.

Four states and two thousand kilometres later, Samuel and I finally arrived in Las Vegas just in time for Father's Day. The son who once burnt toast for me on this day was now a "foodie" and an economist with the interest and the means to treat me to a Father's Day dinner at Gordon Ramsay Steak in Las Vegas for the best Beef Wellington I had ever tasted.

On the very last day of our trip, we returned the shiny convertible to the rental agency, which marked the end of a memorable trip but also an important stage in the process of sharing and redefining our relationship in the context of ALS.

It's tempting to think that life would be so much simpler if my battle with ALS were a duel. That way I could focus on dealing with the bad guy. ALS could be like the rusty maniacal semi-trailer truck in *Duel*, and I would battle it on my own. But real life is both more complex and more rewarding. I wasn't the only one with ALS. Christine had known from the get-go that my ALS was also hers. Yet I had underestimated the extent to which the rest of my family, my friends, and my colleagues were also dealing with this.

Under the blistering Arizona sun, I was reminded that mine were the eyes Samuel had looked into on the day he first saw the rays of the sun shining through a hospital window. I was the father he'd observed and followed for most of his life, and I was the father he was counting on to be there when he got married and graduated with his PhD. Believe me, I was counting on it as much as he was, and I hadn't given up hope quite yet. Maybe I'd seen too many Hollywood movies, or maybe it was just denial, but I still harboured the quixotic hope that I'd somehow win my duel, boosted by the knowledge that, unlike the fictional David Mann, I was backed by a winning team of family and friends.

Chapter 6

Dealing with Death and Sadness:
The Luckiest Man

I can't always be happy. I can't always be sad. My disease is named after the man who moved millions with a speech that defied sadness and despair in favour of gratitude and acceptance. What could I learn from my experiences dealing with death or the prospect thereof? I had lost loved ones and was by my youngest son's side as he struggled to stay alive. Where was I to put sadness and despair? More important, how would I release it?

On July 4, 1939, in front of more than sixty thousand fans at Yankee Stadium, Lou Gehrig didn't even mention ALS. Rather, he euphemized it as a "bad break": "Fans, for the past two weeks you have been reading about the bad break I got. Yet today I consider myself the luckiest man on the face of the earth." Less than two years later, he succumbed to the disease that now bears his name.

The first baseman, known as the Iron Horse—the man whose streak of 2,130 consecutive games could be broken only by ALS—struggled to maintain his composure as he addressed that crowd of adoring fans. As he spoke, he hung his head between sentences and fought back tears. I know about the pain he felt as he spoke those immortal words of courage and gratitude, as he homed in on the positive: "So I close in saying that I might have been given a bad break, but I've got an awful lot to live for."

No doubt he believed every word of that simple yet eloquent speech, but I can't help but wonder how he felt after the game and fireworks were over, when he was alone again. My approach is similar to Lou Gehrig's last stance: I focus on living and vow to give ALS a good fight. Yet behind a frontline of determination, I keep sadness and despair tucked safely away like a caged beast.

The more I keep this under wraps, though, the more it's going to hurt. The problem is this: I'm a formidable fighter armed with determination and sometimes shielded by blind optimism. And I can rationalize regret. But what about sadness and despair? What have my experiences with death and the struggle to stay alive taught me about my ability to deal with these inevitable and essential parts of this journey?

The Altiplano on the Road from Oruro, Bolivia, July 2004

On the horizon, a dust devil swirled, dancing across the dusty plains. In the foreground, vicuñas—animals that look like a cross between a deer and a llama—grazed in fields spotted with tufts of golden brown grass—*paja brava*—that constitute the main forage on this barren landscape. As I drove back up the slope, I once again saw the familiar dogs along the side of the road. They were hoping to get their next meal cast from the window of one of the shiny gas-powered vehicles transporting humans across this plateau on their way to and from the urban centres of La Paz and Oruro.

In just a few minutes, I would see the snow-capped

Andes on the horizon, signalling my approach to El Alto, Bolivia's second largest city, perched at the edge of the high plateau at 4,150 metres, just above the valley that is home to Bolivia's seat of government: Nuestra Señora de La Paz, or simply La Paz.

The 4x4 vehicle I was driving had no radio. It was at least fifteen years old but was rugged and still running strong. The steering was loose, though, and I had little faith in the brakes and tires. As I headed back to La Paz, the truck twisted and turned up the winding road out of the valley.

I held the wheel deliberately and securely, compensating for uneven pavement on this stretch of highway and a steering mechanism that was worn from years of navigating bumpy village roads and the plains of Sajama National Park. I felt a good two inches of slack in the steering as I drove.

That day, there was more traffic coming from La Paz than usual. It had slipped my mind: This was Friday, and many people were heading out of Bolivia's largest urban centre to spend the weekend with family in places such as Potosí. Although my lane was relatively free, oncoming traffic was heavy. I had to be careful of passing cars coming into my lane.

As usual, at every kilometre or so, dogs waited by the roadside. On my first trips on the high plateau, I had taken note of the dogs, which I affectionately referred to as the *Amigos del Altiplano*. On this lonely road, I sometimes felt they were my only friends—the only ones who truly appreciated my presence here. They sat patiently at the side of the road, waiting for travellers to throw them scraps: remnants of a salteña—a sweet and savoury Bolivian pastry stuffed with meat and potatoes—or maybe a chicken bone. On a lucky day, that is.

My thoughts wandered from work to these patient high-plateau dogs and back to the road. I gripped tighter at the steering wheel as a gust of wind rocked the high-set vehicle. I reduced my speed rounding the bend. The truck lost power as I headed up the slope. When the road levelled off and sloped downward again, I accelerated, shifting back into fourth and then fifth gear.

Ahead of me at a good distance on the right side was a mangy old mutt; on the left was a row of vehicles making distance between themselves and the busy capital. At that moment, a passenger in a minibus tossed some food right into the middle of the oncoming lane, and the scruffy canine scurried out to harvest his catch for the day. I expected him to quickly scoop it up and return to the side of the road. But that day's treat must have been more complicated or confusing than usual or much more delightful than expected, as he shifted his attention from the busy road to his long-awaited meal.

I sounded the horn and geared down, but the dog remained focused on his coveted leftovers on my side of the yellow line. I blew the horn again and passed that critical point of no return. I pulled the vehicle as far to the right as possible to drive around him, but at almost that same instant, the dog decided to head back to the side of the road. Without any notice or warning, he ran right in front of the truck.

I felt the truck strike the poor creature. I could feel the crushing of frail bones under the weight of the heavy vehicle as the front left wheel ran over his body. Then I swear I heard a pitiful whimper as the back wheel crushed him a second time. The vehicle bounced as if it had hit a speed bump without slowing down.

I pulled the truck to the side of the road and controlled the shaking just enough to find the force to pull the hand-brake. I buckled forward, touching my forehead to the top of the steering wheel. My heart sank. I tried to swallow, but the lump in my throat made it difficult.

Looking back in the rear-view mirror, I saw the crippled creature limp and fall on the shoulder of the road. Then I saw the dog's legs shudder as he collapsed on his side to die. There was a last jerking movement and then no more.

Jewish General Hospital, Montreal, May 2013

As I paced the waiting area at the Jewish General Hospital while waiting for the surgeon to emerge with news of the operation, my fear of losing my youngest son was not mis-placed. Alex was going under the knife for the fourth time since he was born.

I pulled out my cell phone to make calls to inform fam-ily and friends. It was my duty, but it was also a conven-ient way to occupy my mind while the surgeon and his team—as well as factors beyond the control of health pro-fessionals—determined the fate of a young man with strong will but a life-threatening condition with less than a fifty percent chance of survival. He had a shelf full of chess trophies and medals. Yet, unbeknownst to me, the Grim Reaper had already put him in check. Alex was al-ready in septic shock and had been administered Levophed before he was rushed into the section reserved for cardiac emergencies. His heart had stopped beating.

Eighteen years earlier, Alex had started his life this way. Less than twenty-four hours after birth, he was rushed by ambulance to the neonatal intensive care unit at the Children's Hospital of Eastern Ontario. In his first year of life, he spent more than two months in the hospital and underwent surgery three times. From birth to age one, and again at eighteen, doctors sliced and prodded him, and cut away sections of his intestines. His abdomen bears three discernible scars, but there are others we can't see.

If anyone should understand what it means to battle against your own body, it's definitely Alex. I regretted for both of us that we had that in common. Last year, as I told Alex about my spinal tap, I recalled his at the age of barely half a day. It was to be the harbinger of the health challenges he would face. He spent a good part of the first year of his life struggling against his body, often hospitalized with Christine and me at his side at all times.

He battled a congenital condition known as Hirschsprung's disease—the underdevelopment of the nerve endings of the colon—a malady that was resolved through a series of operations. Despite the serious potential for disability, Alex managed to pull through, demonstrating a level of resilience that was simply off the charts.

Then, on May 19, 2013, at age eighteen, he faced yet another challenge. Just as my body had more recently turned against me, his turned against him, creating adhesions that would block his small intestine, causing his bowels to seep into his body and plunging him into septic shock. His heart had even stopped for a moment. He had died but was resuscitated.

After that, his chances of survival were still below fifty percent. Yet somehow he pulled through. We sat by him for nearly a month, watching him struggle as doctors and nurses connected him to machine after machine. While he was intubated and in an almost comatose state, doctors pumped him full of drugs, poked and prodded him, and drained fluid from his infected abdominal cavity and around his vital organs. When he was released nearly a month later, he was still barely able to eat, and his bones protruded where muscles had once prevailed.

Montreal, December 2014

A year and a half later, Alex had regained his strength and some of the weight he'd lost, and I was the one facing the battle to survive, against even more daunting odds.

I was touched by Alex's reaction to my news. First, when his mother and I had asked him to sit with us in the living room, he sensed it was coming and prepared for the worst. Alex's concern was for my mind. As I mentioned earlier, he wanted reassurance that it would still be me amid this body of muscle that was destined to melt around me like butter on hot toast. The rest, he told me, we could deal with as long as my mind didn't melt with the muscle.

The child who had struggled to survive not once but twice had become a young man with the wisdom to focus on what's most important and to cast aside the rest like an orange peel. The days that followed were filled with warm smiles; frequent, unsolicited hugs; and, Alex's favourite, kisses on my bald head.

Although he didn't know it yet, Alex emulated the spirit of Lou Gehrig's inspirational speech. He was indefatigably positive, and he couldn't tolerate negativism. He'd react to even the slightest whiff of defeatism or self-pity. It was a challenge, though, as I couldn't stop myself from occasionally wandering into those darker corners of my mind.

Although Alex and my lamented *Amigo del Altiplano* had little time for second-guessing, I had lots of time for regret. What did I regret? I regretted the gradual loss of capacity, and I regretted the loss of the life I had planned. I was supposed to bike until I was eighty. I had secretly cultivated an image of my ageing self: wrinkled, perhaps, yet still biking up Mount Royal; travelling the world; volunteering; and using my age and wisdom as activist assets just like the Raging Grannies. Instead, I clung to the hope of being able to walk longer than most people living with ALS. I hoped to make it to Italy and still make it down the street to an outdoor café.

I assured Alex that I would do everything I could. Sometimes that alone helped me focus on the positive. I read, researched, asked questions, looked for answers. I remained active and went to yoga. I took my medicine, riluzole, to slow the progression of the disease and others to manage symptoms and help my body repair the wear and tear of cramping and weakened muscles. I took an Ayurvedic medicine that allegedly protects neurons and strengthens the body's ability to resist the progression of ALS. I cut down on fish because the mercury level in my blood was too high. I ate more organic food and focused on certain antioxidants. I even had my fillings removed, as they contained a high percentage of mercury. I had also read studies indicating that weight gain is good, so I gained about twenty pounds.

I also avoided anything that might do more harm than good. Regardless, I always consulted my neurologist first, and I followed the advice of professionals. I had regular physiotherapy, chiropractic treatments, and treatments from other healthcare providers, including monthly meetings with an interdisciplinary team, regular appointments with a psychologist, and sessions with an occupational therapist.

By July 2015, I already had two thick binders full of information, prescriptions, notes, paperwork, and follow-up. I even tried acupuncture because I believed it had a lot of potential for many ailments, but I doubt my brief time as a pincushion really made any difference. In short, I decided to do everything I could to prolong the quality and duration of my life. Still, I knew that it wouldn't be enough. In fact, some or most of what I was doing might not even help. But I'd try.

I considered myself fortunate. If I had to choose between Alex not being resuscitated in 2013 and my developing ALS, there would be no question of my choice. I would choose ALS. *I know…I know.* That's a ridiculous thing to say because the two aren't at all related. Ridiculous. But these were some of the thoughts that pitter-pattered around my overactive mind.

Norman and his youngest son, Alexandre, in Montreal (2016)
Photo by Marie-Christine Tremblay

Regret makes more sense if I think about incidents such as the one in Bolivia. I still wonder if I should have reacted differently behind the wheel. Maybe, just maybe, that dog would have completed his meal and his day instead of limping away to die.

Likewise, I couldn't help but wonder if there was something I did that contributed to my diagnosis of ALS. I wondered if I was carelessly exposed to heavy metals. Maybe I was exposed to asbestos or lead while doing renovations. Perhaps living overseas put me in harm's way. Maybe the exposure to pollution in Kathmandu or New Delhi increased my chances. Some might argue that multiple inoculations or the DEET I applied while living in malaria-prone areas made me more susceptible to ALS. Probably not, though.

Besides, nobody really knows what causes ALS. It's more than likely that environmental factors are only part of the equation. Yet I just couldn't help but wonder.

Mostly, though, my regret wasn't about the past; it was about the future. I wondered if my own positive thinking were lulling me into denial. I'd sometimes imagine I was that mutt on the road between La Paz and Oruro. I could see that meal tossed onto the road, and I'd spring into action. Some passenger would leave me a generous portion of chicken and potatoes, and I'd push aside the latter with my snout and snap up meaty clumps. Then I'd feel the vibration of a vehicle approaching. I'd then scramble back toward safety, but in my miscalculation I'd be crushed under the weight of the vehicle. I'd instinctively move to the side of the road only to collapse and die.

Was I that dog, focusing too much on the moment? Was my determination my ally or my fatal flaw? Was my insistence on remaining active pushing my body beyond its limits? Did my focus on living in the moment translate into denial of the growing constraints imposed by this callous degenerative disease? Seven months after my diagnosis, I biked shorter and shorter distances, and only occasionally, but I still managed to cycle one last season. And I still worked. Was it too much? Was I setting myself up to be blindsided by this brutal illness?

There have been times when my vulnerability hit me like a sack of bricks. In late July 2015, my left hand started twitching and moving involuntarily on an increasingly frequent basis until I was awoken at 4:45 a.m. one morning by a severe cramp in my left hand and forearm. I wasn't able to go back to sleep.

That morning, I was unable to use my left hand. I put my socks and the rest of my clothes on with my right hand only. I had to ask Christine to button my shirt. I avoided typing, and I used my iPhone with my right hand instead of my computer and keyboard. A sense of panic set in.

ALS twitching and cramps are like tremors when you live on a fault line. They're nothing to worry about in and of themselves. Tremors and small quakes can cause minor damage and cracks, but they're also notices of our vulnerability and of the inevitability of the Big One: the quake that will bring down bridges and buildings. So cramps are both warnings and milestones of my growing limitations. They mark the fact that either I have overexerted myself or I need to increase my medication to better manage my symptoms.

The week before, I had managed to cycle three days in a row, and I should have been proud. My occupational therapist and my physiotherapist had given me some terrific pointers to better mount and dismount my bike and to control my shaky, spastic muscles while starting and stopping. I had also made successful adaptations to my bike, including new ergonomic handles, adjustments to my clips, and a wrist brace to reduce the pressure on my left forearm. I adapted my cycling as well by choosing shorter routes, travelling at a more leisurely pace, stopping to stretch more frequently, and dramatically lowering my gears to keep resistance to a minimum.

Nonetheless, I did manage to overexert my left thumb and forearm while changing gears. I also learned that the allegedly hill-free Magdalen Islands have a lot more inclines than I had bargained for. Finally, I also overexerted my leg while climbing back up from the beach to the road above. It wasn't intentional. Christine was holding my hand, and when she faltered and slipped, so did I.

In the end, rather than celebrate a successful cycling trip, I came face to face with my limitations. Although I could bike shorter distances on level surfaces, my days of cycling up inclines had come to an end. The list of things I could no longer do continued to grow.

All the while, I wondered what would happen when both sides were affected. As it stood, I relied on my stronger right side to remain active. Although my left side was problematic, I could use my right hand to carry objects and open doors, for example. I relied on my right leg to bear the brunt of my weight and lift me up from a seated position while I held my cane in my stronger right arm. Once my right side was like my left side, my list of things I could no longer do was bound to increase exponentially. I wondered how much more time I had before I reached that milestone. Unfortunately, the fasciculations—the telltale twitching so characteristic of Lou Gehrig's disease—had been increasing on the right side, a frightening omen of things to come.

I had more in common with Lou Gehrig than just ALS. Like the Iron Horse of the Yankees, despite my bad break, I was privileged to have lived a life filled with love, a life spent living my dreams. So I managed to forget the aches, the pains, and the setbacks, and I reminded myself that my bucket list was relatively short because "life is too short" had always been my mantra. I had great friends, children of whom I couldn't be prouder, and a wife who—as Lou described his own life partner—"has been a tower of strength and shown more courage than you [or she] dreamed existed." I couldn't ask for better support in my time of need. I was thankful for my friends, my family, my colleagues and board members, the ALS clinic at the Montreal Neurological Institute and Hospital ("the Neuro"), the ALS Society, and the rehabilitation centre that, despite our bumpy start, was an amazing ally in my struggle to remain as self-reliant as possible as long as I could.

There was no dearth of reasons for hope and optimism. The Ice Bucket Challenge had turbocharged research, and there were presently a record four new medications going into clinical trials in Montreal in the coming months. That, according to Dr. Angela Genge at the Neuro, was "more progress than we have seen in decades." Inspired by the words of a man who personified determination and focus, I focused on the positive and kept sadness at bay at a time when we were finally giving ALS a run for its money. Surrounded by so much love and support, I persevered. I gushed with positivity and hope, and I changed my Facebook status to "the luckiest man on the face of the earth."

Yet experience has proven that I have trouble summoning certain emotions. Positivism is great, but it can also be a clever ploy to block inevitable bouts of sadness and random waves of despair. After my mother died, I spent tearless days planning events, accompanying her surviving spouse as he prepared the funeral, and dutifully organizing family gatherings. I delivered a flawless eulogy that would have made her proud, and I put on a brave face for family, friends, and acquaintances. Then, when all had been taken care of, I loaded the car with family and luggage and headed back from Waterloo, Ontario, east on the 401.

But I didn't get far. Just east of Toronto, it overcame me like a tidal wave of emotion. I took the first exit I could see and stumbled out of the vehicle, leaving the family behind to get coffee and donuts. They returned to find me curled up on a park bench, sobbing. Since they had never seen me cry before, they didn't know how to react. In fact, they weren't even sure whether I was laughing or crying, and it took some time before the tears stopped.

Previous drafts of this chapter ended on an upbeat note, buoyed by Alex's militant positivism. But then I caught myself hiding behind the keyboard. Sure, I felt like the luckiest man on the face of the earth like Lou Gehrig did, but I was also goddam unlucky, and I couldn't hide for long behind spin and prose. The longer I forewent facing the sadness and despair, the more it was going to hurt. I just wished I could find the safety valve because I feared the consequences of opening those floodgates. Perhaps the first step (and maybe there were eleven more) was just to write down my admission that I had to work on releasing those waves of gloom and despair. That, my friends, is the truth about how the luckiest man addresses death and sadness.

Chapter 7

Kindness Conquers All:
Christmas in August

My daughter, Émilie, my middle child, exemplifies the importance of simple gestures of kindness. In the most difficult moments, her kind acts have kept fear at bay and filled my heart with positivity. In an ideal world, we all take the extra time to be kind and to savour each act of kindness. They aren't nice additions to life; they are the very essence of it.

Ice Bucket Challenge 2015, with family
Photo by Alexandre MacIsaac

August 2015 marked the attempted return of the ALS Ice Bucket Challenge, which had probably been the most successful viral fundraiser of all time. It had propelled ALS into the public consciousness and, in Canada alone, injected $26 million into research to find a treatment. When the ALS Society launched an encore performance of the Ice Bucket Challenge, my family took part, challenging friends and colleagues to join in.

Like greeting cards at Christmas, videos poured in from friends and colleagues in Montreal and a half dozen other cities. Meanwhile, a friend's nostalgic message took me back to my first Christmas abroad, and Émilie returned from China after a year away. She shared with me a mixed CD, a private open-air concert, and letter that I present to you in these pages. I received so much in one month that it was like Christmas in August!

The Gift of Memories: Sand 'n' Claus

I spent my first Christmas away from home in 1983 along the coast of the Horn of Africa, some twenty kilometres south of Mogadishu, on a treeless, windswept beach where gentle waves caress fine sand. That beach is called Shark's Bay, and I would have been hard pressed to find a better place in all of Somalia to spend the holidays.

Nor could I imagine a better Father Christmas than Shaacir. Sure, there were a few superficial constraints that made him very different from the Santa Claus of artist Haddon Hubbard Sundblom, popularized by the likes of the Coca-Cola Company. Although he was jolly and as plump a Somali as I ever met, he was certainly not what I would describe as a rotund figure with red cheeks and a pinkish hue. However, let's be clear. Our image of Santa Claus has evolved over time from Sinterklaas riding a goat to a Coke-guzzling reindeer musher from the North Pole. So, my 1983 East African Santa suited me just fine.

Shaacir donned red pants, a reddish pink shirt, and a mock beard fashioned from shredded white plastic bags. He topped it off with a dark red tinfoil hat. Granted, it wasn't the best Santa outfit. Yet, despite his sartorial shortcomings, this gentle soul embodied for me the compassionate, generous spirit of Saint Nicholas.

The wild boar roasting on a fire on the beach was a unique and tasty Yuletide feast. Our Christmas tree was a thorn bush decorated for the holidays with paper snowflakes and angels as well as assorted colourful shapes and a few red and white candy canes brought from Canada for this special occasion. It wasn't much, but it succeeded wonderfully the same way Charlie Brown's pathetic tree attained perfection, embellished by a few requisite ornaments and a lot of determination and joy. Under that tree were a few wrapped gifts, a watermelon, a guitar, and a basket.

I remember having spent most of that day lying on the beach and romping in the Indian Ocean, enjoying the soothing, warm waters and the sand between my toes. Toward the end of the day, a few of us got caught out by the tide rapidly coming in. As we rushed back to shore, I felt a large fish brush up against my leg. I'm glad that wasn't a shark, I thought.

As the light changed, so did the colour of the sand. I remember taking a walk out into the desert away from the beach to take pictures at dusk against the backdrop of the beautiful red dunes.

A twenty-year-old Norman walks over sand dunes near
Shark's Bay in Somalia, East Africa (December 1983)
Photo by Jo-Anne Bund

It was like August at Christmas, and I have been thinking about that Christmas ever since my friend Jo-Anne,
whom I haven't seen in more than three decades, sent me
a picture and a brief but nostalgic message that took me

back in time. She reminded me of the day we shot that photo "on the red wavy sands that stretched into the distance, with the sun casting long shadows, and you and I laughing and laughing while trying to get you to strike a pensive pose." She recalled our days together at the Jowhar Agriculture Centre: "sitting across the table from me, telling me your stories while we share an overly sweetened Somali tea in a glass that is too hot to hold."

Who would have thought that an old snapshot and brief message could mean so much? Indeed, it was as if the theme of August were sharing and strengthening the ties between me and family and friends. So many friends took the time to get in touch or visit. It's as if the barriers that separated us—time and space—had been overcome. And nothing was better than reuniting with my daughter, who had spent that past year on the other side of the world. So let's go from twentieth-century Africa to twenty-first-century China.

Beijing, December 2014

Émilie was the last to be told about my diagnosis. She wasn't the youngest, but she was the farthest away. Although we spoke almost daily on FaceTime or Skype, it wasn't the kind of news to share over the Internet or the phone. So we waited until we'd see her on the trip we had planned to China over the Christmas break. It was bound to put a damper on our trip, but there was no other way.

In the days leading up to my departure to China, and on the flight to Beijing, I imagined it in my head. I pictured her cheeks turning red, her eyes watering, and her voice cracking, followed by her arms reaching out and around my neck as she melted into my arms. It would be like attending my own funeral.

Émilie was calm and happy as a baby. She'd sleep so long that her mother would sometimes grow impatient and worried and would wake her in the morning. More than once, Émilie fell asleep in her highchair during mealtime. I have etched in my memory the image of her enjoying the wind in her hair as we walked along the Ottawa River. She would close her eyes and turn her face toward the gentle breeze to feel the air flow through her soft blonde curls.

Now she had that same attitude toward the world that was her oyster. She revelled in the little things in China: the subtle and not-so-subtle cultural differences, the food, and the faces. She shared her stories daily like a personal blog delivered live over FaceTime.

My news was unlike a gentle breeze though. Rather, it was abrupt and lacking in subtlety. So I feared delivering the news almost as much as I feared the news itself.

Émilie greeted me at Beijing International Airport with her characteristic enthusiasm and good humour. She chatted incessantly about her experiences since our last FaceTime exchange some thirty-six hours prior: the train, the airport, her work the day before, and her apartment back in Luoyang. I often joked that for each hour she experienced, she took two hours to recount it. But I just loved to hear her stories.

We had a long wait for Christine and Alex to arrive separately from Canada, and since their flight was further delayed, we ended up waiting more than twelve hours. Thank you, Air Canada, for extending our father-daughter reunion.

Fortunately, this airport had everything, including overpriced Starbucks coffee and the offerings from seventy-one other food outlets in addition to other shopping and services. This was post-Olympics Beijing, not the People's Republic of the Cold War. Terminal 3 is 1.7 million square metres of jet-set magnificence.

After hours of chatting and looking at her photos of China, her photos of her trip to Taiwan, and the videos and slideshows she had carefully created around each of her adventures since she had arrived on the other side of the world, we headed upstairs to the "Global Kitchen" for Thai food. We sat at opposite ends of enough aromatic and spicy dishes to feed a family of four, and we talked and ate until there was none left. Émilie, slim and healthy, mentioned such overindulgence more than once.

I then started thinking of when I'd tell her the news. Now or later? Part of my brain told me *never*, but we're not really that kind of family. *Cards on the table.*

We finished lunch and agreed to yet another cup of java. Then, as we headed down the escalator, just as I could see the Starbucks logo—that Seattle siren who lures caffeine addicts into comfy chairs— Émilie asked about my health.

"How's your health, Papa? Did you ever get more results from those tests?"

I didn't want to tell her on the escalator. "I got some results, and I'm waiting for more, but let's talk about that later."

I brushed off the comment with a shake of the head and a squished-up mouth, an expression that said, "It can wait." But it couldn't.

There was more caffeine. More videos. More stories of China. Then, somewhere toward the end of a slideshow, I spotted an opportunity to segue into this uncomfortable discussion and address the elephant in the room. It was my elephant, and Émilie didn't see it coming.

Our two-week trip to China became a combination re-union, visit, and period of coming to terms with a new reality. We had multiple opportunities to talk, share, cry, and hold each other. I found extra time for Émilie because I knew I had to leave her on her own after two weeks to deal with this in her apartment on the other side of the world. There was always FaceTime, but that was no replacement for being there in person.

For me, our exploration of China—of the Longmen Grottoes, the Terracotta Army, the Xi'an night market, and so much more—became a symbol for us, of all we could still do together, living with ALS, like countless others facing life's biggest challenges. On the Great Wall of China, I crossed paths with a woman who was walking with crutches. She was accompanied by her husband, just as I was accompanied by Christine, who held me steady on the stairs and over uneven terrain. I wondered about *their* story. I guess everyone's got a story.

I cherished these moments with Émilie. Our bus ride together out to the White Horse Temple on municipal transportation was much longer than we expected, but I didn't mind at all. We just talked and talked, and we held hands and looked at China around us. We were floating in a sea of people, watching the waves calmly swell with the tides of humanity.

Although the sights were amazing, even more important was the fact that we were visiting these places together, making memories and living adventurously as we had always done. We were more aware than ever of the value of this time together.

Norman and his daughter, Émilie, at the Xi'an night market in Shaanxi Province, China (January 2015)
Photo by Marie-Christine Tremblay

Eight months later, Émilie returned to Canada. While it was great to be back together, it wasn't always easy to adjust to our new reality. There were moments where we just didn't know how to face it. Émilie's visit with me to the rehabilitation centre brought her to tears, and there were times when she needed to express her anger and frustration over this cruel twist of fate and its impact on her life.

When we celebrated her upcoming twenty-third birthday before she departed for Quebec City, she was the one showering me with priceless gifts. The first was a mixed CD. She always had a knack for communicating through song. The CD contained a couple of songs I used to sing to her. She recalled that I have a beautiful voice, thereby demonstrating that love is not only blind but also definitely deaf! It also contained some songs featuring lyrics that made her think of how she imagined I was feeling, and others that brought back memories of special times we'd spent together. It was a great gift as well as a throwback to the era of mixtapes. I listened to that CD over and over again, paying close attention to the lyrics and understanding a bit more each time.

Second, Émilie dusted off her guitar, summoned her vocal chords, and played me a private concert of assorted tunes on our backyard patio. What can I say? Each note was flawless to my ears. My heart swelled.

The third gift—and probably the best of all—came three weeks later in the form of a letter from Quebec City. I present it to you here, as is, because it read just perfect to me:

Dear Papa:

Today I thought about you. I thought about you when I put on my bike helmet at 8:30 a.m. I thought about you when I made a hand signal that I was turning right on the bike path of Laval University as the woman in front of me botched all efforts to make hand signals. I thought about you when I stopped on Samuel de Champlain Boulevard to watch the runners participating in the Québec City Marathon. Their families watched them and videotaped them as they ran past. Some of the runners joined their families on the bike path along the road. They were so proud.

I thought about you when I saw two runners, a father and his teenage daughter, holding hands as they triumphantly crossed the finish line, with Mumford & Sons playing in the background.

I thought about you when I heard the blended sounds of wheels against the rock dust trail and the waves breaking against the shore beside me, reminding me of the Confederation Trail on Prince Edward Island.

I thought about you when I stopped at the Old Port of Quebec and a father in the parking lot adjoining the bike path said to his child, "Next time, when the weather's better, I'll take you on the Quebec Bridge."

I thought about you when I saw one of the runners crying because she couldn't run any farther. A family member walked along side her, expressing compassion for the disappointment she was feeling. It reminded me of the time I was following you, biking through downtown Montreal, and I just couldn't follow anymore because the incline was too steep. But you stayed by my side, reassuring me. And then I thought of you when I conquered four steep inclines in a row without ever setting my foot on the ground. My lungs were about to explode.

I thought about you when I reached the 50 km mark.

You could probably never do this 50 km ride with me. (Anyway, it's so friggin' cold in Quebec City that the bike path will close in another four weeks, so neither will I before May comes around again!) But I want you to know that today you were with me. You should also know that it's all thanks to you that I am able to experience these pleasures, that I discovered the wonderful world of bike paths.

It's as if everyone's out celebrating today, either on the terraces of Old Quebec, on the paths along the Saint-Charles River, or picnicking at Beauport Bay. Québécois music and popular summer tunes intermingle, motivating my legs to continue pushing even farther.

All that can't change the fact that my love of biking is yours. And I feel like I'm stealing it from you. I want to talk to you about the pleasure I get from biking because I know you understand it. But I'm also afraid that it'll make you sad. I have already mourned going spinning with you, but I feel that today I am mourning going biking with you.

Life's funny that way: It would have been so unimaginable two years ago that I would enjoy a day like today. And I owe it all to you.

Merci, Papa.

And thank *you*, Émilie. Thank you for Christmas in August.

Epilogue

"There but for the grace of God go I."
—John Bradford

Is the name of that beach—Shark's Bay—and the statement that a "large fish" brushed up against me still trotting around in your head as you wonder if perhaps that idyllic beach wasn't imminently dangerous? I must admit that the thought crossed my mind too.

What's in a name? Why's it called *Shark's* Bay anyway? Back in 1983, a much younger, more invincible version of myself asked those around me that very question as we arrived at that alluring beach. The first answered, "Just a name." The second told me that the way the waves hit the rocks just offshore was reminiscent of shark fins. I wasn't convinced, but the fine white sand and salt water beckoned me, so I plunged into the warm Indian Ocean without a care.

Everyone knew you ought not swim farther north up that shore on the beaches of Mogadishu, where the camel entrails from the abattoir were discharged into the sea, attracting a frenzy of ravenous Zambezi sharks. I too had heard the stories of countless attacks in those shallow waters. In fact, the next year, upon arrival in Mogadishu, two Germans headed directly to the beach, too early to hear the standard warning that all foreigners receive soon after arriving at this harsh posting. They didn't live to tell the tale.

Yet I learned decades later that Shark's Bay was also the theatre of shark attacks on human bathers, including a doctor from Médecins sans Frontières who lost a leg in 1984 and a little girl who was fatally wounded soon thereafter.

The lesson I take from this is that life is full of perils and risks. We sometimes don't worry at all when we're actually in serious danger. At other times, when peril appears on the horizon, we rush to it without thinking like a fly drawn to flypaper. So maybe we're better off—with the notable exception of beaches with names containing the word *shark*—casting aside fear all together. In any case, we should all live each day as if it's our last, and it helps when we're reminded of everything there is to live for. That's why even the most modest expressions of sharing, caring, and solidarity are so important. And that's why I'm so grateful for Christmas in August.

Chapter 8

Confronting Our Fears:

Three Stories

Norman at Notre-Dame-des-Neiges
Cemetery in Montreal (2015)
Photo by Marie-Christine Tremblay

Fear is an issue I tackled in October 2015 as I approached
the first anniversary of my diagnosis. It was October 31st,
a fitting time to talk about it.

For many, Halloween presents an opportunity to dress up in amusing, scary, or sexy costumes. Children go trick-or-treating, while those who have outgrown this costumed sugar rally may instead attend a party or celebrate by watching blood-curdling horror flicks.

There are festivals of the dead in many cultures, and it is widely believed that our secularized version of Halloween evolved from pagan roots. The Gaels celebrated Samhain, marking the harvest and performing rituals to appease the dead. Celebrants wore masks and other disguises to mimic these spirits. Halloween has since replaced Samhain as our autumn death-themed festival.

We don't see much fear amongst the young candy hunters, however. Nor do we see fear amongst costumed partiers, as their alcohol-infused brains are typically focused on other primal needs. So, in the spirit of really facing our fears on this occasion, let's look at three real-life examples of fear and how we face it.

Three Real-Life Cases of Fears

The first case is about how Michel met the Grim Reaper, who came to him disguised as cancer. On August 26, 2014, Michel turned sixty-six, just a few days after he officially went into retirement. Unfortunately, the eve of retirement coincided with some troubling news. An appointment. A mass on the pancreas. An ultrasound. Metastases on the liver. And, on the day before his birthday, a biopsy. Then, on September 4th, the fateful result and devastating prognosis. Cancer. Three to six months to live. On that fateful day of diagnosis, he was expecting details on the magical medical intervention that would save him. Instead, he was given a timeline, a horizon that he could at best stretch to ten months with chemo.

The second case is about death with a side dish of total loss of muscle control, and it's my story. It first reared its ugly head via an online symptom checker, followed by a Google search and a series of truly horrifying YouTube videos of emaciated, wheelchair-bound victims intoning with slurred speech the sad, sad stories of their downward journey to loss of autonomy on the way to certain death. My story involved the shock of the initial diagnosis, but it became less sad as I came to terms with my condition. Yet there were lingering fears, so I avoided attending meetings with fellow ALS sufferers organized by the ALS Society. I feared meeting in person the scary future I had viewed through YouTube.

The third case is that of a slight boy with soft features and straight chocolate-brown hair. He had frequent nightmares and lived in fear of his father's outbursts of rage and violence. Decades later, he could still feel the sting, both emotional and physical, of his father's slaps to the back of his head as he rounded the bannister, of running upstairs to escape the wrath of the one who, as he learned later in life, was supposed to protect him. "Go—to—bed!" His father would roll his tongue back against his top teeth, exposing the veins underneath. The boy always wondered if he might one day bite it off.

His father would lash out with expressions that he still hasn't forgotten to this day. His father spoke of "the horrible death of a thousand pigs," which made no sense but evoked images of blood and squealing swine. He learned later in life that this was a biblical reference. The more enduring expression of anger and impatience, though, was much more direct: "I brought you into this world; I'll take you out of it!" That one was little more than a lyrical death threat.

He knew these were more than words, and he couldn't erase the image of his older brother cornered and curled up in the fetal position, repeatedly kicked by his enraged father with his tongue curled back.

Facing Fears

How have our three characters faced fear?

Let's start with the young boy afraid of his father's fury. For him, running and hiding was probably an appropriate response. At the age of ten, he undertook the project of cleaning up the basement. There were boxes everywhere, so he piled them up neatly and purposefully, building three walls of boxes behind which he created his own secret hiding place. He connected a garage lamp to an extension cord for lighting. He covered the floor with an area carpet and the walls with sheets. He also had pillows. At the back were two empty boxes that were his secret entrance.

When the shouting became intolerable, he had a place to escape the chaos. He would take his dog with him. She was a lot like him. She was a stray, and she often had nightmares from the abuse she experienced before she was rescued by the boy and his siblings. But together they were safe. He would hug his dog and read his books. And when the shouting finally subsided, and he heard voices asking where he was or calling him to dinner, he would turn off the light and emerge from his hiding place. He mostly avoided using the stairs to ensure that nobody suspected he had been hiding downstairs. He would instead escape through the basement window and reappear at the back door to make it seem as though he had been outside with his dog, oblivious to the conflict that had taken place.

But what about Michel, who faced death by cancer? He was also going somewhere, but he wasn't running away.

In mid-September, while I was at his old stomping ground around Lake Titicaca, Michel was in Havre-Saint-Pierre, Quebec, preparing for a bucket list journey to Las Vegas. The excitement was palpable as he packed his suitcase to fly south with his girlfriend and family members to see Céline Dion live in concert. Little did he know, his niece had contacted the singer's agent to follow up on the letter he'd written to Céline a week earlier.

So, on a Saturday night in September, one of the best-selling music artists of all time descended from the stage as she sang "That's the Way It Is," took Michel's hand, and serenaded him. Stoked like a groupie, Michel was grinning ear to ear as Céline looked him in the eye. She then rested her head on his bald head before returning to the stage to finish the number.

Those were the fifteen minutes of fame (or less) for this psychologist from Shawinigan. It was a Kodak moment worthy of the good news portion of the French CBC, Radio-Canada, and *Le Journal de Montréal*. The media have a way of boiling most stories down to one very narrow incident, but there's more to Michel than being serenaded by Céline Dion.

Michel focused on making the most of his endgame, and he posted photos of himself smiling during the last year of his life. Yes, smiling. Smiling as his grandchildren shaved his head. Even smiling through chemo. Smiling and living. He shared the experience of living this last chapter with others. He did interviews and philosophized on it.

When he prepared to depart for Las Vegas, he wrote on his Facebook page, "I know that at any moment the bell could ring, calling an end to recess." Yet he wanted to "make the most of this grand departure."

And I wasn't surprised. I never saw Michel frown. He had a face with skin like the surface of a volcano, but his eyes sparkled and his smile was contagious. I first met him in Bolivia and then saw him again in Peru, where he dedicated himself to bettering the lives of alpaca producers. This was when he fell in love with Peru and met Esperanza. (Would it be too obvious to point out that this optimist fell in love with a woman whose name means "hope"?)

Michel was at the end of his life, and I don't claim to have known him as well as I wish I did, but he had a positive influence on me.

On September 4, 2014, I was floored by Michel's announcement on Facebook that he suffered from advanced, incurable cancer. I couldn't even find the words to comment on his post, and I certainly couldn't "like" it. Yet, less than three months later, after I'd received my own life-altering diagnosis, I realized the impact on my own life of this friend whom I had known only south of the equator in the Andes. Michel's post and his choice to live the end of his life openly and to the fullest incited me to come out of the closet on April 18th of the following year and announce my struggle with ALS to my friends via Facebook.

More than a year after Michel's diagnosis, I found myself in Peru with Maria, a mutual friend, and we posted a photo on his Facebook page. "Even the alpacas are thinking of you!" We wrote in Spanish. Tongue in cheek, I tagged the photo of the adorable beige alpaca as Michel.

Maria Guay Cartagena and Norman in Puno, Peru
(September 2015)
*Photo by Centro de Apoyo e Investigación para el Desarrollo
(Centro CINDES), Peru*

I posted this photo on September 19th and patiently waited for a reply, but weeks later, with not a single Facebook post from Michel or Esperanza, I began to fear that maybe Michel would never see my post, meaning that not only had the bell rung and recess was over but also the bell had tolled one last time for him.

And that brings me back to my story. Whether or not he

had already passed on, I thought, he had taught me that there's nothing depressing about sharing this stage of his life. On the contrary, he had been a catalyst for my coming out.

Still, though, I hadn't mustered the courage to truly face my fears. For months, I had found excuses to avoid going to the meetings organized by the ALS Society where I could meet other people living with Lou Gehrig's disease. I imagined myself surrounded by dying people in wheelchairs, struggling to breathe, sharing recipes for food they could manage to swallow, as they wasted away before my eyes. I dreaded seeing my future in the flesh, and I feared I wouldn't fit in.

However, I finally took the plunge and attended one of these meetings. Three other people living with ALS were there along with five caregivers. During the first part of the meeting, there was indeed a lot of talk about the challenges, and several of the caregivers wanted to talk about recipes. Luckily, I was the last to introduce myself, and the tone changed considerably when the caregivers left the room to continue their discussion.

The conversation that ensued was anything but gloomy. We shared our stories and enjoyed this unique space to talk about our challenges and issues. The most "experienced" person in the room was Ginette, an exceptional fourteen-year ALS survivor with a gentle demeanour and infectious laughter. Gérard (a pseudonym) was a witty, rascally 74-year-old diagnosed six years ago. His banter was quick and comical, and it reminded me of Jonathan Winters. The third participant was Adèle (also a pseudonym), a retiree who was approximately where I was in terms of the development of the disease but who was not as open about her symptoms and complained that her spouse and caregiver worried too much.

The meeting was nothing like I'd feared. There was a strong feeling of solidarity and open sharing like you can get only from informal group therapy. And there was a lot of laughter. At one point, when the social worker had left, we struggled to understand Ginette, whose slurred speech was difficult to decipher without assistance. Whenever she repeated a word we didn't understand, we all tried to guess it like some sort of game of ALS charades. Ginette took the challenge in stride and with good humour, laughing as we struggled to communicate. At that, Gérard retorted, "Okay, we can't understand, but that's no reason to laugh at us!" That only made Ginette laugh harder.

It's All Interconnected in the End

An emaciated sixty-six-year-old psychologist from Shawinigan with a passion for alpacas unknowingly encouraged me to follow his example and open up about my challenge and my endgame. I know that Michel was keen to pay it forward, but he probably didn't know that he had played such a role in my life.

That month, I finally went to an ALS meeting and met survivors, not sufferers. I used to fear these meetings, but now I couldn't wait for the next one! Sure, I know that these meetings are biased and that those who attend them tend to be doing comparatively well while those who suffer or have lost their autonomy remain at home. Still, it's a reminder that our fears—no matter how grounded in fact we *believe* they are—are often unfounded.

Then there was the cherry on the sundae. A full month

after I posted that photo of a Peruvian alpaca on Facebook, Michel finally liked it. He then went on to invite me to like a page about a community enterprise that made slippers out of pure alpaca wool. Michel was back with a passion that continued to defy the prognosis that he would be six feet under before the snow melted. Instead, the snow melted, the summer came and went, and Michel was still fighting.

On the weekend before Halloween, when we festively challenge fear and the taboo of death, I said thank you to my mentor in optimism and dying well. Michel helped me revive the notion that I might just be brave. Knowing full well that I'm probably not, I continue to pretend I am while focusing on the winning battles and enjoying the blissful illusion of bravery.

And the boy? After a long period of rebellion, and once he had learned that enraged men are unfortunately as common as an old shoe, he reconciled with his father, and he leaned on the resilience and reliable love of his mother. That boy learned to be brave.

Someone once told him, "Even if you aren't brave, pretend to be brave. No one will know the difference." (It's like that H. Jackson Brown quote from *Life's Little Instruction Book*: "Be brave. Even if you're not, pretend to be. No one can tell the difference." I heard something similar when I was young, and after decades of faking it, I think I have fooled everyone—even myself.) So he learned when to hide and when to confront his fears. In his younger years, he trained in karate. As he grew older, he grew more confident. He learned to walk confidently and to scan his environment for enraged men, ready to confront any and all potential threats. He travelled the world with remarkable energy levels and seemingly limitless endurance. He had developed coping abilities, and there wasn't a problem he couldn't solve. He no longer needed to avoid troubles; instead, he developed the courage and fortitude to face them head on and turned them into opportunities. He was confidence personified.

Yet, he still faced that demon, that reflex to run and hide. At every turn, despite the courage he had developed, the boy within called upon himself to seek a hiding place, to protect himself from the hostility of the outside world, with his dog and a book that took him to the peaceful inner world of his mind. So, decades after he had metamorphized into a bold man with the capacity to face his fears, he still needed to cross paths with Michel, to open up and muster the courage to attend that ALS Society meeting.

Forty-two years later, I was once again alone with my dog. This time, it was a little Bolivian mutt, a mixed breed I got in La Paz and brought back to Canada. In many ways, I still felt strong, but in some ways I feared I'd come full circle, and I longed for a hiding place again. ALS had made me vulnerable again. Nearly a year after my diagnosis, I sometimes felt optimistic. Then, suddenly, as I struggled to make it down the stairs after a visit at my sister-in-law's house, I felt a sinking sense of doubt. That's when I needed inspiration from the likes of Michel, who defied his death sentence of cancer to attend a concert in Las Vegas, or from the likes of my sister-in-law herself, a three-time cancer survivor.

We face our fears together. Just as Halloween returns each year, dealing with our fears is a recurring theme we must revisit regularly. It's a part of the human condition.

Chapter 9

Perspective and Humour:
The Bright Side of Life

When we face life's biggest challenges, we often concentrate on the end goal to the detriment of living in the moment. That's understandable but unfortunate because if we dare open ourselves up to beauty and perspective in times of hardship, we will be rewarded with the best that life has to offer. Like the sunset at the end of a glorious day, beauty is to be found at the cusp of darkness. And if you're really lucky, you might also find humour in your predicament and end up rolling on the floor laughing.

Norman photographs a sunset over the Grand Canyon
(June 2015) *Photo by Samuel MacIsaac*

"The world is a comedy to those that think but a tragedy to those that feel."
—Horace Walpole

When I was a boy, I used to fill the bathtub, lie down, tilt my head back into the water until my ears were submerged, and just listen. Under the water, the sounds from my immediate surroundings were muffled. Once, when I dipped my head in, the radio in my sister's room was transformed from a sound that defined my environment into a faint rumble. Yet, distant sounds from the farthest reaches of the house became decipherable, resonating through the frame and plumbing of the house.

I could hear my mother turning on the water and crossing the kitchen to open the fridge door. I could hear my father as he exited the side screen door, letting it close behind him, generating a chorus of rattling that underscored his hasty departure. As I emerged for a breath, I could hear the car door slam, followed by my father's car starting and gravel slipping under the tires as he impatiently sped backward down the driveway toward the street. Then I heard footsteps up the stairs and the voice of my mother calling me to get out of the bathtub. "Dinner is almost ready!"

Decades later and on the other side of the world, I revelled in another unique perspective as I rode on a rickshaw through the bumpy back streets of Kathmandu from Thamel to Asan Tol. This time, while I was perched high on the seat of a cycle rickshaw, my Walkman blocked out the aggressive sounds and put me in touch with other sensations: smells, expressions, the flow of people, the clutter of overhead wires and signs.

My senses delighted at the spectacle of colours: green vegetables next to baskets full of purple flowers; multi-coloured topis, the typical brimless hats worn by Nepali men; and market stalls with piles of spices and coloured powders for tikkas just outside the small temple in the heart of Asan Tol. A woman in a sari sat cross-legged on a mat beside her goods, counting small notes. She took stock of her day's intake of rupees before rolling the small stash into the fold of her sari. Her blouse was held together with a safety pin, a sure sign that her earnings barely sufficed to ensure the livelihood of her family.

An energetic young man took out a bowl made of leaves and removed the lid from a boiling cauldron. With a large ladle, he scooped out several momos (Nepali dumplings) as his client licked his lips in anticipation and pointed to a red sauce in a large plastic container. His young wife was wearing an orange shalwar kameez with purple, green, and red shapes and a grey shawl, which she pulled over her head at the sight of the client. She opened the plastic container and scooped out the sauce while her husband passed her the bowl of steaming momos.

A small dog was on a balcony above, barking at a truck below. I wouldn't have noticed him, and his bark was likely too faint to hear above the daily cacophony of Kathmandu's Asan Tol bazaar, but with the sound blocked out, I could *see* him bark. I also felt every pothole in the street as the rickshaw negotiated its way through a sea of humans, cows, and vehicles ranging from a single large Tata truck billowing a cloud of black smoke to a Hindustan Motors Ambassador car that looked like it was straight out of the fifties.

Then there were the motorized three-wheeled taxis and autos as well as the rickshaws, like the one I was riding, powered by a dark-skinned sarong-clad little fellow who wiped the sweat from his brow and bent forward as we rounded the bend into the small laneway and began to move up the gentle slope past a popular shop filled with sweets. Women and men pushed their way into the door, past customers who exited with gelibi and other South Asian treats.

Perspective. We can see our world in countless different ways.

I could finally add the perspective of the overworked, stressed urban masses, their gazes focused on 4.7-inch screens—or perhaps upsized, upgraded 5.5-inch screens— while the sun shines above them and the spectacle of the urban jungle is deprived of yet another spectator, indeed another participant. But I'm not sure that's as much a question of perspective as the lack thereof. Such is the blithe indifference of the masses, and I'll come back to that eventually.

The Perspective They Expect

In November 2015, I made my first media appearance, on a television morning show, as a person living with ALS. I wasn't nervous, but I visibly struggled to contain my emotions. I described ALS as an inevitable downward slope. I explained what the massive investment in research meant to me.

I was doing my job as a volunteer spokesperson for ALS, alongside the chair of the ALS Canada Board of Directors. I spoke openly and honestly. If anything, I may have understated the issues in some ways. I talked about the contrast with 2013, when I could bike 150 kilometers in a day. "Now I no longer cycle." I didn't mention that I could walk only short distances or that I couldn't take the subway anymore because I couldn't make it down the stairs.

Still, following that interview, I couldn't escape the thought that this was *not me*. I didn't dwell on the negative, nor did I accept "the inevitable." I wanted to yell that I'd fight this to the end, that I just wouldn't accept that I had less than four years left to live. I didn't even want to even hear about "the inevitable," and I certainly didn't want anyone feeling sorry for me. So, although the interview went very well, and I received a lot of positive feedback, I needed to analyze the feeling that this somehow wasn't consistent with the way I wished to address this issue. Was it because I was kidding myself? Was I still in denial?

So I asked myself two big questions. First, when I focused on alternative perspectives, was I simply evading the cold, hard reality of it all? In other words, was looking at apparent misfortune from a completely different perspective little more than a clever form of denial? Second, should I do more ALS interviews?

The Perspective She Taught Me
This takes me back to the mid-seventies, to a time when I had put hiding in the basement behind me and looked forward to family time.

For a while, it seemed like everything was perfect. We were a family again. We had a new dad, we actually owned our own house for the first time ever, and there was a nearly nineteen-foot-long Ford LTD Country Squire station wagon in the driveway with my hockey equipment in the back.

This, I told myself at the time, was the way it was supposed to be. This was happiness. My mother was happily married. We managed family issues through weekly "family council" meetings, during which we all took turns chairing. We played **euchre** as a family on Friday nights. My new dad was even the assistant coach of my hockey team on weekends. Life was good for this happy, young teen.

Unfortunately, this **Brady Bunch** period was to be short-lived.

I thought it had started when my new dad, a millwright at the local Carlsberg brewery, was summarily laid off. It turns out, however, it had started much earlier when we were still basking in the bliss of our newfound middle-class family life. Looking back, in the days when I used to sketch and paint, I remember noticing that my new dad had a drink in his hand in every one of my drawings. Although it didn't strike me during the Brady Bunch years, he had a drink in his hand every day—at every euchre game, at every family council meeting. Always.

So, like a predictable Hollywood movie, my unprecedented happiness was followed by a series of tragic events. Sunny days were followed by dark, ominous rain clouds and violent storms, one after the next.

Hockey and euchre were quickly replaced by violence and nights with my mother at the women's shelter, or staying with the only neighbours who would have us without judging us. Family council meetings were replaced by 911 calls and court orders. But court orders weren't always effective, and my new ex-dad came back, kicked down the door, and came to collect the television and his rifle. When I confronted him at the top of the stairs with a screwdriver as my weapon of choice, my mother broke down in tears, pleading me to let him pass. And I did.

I remember the words of the police officer who towered over my mother in his sturdy police-issue boots. "We've seen this scene a hundred times, ma'am," he lectured. "He's not going to change, and you have to protect your family." I figured she was too shaken to be ashamed, but I was too young to know the half of it. Yet I wasn't too young to understand my mother's resilience. I wasn't too young to understand that she gave love a chance. I wanted the Brady Bunch back as much as she did.

After the dust had settled, once the man had left for good, my mother was alone again, saddled with the debt he had accumulated sitting at the end of a bar, drowning the hope he had generated in the people he once loved. He drenched his liver in rye or gin until there was no bar tab to be had and the only way to get a few more drinks was to hawk a television and a rifle.

It almost ended there for her. She had a major heart attack shortly afterward. I was seventeen by then, and I drove her to the hospital myself in record time, paying no heed to red lights or speed limits. The very next morning, I drove back to an empty house.

For weeks, while my mother was in the hospital, I paid the bills, took care of the house, and took out the garbage. Only later did I learn that my mother's chances of survival after that heart attack had been so slim. I had no idea how close I had come to being truly alone.

Most of all, though, I remember the way my mother looked at me when she grabbed my hand as I sat beside her in the hospital and she told me how proud she was of me. Sure, I have memories of feeling alone in that house and, before that, of walking alone from the women's shelter to school without ever telling a soul of my predicament. But more than anything, I remember that the contrast between the chaos and peril around me just seemed to make my mother's love shine brighter. Amid all the adversity, her love was unwavering. And that was enough for me. Indeed, it was everything for me.

I had the perfect family all along, before and after my "new dad" had come and gone, and it had nothing to do with the woodie station wagon, homeownership, and Friday night euchre.

I learned another lesson about perspective. While the happy times are best, the most arresting beauty is found amid hardship and turmoil. In times of crisis and struggle, when surrounded by unrest and nastiness, the contrast is stronger, and love and beauty become clearer. So, like the intense green eyes of that famous Afghan girl named Sharbat Gula, captured by National Geographic Society photographer Steve McCurry amid the turmoil of a refugee camp in Pakistan, or like the flower that breaks through a crack in the sidewalk of the impoverished east end of town amongst disparity and decay, that beauty is intensified by the contrast.

The Funny Perspective
There's more to perspective than learning to appreciate

the beauty that shines in the darkest moments. It's also about finding humour despite it all. Those who know me are familiar with my unique sense of humour, but maybe now they understand its deeper roots. Those who know me also understand when I tell people I was tempted to subtitle this chapter entry "Crucifixion Is a Bitch, but the View Is Amazing."

First, though, let's establish the far-from-humorous context. ALS is an infinitely depressing disease. It is, after all, an incurable, degenerative disease. It's a downward slope.

At Hôpital Notre-Dame in Montreal, they didn't track my progress but my degeneration. First, they took my weight. I hoped I wasn't losing weight. Then they went down their depressing checklist. Could I *still* eat on my own? *Still* dress myself? *Still* wash myself? *Still* stand in the shower? *Still* make it up and down the stairs? *Still* breathe unassisted at night…? The operative word that resonated in my head like a parent's criticism was *still*. Still.

The nurse asked me about drool, swallowing, depression, and suicidal thoughts. This was ostensibly a checklist of my seemingly inevitable and undeniably depressing future as an ALS sufferer.

There was no room for improvement. Even with cancer, against a backdrop of chemotherapy and countless other agonizing treatments, there is the specter of potential improvement up until the last stage. Is the tumour shrinking? Is the cancer going into remission? Is the pain subsiding or the overall condition improving? But not with ALS. There is no direction but down, and the faint hope is that the slope might be less steep, or that there will be a plateau, some respite in the inevitable journey into greater and greater disability, loss of autonomy, and eventual death. I hope my Catholic brethren will excuse me for calling it a long, drawn-out crucifixion.

Which brings me to Monty Python and their unique brand of absurd, stream-of-consciousness comedy.

I think one of the best movie endings ever has got to be the one in *Monty Python's Life of Brian.* The 1979 film, a comedic romp through the life of one singularly unambitious man who reluctantly becomes a cult leader and saviour, ends with Brian crucified on the cross, flanked by several other men, also hanging on crosses. It's a familiar scene to anyone acquainted with the basics of Christianity and the life of Jesus of Nazareth.

Despite being sentenced to die on the cross, one of the men encourages the other men to break into song, and they all join in a cross-bound chorus line, cheerfully belting out a tune atop a barren hill. "Always look on the bright side of life," they sing. It's a silly, optimist tune, befitting of this awkward satire marketed in Sweden as "So funny it was banned in Norway!"

Adoring fans rave about *Life of Brian*, and many praise it as the greatest comedy ever. Yet, it finds its humour in the most important tale in Christian mythology, the crucifixion of Christ. This is why it has always been as controversial as it was successful and popular. As funny as it is for so many, it is deeply offensive to others.

Similarly, it appears to be universally accepted that jokes about a disease as serious as ALS simply go too far. Quoted in *The Wrap*, the ALS Therapy Alliance released a statement in response to a joke about ALS in the Hollywood comedy *Ted*, the story of a man and his pot-smoking talking teddy bear. The Alliance stated that "the disease, which has no cure, is not something to be made fun of" and argued that "the film sends the wrong message." According to the organization, "ALS is no joke." And they're right.

But, still, I like to laugh, and I laughed throughout the movie *Ted*. I don't want to minimize anyone's right to be pissed off, though. That's every ALS patient's and caregiver's right. It's our disease, and if we want to moan and groan, or scream and protest, or demand an apology or reparation, that's also our right. It's a free country.

And it wasn't much of a joke. The offensive words were simply "I hope you get ALS." Notwithstanding the offensive nature of the joke (and let's be crystal clear that it was low even for *Ted*'s stoner, sophomoric humour), my critical inner voice can't help but ask if any notoriety isn't good for such an underrecognized, hideous disease. Isn't it good to raise awareness that ALS is everyone's worst-case scenario, a terminal, incurable, degenerative diseases that cripples, strangles, chokes, and kills?

Those who know me also know that I like to make jokes about everything. In the true spirit of *Monty Python's Life of Brian*, I do believe in looking on the bright side of life, so I told my wife and son I wanted to start a website of ALS jokes. If nothing else, it would be cathartic. My wife, who knows me all too well and has heard all of my jokes over and over again, responded with the best ALS joke ever: "Your career as a stand-up comic will be short-lived!"

I laughed hard, and I still laugh when I think about that joke—the best joke she has ever made. I even told the social workers at the ALS Society that joke, and in the context of a discussion about being open and learning to laugh in the face of adversity, my wife's joke was again met with laughter and approval.

Even the suggestion of making light of ALS is therapeutic, so I don't hesitate to mention the lighter side of the heaviest of subjects. Those days, in the back of my twisted mind, which is like my own personal Just for Laughs comedy festival, I'd been thinking of Monty Python's legendary sketch "The Ministry of Silly Walks" as I struggled with my own increasingly awkward gait and the time it took me to do simple tasks such as button a shirt or dress to go outside in the winter. "I'm sorry to have kept you waiting," I thought, remembering that sketch, "but I'm afraid my walk has become rather sillier recently."

I also rave about the ALS cloud's silver lining. I have my very own list of silver linings: Montreal has Canada's best ALS clinic. The Ice Bucket Challenge has resulted in $300 million in new funds for research. ALS is gaining attention, and meaningful progress is around the corner. My neurologist is at the cutting edge of the latest research. The list goes on.

I'm like a knight heading out to battle hopeless odds but with faith and conviction. I rave about my new sword, my shiny new armour, the indefatigable esprit de corps of my comrades-in-arms, the king's blessing, and the queen's inspiring message. My weapons are medical and paramedical services, my family, and my friends.

Don't get me wrong. I definitely have an overactive imagination, but I still have a filter, so I mostly keep my own odd ideas in my own little head. I will probably never put to paper that incongruously bizarre script I have in my head for a sitcom about some wheelchair-bound jokester and baseball enthusiast from Manhattan who's strangely reminiscent of that wacky Lou Gehrig. But I will sometimes escape to that imaginary world to gain new perspective on the world around me. Such are the lessons in perspective from the comically absurd.

The Positive Perspective

As I have said, this is my journey; I didn't choose it, but it's a journey nonetheless. I reserve times to damn the disease, scream at the sky, and simply cry, but it's much better to focus on the wealth of new perspective in contrast to the carefree (yet often too petty) existence of the masses around me in the Western world.

It's a lack of perspective that can allow our attention to be drawn toward showmanship, fashion, minor annoyances, and trifling irritations. Take, for instance, the young woman with the glum expression on her face and blue streaks in her hair at the reception counter at the dealership where I go to pick up my car after repairs. She's visibly annoyed by her state of affairs, having to work on a Saturday morning. From the sound of the telephone conversation I interrupted to ask for my bill and my car keys, she's even more peeved by her entirely unsatisfactory boyfriend.

If contrast makes beauty stand out in those dark moments, perhaps our carefree existence camouflages true beauty behind fast talk and flashy celebrities. Blame the Kardashians, blame reality television, blame Katy Perry… . (Okay, maybe not Katy Perry.) Blame consumerism. In the end, though, there's only one person to blame if you've lost sight of the beauty in the world—the person in the mirror.

Maybe that's why practicing compassion is one of the keys to happiness. *Perspective.* So if your untroubled life has blinded you to beauty, perhaps you need to open your eyes to poverty, injustice, violence, and bigotry. Or maybe the court jester of the consumer world—comedy, that is— is another viable introduction to perspective.

I don't actually know what might work for others. For me, it seems to help when I focus on the beauty amid adversity; consciously seek new, positive perspectives; and laugh, especially at myself. This is why I don't feel like an ALS "sufferer." Sure, I have challenges, frustrations, and discomfort. So does everyone. Sure, most of the plans I once made are no longer feasible. Sure, sure, sure. But when I'm with friends and family, I'm living like everyone else. In fact, I see a lot of people who don't seem to be enjoying life nearly as much as I am.

I would often drive past Notre-Dame-des-Neiges Cemetery on Mount Royal, passing within a few hundred metres of where my mother's ashes are buried. She was gone, but her spirit remained in me, and I felt an inner strength that focused on the positive. It was as if life had trained me to cope. That's why focusing an entire interview on the challenges, and placing all of my hopes on the research, on the efforts of others, just wasn't in tune with my usual approach. That doesn't mean I wouldn't do any more interviews. On the contrary, I looked forward to taking on that mission to raise awareness about ALS, but next time I'd do it knowing that this was only one side of me, and I'd do it with the confidence that I could continue being happy and positive with my own weird sense of humour.

I wouldn't crack jokes at my next interview either, but my daily life would continue to be peppered with humour, including some really bad jokes—because they're my specialty—and some jokes that are way over the top. Buoyed by a life full of experience in coping with adversity, with blind confidence that beauty and love are only intensified amid calamity and struggle, and inspired by the irreverent satire of Monty Python, I would continue to look on the bright side of life. But that's just my perspective.

Chapter 10

Serenity with Eyes Wide Open:
A Perfect Christmas

I have one reservation about the label "optimist." It's the assumption that I believe in a favourable outcome. I prefer to see myself as a "bright side" guy capable of focusing on the positive, rather than someone who blindly believes in the best possible outcome.

It's a bit like Christmas.

We can never relive the magic and wonder of our childhood Christmases. As a boy, I saw one version of Christmas with the expectations created for me by society. As an adult, though, my December 25th often rejected the traditional list of what makes this holiday "perfect": the white Christmas, the perfect tree, the perfect gift. Still, long after my childhood version had been debunked, and even when the reference points had changed, I could still derive serenity and joy from Christmas, even in the middle of the desert or while feasting on Peking duck with family in Beijing.

Living with the worst news is a lot like that. So many hopes and expectations have been dashed, but life is still awesome. You just have to look beyond your previous plans and expectations and instead focus on what's really important.

This was what I was thinking about during my second Christmas after my diagnosis.

Norman and his siblings in front of the Christmas tree in
Kitchener, Ontario (circa 1970)

Photo by Anthony MacIsaac

The boy with straight chocolate-brown hair sat motion-
less on the floor in the dark living room, looking up at the
Christmas tree he had decorated with his mother and his
siblings. He loved to gaze at the star on top. He particularly appreciated the tinsel streamers, the sparkling lametta
that flowed down the tree like icicles, accentuating its tri-
angular shape. He would focus on a single ornament, then
lean back and take in the whole tree. Never mind that this
was an artificial tree, or that a more critical witness to this
Christmastime scene may have noticed that the paint on

several of the light bulbs was badly scratched and white light shot through the scuffs where it should have been translucent red, green, yellow, or blue. Never mind because the details meant nothing to the boy, who still believed in Santa Claus.

The boy knew serenity even before he learned to use the word. This was right up there with kicking your way through knee-high leaves and then, with total abandon, jumping into a multicoloured pile of autumnal bliss. Or lying on your back in thick green grass and gazing at the stars in the night sky. But this was more. This was Christmas, and it was magical.

It's worth mentioning that this boy sitting alone in the living room was generally afraid of the dark, yet there he sat cross-legged, quiet and without a fear or worry in the world. It would soon be Christmas, and in that instance, his world was at peace.

He sensed a presence, so he turned his head away from the Christmas lights for just a second, looked over his shoulder, and saw his mother beaming with a smile he would never forget. He smiled too and then turned back toward the tree. When she approached quietly just to stroke his hair, he said nothing, but he would remember that moment forever as one of the purest expressions of love he ever experienced without a word spoken. And as she returned to the kitchen to resume Christmas preparations, he looked over his shoulder and saw her wink at him before she left the room.

Christmas and Consumerism

Subtly, through the work of Charles M. Schulz, I was introduced at an early age to the critique of the holidays as a consumer trap and to the struggle between the true meaning of Christmas and commercialism. This clash is not new. Long before *A Charlie Brown Christmas* was released in 1965, the true meaning of Christmas had already been a topic of hot debate. For instance, the Puritans were against the boisterous pagan festival so much so that, in England, it was rendered illegal to celebrate Christmas during part of the seventeenth century.

By the twentieth century, the new criticism of Christmas concentrated on commercialism. Rather than bringing serenity, it is commonly argued that the holiday season often brings stress, increases demands on our time, generates consumer frenzy, and condemns us to starting the New Year heavyset and burdened with debt. In *A Charlie Brown Christmas*, Charlie Brown faces the holiday blues, a feeling of being left out, and even despair at the sight of Snoopy's doghouse, decked out for the holidays, with a first-prize ribbon for a decoration contest.

This adorable Christmas special, engrained in my cultural landscape along with *How the Grinch Stole Christmas!* and *Rudolph the Red-Nosed Reindeer*, features Linus's lispy soliloquy, recounting the birth of Baby Jesus from the Gospel According to Luke and ending with, "That's what Christmas is all about, Charlie Brown."

Dare I mention that this wonderful message was commissioned and sponsored by the Coca-Cola Company, the renowned maker of the sugary black waters of capitalism that contributed to redefining Santa Claus and somehow even managed to market the illusion of polar bear cuddliness? But I digress.

Alex's Christmas Tree

It wasn't until my own children reached a similar age that I understood what my mother must have felt that late December evening in 1970. Twenty-seven years later, *I* was the parent. And although we lived at the opposite end of the world, celebrating a Western, ostensibly Christian, festival in a Hindu kingdom, the feeling was the same.

It also reinforced Schulz's theme that Christmas is about so much more than the material aspects, and the cherry on the sundae was my youngest son's contribution to our 1997 Kathmandu Christmas.

Perhaps you thought Charlie Brown's tiny, sparse tree was pathetic. Maybe you've criticized the imperfections of the same artificial trees and gaudy decorations of my youth. Regardless, these were both surpassed in meekness by our far more humble Nepalese version of a Christmas tree. In 1997, Alex had made a paper Christmas tree in arts and crafts at his school in Kathmandu. We placed it on a simple bamboo table and surrounded it with a variety of gifts we had purchased locally.

Finding gifts for the season was another challenge. I had wondered how I would find suitable gifts in a country with no department stores and no shopping centres. With three young children, Toys "R" Us had become as big a part of Christmas as the jolly old elf himself. Yet, in the end, far away from the influences of the commercial world, where children learn to transform remote desires into needs, we all rediscovered the simplicity and joy of receiving something completely unexpected rather than just satisfying false needs created by the constant bombardment of 24/7 marketing. It's amazing how open children can be to any type of gift when you simply take them away from the sugar-coated images of corporate America.

It's generally cold and humid in late December in Kathmandu, and that year was no exception. So, on that morning of December 25th, Papa and Mama Christmas got up early and placed all the heaters we possessed in the living room so that it would be warm enough to celebrate Christmas morning in our pyjamas. We basked in the warmth of our comfortable living room while the children experienced their first Christmas gifts that weren't just the fulfilment of expectations created by countless commercials.

Although there was no snow, it was as magical as any Christmas could be, and the big gift, the pièce de résistance that my children would never forget, was the gift of three snow-white rabbits in an oversized cage that we had built just for them.

Just to prove that different can also be great, we also attended Mass at a Catholic church where a band of musicians played Christmas music while seated cross-legged on the floor. They played traditional South Asian instruments, including a tabla and a sitar.

The children also attended a party at the American Club in Kathmandu, where Santa Claus arrived ho-ho-hoing from atop a three-wheeled cycle rickshaw. This was followed by our departure the next day for Chitwan National Park, where the children enjoyed Boxing Day in the jungle. *Perfect.*

Stuffing with Your Peking duck?

Fast-forward seventeen more years to our 2014 Christmas in Beijing—not atop an Asian elephant but rather with a view of the city from one of the Chinese capital's countless high-rise apartment buildings.

It was yet another original Christmas, this time with exotic animals at the Beijing Zoo and a Boxing Day stroll along the Great Wall as well as visits to Tiananmen Square, the Olympic site, and the Beijing Temple of Confucius.

On the culinary side of things, Peking duck was a welcome substitute for the traditional Christmas turkey dinner. On the artistic side, *The Nutcracker* ballet was replaced by a kung fu performance unlike anything we had ever seen. In terms of transportation, we swapped a road trip down the 401 for 320 kph bullet train rides to Luoyang and Xi'an.

Perfect.

Norman flanked by his wife, Christine; daughter, Émilie; and youngest son, Alexandre at the Great Wall of China (Boxing Day 2014)

As our visit drew to an end, we enjoyed the New Year at Émilie's apartment in Luoyang and a Skype call to Ottawa with Samuel, who had to work during the holidays.

And that was it. After the party was over and everyone had turned in, I sat alone in the dark.

Not so perfect.

The Christmas Blues

I'm not saying I didn't miss those Christmas lights.

There was no Christmas tree in Luoyang, and the serenity of Christmas was replaced with worry and the uncertainty that came just a month after my diagnosis. Instead of Christmas lights, there was only the glow of the 1.3 megapixels on my computer screen, with my Internet browsing history chock-a-block with sites about ALS. At that moment, it seemed that nothing remained of the boy with chocolate-brown hair who found serenity in front of a fake fir garlanded with tinsel and glowing with multi-coloured Christmas lights. I was far away in terms of geography, years, and especially peace of mind.

Here and now, I reminded myself.

Nonetheless, there I sat in the dark at 1:30 a.m. in front of my laptop, reflecting on my sad, new take on this annual passage to a new calendar year.

Tick-tock. I could pretend I didn't hear it, but it was still there.

For some time I had attributed the aches, pain, and stiffness to some minor injury, and I'd explain away my symptoms. *Maybe I'd overdone it. Maybe I stretched something. Maybe it's my sciatica or those herniated discs. This is probably just what fifty feels like. Fifty-one feels infinitely worse....*

But now I knew the cause. Unfortunately, those aches were the bell that tolled for me, under the banner of those three fateful letters that accompanied me wherever I went.

I popped an over-the-counter sleeping pill I usually reserved for the first couple of days of getting over jet lag. This time they weren't for jet lag; they were for blocking out that nasty ticking sound.

Tick-tock.

How long was I prepared to toss and turn?

I folded my laptop and slid it back into my bag as if I were filing my worries in digital format.

Fast-forward to my second Christmas after diagnosis, December 2015.

A year later, just before Christmas, the holiday blues were momentarily back.

Despite the season, my optimism once again momentarily lost ground to the sense that I had been kicked while I was down. I thought I was going to take part in a clinical trial of a new drug, masitinib, to fight ALS. In its place, the screening for the test revealed further complications, latent tuberculosis, resulting in a prescription for yet another medication to deal with yet another medical issue. So I felt like I was going backward instead of forward.

I wished I were dreaming of sugar plums and Saint Nick, but as the holidays began, Christmas couldn't quell the noise in my head. Although the disease had been progressing relatively slowly, there had been a constant stream of challenges and a need to constantly plan for the next stage. It was like retirement planning, but instead of Freedom 55, it was Thralldom 55. Christine and I had spent the first part of the fall meeting with contractors and city officials to plan the adaptations to our house. This turned out to be more complicated than we expected, so we spent the latter part of the autumn considering our plan B: exploring the real estate market and visiting condominiums.

It would have been easier if I could have just gone back to my youth when Christmas solved everything and even temporarily cured me of my fear of the dark. But I couldn't. Instead, I reminded myself of the big picture and all the positive aspects of my first year living with ALS. That year, I had met a lot of people living with this merciless ailment, and I must admit that I had been relatively fortunate. At the ALS Society Christmas brunch, I met so many others facing bigger challenges, including people diagnosed after I was who were unable to walk and could scarcely talk or move their arms.

The Meaning of Christmas

Maybe the blues are par for the course. In fact, maybe Christmas is all about fighting the blues. After all, despite its Christian significance in the Western world today, it's a festival that evolved from the celebration of the winter solstice. It's about overcoming depression by getting together and finding warmth and light at a time when these two critical elements are in shortest supply. It's about the hope that the days are now getting longer and that we can make it through the winter together. This is the time of the year in countries with harsh winters when we tend to isolate ourselves, to withdraw and to retreat into the darkness. Long before Christmas had grown into the favourite Christian festival of all, it was already about openness and warmth.

It's also a time to share and to remember that, although Christmas brings joy to many, others are alone with their troubles. Just as hardship seems to accentuate beauty and love, a holiday based on family and friends can also make loneliness and isolation all the more painful. Sometimes when the holiday season coincides with illness, death, or adversity, the holidays can be a sad reminder of what we've lost.

So it's a time to think of all the people here and around the world who are facing hardship and isolation: the homeless facing the winter chill, the survivors of human trafficking, the farmer in Sub-Saharan Africa or the Andes facing the consequences of global warming, and the mother trying to make ends meet in a consumerist world that bombards us with the message that Christmas is about gifts and that *stuff* will make us happy.

Just to be clear, I'm not thinking of that godawful Bob Geldolf tune "Do They Know It's Christmas?" Apart from its patronizing "save the world" neocolonialist tone, that ridiculous song isn't about any Africa I know, since it's an Africa where it doesn't snow, where "no rain nor rivers flow," and where the people don't know it's Christmas. Yet, it *does* snow in parts of Africa, there *are* plenty of rivers and lush landscapes, and Christianity *is* one of the leading religions on the continent, with an estimated 380 million African Christians. *So I'm pretty sure they know more about Christmas than Bob Geldolf knows about Africa!*

End of rant. Back to Christmas.

Perfect Moments, Perfect Memories

As I sat in my living room writing this piece, there were three visible sources of light. One was the glow of my computer screen, another was the flame in the fireplace, and the third was the subtle golden glimmer of the Christmas tree at the bottom of a winding staircase.

I exhaled a shuddering sigh, put away my computer, and sat for a moment in front of that tree. Unlike the tree than enraptured me as a child, this one was real, and the lights were more discreet golden LED lights. There was neither tinsel nor garland on this tree, as we had opted instead for a more natural look.

The scent of the tree intermingled with the delicate scent of the wood fire. I looked at the decorations one by one. There was a miniature Christmas stocking for each of my children as well as ornaments marking each of their births. There were decorations I'd inherited from my mother, of that same tree that had inspired the yuletide serenity of my youth, as well as decorations from all the places we had lived and travelled, ranging from a hot-air balloon from Gatineau to miniature people in traditional garb from India and Nepal. At the base of the tree was a nativity scene from the Andes, with María and José in typical Bolivia apparel and with Baby Jesus flanked by a llama and a sheep as well as three barefoot wise men sporting a poncho and a chullo (a hat with ear flaps) and bearing gifts: a lamb, potatoes, and a horn in the shape of a snail. This tree meant so much more than tradition or aesthetics. It was like a photo album; it was a portrait spanning a quarter of a century of our life as a family.

I then recalled my mother's fingers stroking my hair and the twinkle in her eye as she winked and headed back to the kitchen to prepare my favourite treats for the holiday season. And with that memory, at that perfect moment, I was overwhelmed by everything I had received and continue to receive. I don't believe in Santa Claus, and, frankly, most of what I've read in the Bible seems hardly more credible. Yet the days *were* getting longer, and I could still appreciate the beauty of the snow even if ALS had rendered me hypersensitive to the cold.

Sure, there was still a part of me that longed for the facile serenity of the young boy sitting in front the tree, dreaming of Santa and his reindeer, but there was no going back, no way to unlearn what I'd learned. There was no way to *un*smell the dead bodies along the road after Typhoon Haiyan or to *un*meet the two young women dying of tuberculosis and AIDS after a harsh life during which childhood was replaced by sexual slavery. Nor could I *un*-witness the resilience of the survivors of that typhoon or of the brave women who overcame worse abuse than you or I could even imagine and who now lead the battle against human trafficking. So, although I'd borne witness to suffering and tragedy, I'd also met real-life heroes, and my childhood naiveté had been replaced by awareness.

Awareness doesn't preclude serenity. On the contrary, it can (and should) increase our appreciation for the peace and joy of the season. I have accumulated so many more memories than that boy, and that boy is still part of me, seeing the beauty in the Christmas tree. Yet now I focus on the moments and the memories rather than the myth and the magic, and that's why our tree is now so much more meaningful. In a world of imperfection, that tree is a reminder of so many perfect moments, of a life well lived, and of a life worth continuing. And that too is a perfect Christmas and a beautiful life, even with ALS.

Chapter 11

Self-Image:
The Superhero Who Fell Off His Horse

Few see the real you; few see the real me. They come to their own conclusions of who we are by observing the way we speak, the way we move. So what happens when my voice fades, my muscles melt away, and my belly protrudes? It feels like Lou Gehrig's disease is taking away all that defines me. Piece by piece.

This is the story of a superhero who fell off his horse. Well, actually, he wasn't a real superhero, and he didn't even own a horse—nor did he literally fall off a horse. Okay, it's more of a metaphor....

Our story starts with three examples of dealing with perceptions about ourselves, including the story of our "superhero," a father of three—a playful, adventurous child of the sixties—who was believed to have mastered every language on the face of the earth. He criss-crossed the world, carried his children through dust storms and across rickety bridges over deep canyons, and guided them safely through a world of turmoil and social unrest.

Norman beside his daughter, Émilie, on the road to
Kagbeni in Lower Mustang, Nepal (2000)
Photo by Marie-Christine Tremblay

But wait. He certainly doesn't speak all the languages known to humankind. If fact, that same "hero" has been perceived as a halfwit whose delayed reactions appear to indicate that he isn't that bright after all. I'll also tell you how our supposed superhero was also possibly the worst best man ever.

You'll understand that this character has been misunderstood and embarrassed before, but he still wondered if he was ready to face new perceptions of him as he faced the greatest challenge of his life. This is the story about the fear of being misperceived as we lose the physical capacities we rely on as the external expression of who we are.

Perceptions and Misperceptions

It was 2002, and we had already been in Thailand for several weeks. Samuel was turning twelve, Émilie was nine, and Alex was turning eight. As I organized our trip to take us south of Bangkok to Hua Hin, the porter turned to the hotel supervisor to make a comment, and the latter responded in Thai.

Curious as always, Samuel prodded, "What did he say? What did he say?"

"I don't know," I responded. Sure, I had learned basic greetings and formal niceties, but I didn't speak Thai by any stretch of the imagination. But Samuel wasn't buying it.

He turned to his siblings. "He knows. He just doesn't want to tell us."

I tried to explain that I didn't understand, but Samuel would have nothing of the sort. That's when I realized they thought I spoke virtually every language on earth. I guess it's understandable. I spoke the language everywhere we went. In Canada, I spoke both English and French, and when we arrived in Nepal and India, I could already speak the language. Never mind that I was simply asking directions, only developed more complex language skills over time, and never learned to speak as well as I'd hoped. For them, I spoke the language. I could even follow some of the local hill dialects. And when we arrived at Costa Brava on vacation, I could already speak Spanish. So how believable was it that I couldn't speak Thai? According to my twelve-year-old son, *not very*.

Having lived in different countries, and massacred numerous beautiful languages, I also faced the challenges of integrating into the local culture. Like I wrote in Chapter 3 – Nepal and the Art of Letting Go, I had to learn the basics, including how to communicate, the impact of the changing seasons, and the rules of etiquette. My status and how others perceived me was radically different from what I was used to. I may have prided myself in being articulate and witty, but in a totally new cultural context, I was sometimes perceived as the exact opposite: as someone with a strange accent who sometimes said things that provoked mockery.

In 1997, when I was in a village near Pokhara, taking language lessons in Nepali, an adolescent member of my host family called me a "tube light." He was referring to fluorescent lights that flicker for a good twenty seconds when you turn them on. For him, the foreigner who, after a few short weeks of language training, took longer to express his ideas and to understand his jokes in Nepali was slow like a tube light.

Although cross-cultural contexts may be to blame for some of the negative perceptions, on April 17, 1993, I had no one to blame but myself for it.

It started innocently enough at a hair salon with the groom (my brother, Brian), the best man (me), and a couple of childhood friends. I could try to blame it on Brian. He had the brilliant idea of gifting us all beautiful monogrammed flasks to mark the occasion. And what was the deal with the haircut anyway, what, with Brian having so little of it?

Those flasks full of whisky played an important role that day. They just encouraged us to toast this, that, and the next thing. "To Brian…." "To the end of freedom…." "To old friends…." "To the bride, the one woman on the face of the earth who actually wants to sleep with my brother…!" And so on. You can see where this is going, and it's not pretty.

The toasting having started shortly before noon, and the flasks having been refilled more than once, we were well lubricated by the time of the wedding at 4:00 p.m. And rather than opting for coffee between the church and the reception dinner, we maintained our unhealthy pace of consumption. It was a recipe for disaster, and when it came time for the best man's speech, what started off just fine ended up as the absolutely worst wedding speech ever. It was because of one minor detail: one innocent slip-up by the best man with a flask in his pocket and the rich, malty scent of Johnnie Walker Black on his breath.

Like I said, the speech started off just fine. I said some really nice things about my brother, made a couple of jokes that generated hearty laughter, and even toasted the bride in Italian.

Yes, in Italian. Did I mention that we were at the Italian Canadian Club in Guelph and that the bride's family, comprising about seventy percent of those in attendance, were proud Italians? So my modest effort to toast the bride and groom ought to have been greatly appreciated by the bride's family…and would have had I not ended with the following words as everyone raised their glasses: "To Brian and Sandy!"

With that, the toast fell flat. Less than three metres in front of me, my buddy, Frank, motioned to cut it short. I didn't understand until I wrapped up my speech and sat down, only to be informed that I had toasted "Brian and Sandy." Brian's bride was Lucy; Sandy was his ex-girlfriend.

Here's the thing. I had been saying "Brian and Sandy" for years, until my brother met a girl named Lucy and soon proposed to her. Too soon, I guess, for a drunken best man to even realize the gaffe he had made. So in front of a room packed with Lucy's family, I had toasted the groom and his ex. And although the man videotaping—who just happened to be Sandy's father—later managed to edit out the best man's blunder, dozens of confused Italian Canadians demanded an explanation, and I just wanted to disappear.

Identity

So I have been perceived as a hero, a halfwit, and a phenomenally clumsy drunk who turned out to be possibly the worst best man ever.

But do these incidents define me?

First, perceptions are often deeply biased. Certainly, it's not unusual for young children to idolize their parents, and with my own children, this was likely accentuated by extraordinary circumstances. I took them to strange new lands, to countries most people couldn't even find on a map, and I always protected them. I flew them to fascinating new places, and I was always in control.

Christine would typically huddle with them to keep them busy while their father sorted out every detail. While we lived in countries amid civil war or in places facing general strikes, shortages, and violent confrontations, Papa was always there to save the day. Through evacuations and amid shoot-on-sight curfews, and even with trucks teeming with soldiers and police in riot gear barrelling down the street past machine guns surrounded by sandbags, my children didn't worry. Papa spoke every language and protected them from every danger. He was their personal superhero. Until they reached adolescence anyway. By then, I suddenly didn't know anything.

Second, some perceptions, whether positive or negative, are based on ignorance, so they don't reflect reality. Recently, one of my daughter's friends concluded that I was brilliant, and he did so without even meeting me. Émilie had told him that her father had ALS—"You know, Lou Gehrig's disease, like Stephen Hawking." Her friend knew of Stephen Hawking, the genius scientist and author of *A Brief History of Time*, and he was genuinely impressed: "Your dad must be really smart!"

Third, whether or not unnecessary haircuts and flasks full of whisky had a role to play in it all, one single incident does not define me. Nonetheless, it does underscore that misperceptions and embarrassments have been part of my life, and this will likely continue or even increase in the future.

What *does* define identity, especially in a context of rapid change? The *Oxford English Dictionary* defines *self-identity* as "the recognition of one's potential and qualities as an individual, especially in relation to social context." One of the toughest questions to answer is probably this: "Who am I?" Am I the director of a foundation? If so, what happens when I can no longer work? If the fatigue and the mobility challenges have grown, making work impossible? Then I would no longer be the director of a foundation.

I used to be that guy who rode to work on his bike. I was the guy to keep up with on two wheels. I was the slim, fit fifty-year-old guy acting like he was twenty-nine. By 2016, I was the fifty-two-year-old who walked with a cane, who needed a hand to get downstairs, who took more time than everyone else to get ready in the morning, and who laboured to get in and out of a cab. As I followed the recommendation to put on weight, I mourned the loss of my slimmer, fitter self.

I was also a proud homeowner. In November 2015, city workers put up signs for a reserved disabled parking spot in front of my house. As we planned the wheelchair lift, the elevator inside, and the ramp in the back, I couldn't escape the feeling that I was undoing what I worked so hard to build up. I was scarring my house, transforming it from that charming postwar home that we had bought and renovated to an unsightly adapted residence.

Tell Me About Yourself

In the 2003 comedy *Anger Management*,[2] Dr. Rydell, played by Jack Nicholson, asks the meek, indecisive Dave Buznik, played by Adam Sandler, to introduce himself in his group therapy session.

"So, Dave, tell us about yourself. Who are you?" asks the eccentric therapist.

Dave responds by telling him about his job, to which Dr. Rydell objects: "I don't want you to tell us what you do. I want you to tell us who you are."

Dave takes another stab at answering this seemingly straightforward question. "I'm a pretty good guy," he explains. "I like playing tennis on occasion."

But the good doctor interrupts him once again. "Also, not your hobbies, Dave, just simple: Tell us who you are."

Dave is flustered but gives it one last try. "I'm a nice, easygoing man. I might be a little bit indecisive at times... ." He fails yet again.

"Dave," explains Jack Nicholson's character, "you're describing your personality. I just want to know...who you are."

Dave never does manage to answer that question, at least not in group therapy, but the question is a tough one.

The challenge that Dave faces is one we all face. Can

---

[2] Excerpt from the movie used with the permission of *Anger Management* © 2003 Revolution Studios Distribution Company, LLC. All Rights Reserved. Courtesy of Sony Pictures Entertainment.

we define ourselves without reference to our possessions, our appearance, our career, or our status? And what happens when these factors change?

Beyond the Clutter

If identity is the recognition of personal potential and qualities, perceptions certainly play a role, but we can find a true sense of self in the constants throughout time. These are the personal aspects that remain the same no matter what, despite time, location, seasons, or circumstances. No matter how my environment changes, no matter how others perceive me, whether or not at any precise moment I appeared to be a blockhead, a brainbox, or a blundering boozer, I will continue to be the same person inside.

The challenge of perceptions had increased as ALS took its course. Already, regardless of how I perceived myself, the ungainly gait of the man with the cane and an ankle brace contradicted the tale of the carefree, dynamic adventurer.

In 2014, I was the energetic neighbour on two wheels, sporting a bicycle helmet with built-in visor, cycling pants, and cycling shoes, pedalling to work through the urban jungle and taking the challenging route up Mount Royal on the way home. I was dynamic and jet set and was frequently seen unloading wood, drywall, and other building materials or working outside trimming the hedge or pruning the cherry tree in the front yard.

More than a year later, that active, athletic neighbour had become the disabled neighbour. This less fit version of me now carefully made his way to his car parked in a space reserved for the handicapped, having abandoned two wheels in favour of four. My wife became the one who unloaded the groceries, shovelled the snow, and trimmed the hedge. I no longer renovated. The one who used to help others became the one who needed help. I used to glide almost effortlessly over generous stretches of pavement until my legs grew heavy, but such graceful movement became a thing of the past.

The challenge of changing identity is not unique to ALS. It's something we all face. We all eventually get older and slowly lose our autonomy. We can all ask ourselves these questions. Can we define ourselves without reference to our possessions, our appearance, our career, our status? Can we focus on where we're headed, on the dynamic self, even on a daily basis? If we lose our possessions, our job, our status, our looks—all the external features that define us—who are we?

Life is about constant change, with challenge after challenge. Perhaps it's the predictability and the plans we make that are the illusion. In his song "Beautiful Boy (Darling Boy)," John Lennon sings, "Life is what happens to you while you're busy making other plans."[3] Adaptation, although exceptionally concentrated when dealing with ALS, is part of the human condition. This includes adapting to married life, to a new school, to a new job, to a new home, to the inevitable process of ageing, to the role as parent, to losses of all sorts, and to becoming an empty nester.

We can experience these changes at various times during our lifetime. The key to determining who I am—and

---

[3] While people tend to credit this wonderful quotation to John Lennon, who wrote this into a song that was released in 1980, various sources claim that this can be traced back to the fifties in Ireland.

please excuse my Buddhist proclivity—is to focus on the journey and not the destination. In other words, where have I come from and what do I become now?

What defines us is what we carry over despite exterior transformations. I may no longer be able to bike to work, I may continue to grow physically weaker, and I may gain inches around my waist, but can I stay dynamic and youthful in my own ways? Even as my ability to speak fades and my voice fatigues, can my inner voice not find volume and resonate in other ways? If I'm the observer, the dreamer, and the one who's in awe of the simple things in daily life, why should I not remain that person?

A lot is changing on the outside, and that will inevitably influence how I am perceived. Perhaps the day will come when people misconstrue my feeble exterior as a reflection of a feeble mind. *A tube light.* Or maybe some people will expect me to be as smart as Stephen Hawking.

I tell myself that, as my body fails, my mind will soar. As nerves die and muscles weaken, my greatest hope is that my voice will be heard and that I will continue to communicate and spread a little love and sunshine. Indeed, it should come as no surprise that this is what really counts for the guy who spent most of his life in international cooperation, learning to communicate with those around him.

We waste far too much time on what *doesn't* define us—all the clutter in life—so I hope that people can see past the outside stuff—job titles, disabilities, physical weaknesses, and all the other superficial things. I also hope for the strength to face these weaknesses and the misperceptions that come with ALS. Along the way, I might delight you with my wit, and at other times, I might flicker like a tube light. Most of all, I'll try not to drink too much at your wedding.

Chapter 12

Invisibility and the Desperate Search for a Connection

Nearly a year and a half after my diagnosis, against the backdrop of a typically Canadian "scandal" and after thoroughly enjoying *Demolition*, a movie about a grieving widower's effort to demolish his old life, I reflected on my ongoing struggles and especially my invisibility.

In the movie *Demolition*, a recently widowed man, played by Jake Gyllenhaal, writes to a vending company to complain that he did not receive his M&M's despite having deposited the exact amount of money required in the machine. He concludes with the following glib statement: "I found this upsetting, as I was very hungry and also my wife had died ten minutes earlier." Strangely enough, I could relate, as I directed—or misdirected—my own frustration and grief at a petty political squabble.

I imagine that all of those who face their worst news will feel moments of isolation and incomprehension. While politicians squabble and brawl like kids in a schoolyard and fashionable smartphone-toting urbanites cut in front of me as I struggle with a door, I feel annoyed and even bitter. Beyond the self-help recipes, though, we sometimes just have to find a way to voice our feelings, even if it's as desperate as calling the vending machine company to complain that your M&Ms got stuck in one of their machines.

Photo by Norman MacIsaac

Elbowgate

The third week of May 2016 in Canadian politics was dominated by a very Canadian scandal. It involved Liberal Prime Minister Justin Trudeau accidentally elbowing New Democrat MP Ruth Brosseau in the House of Commons and then apologizing unreservedly.

Let's point out the obvious. First, apparently many Canadian parliamentarians have never been to Asia and have never travelled on crowded public transportation, where they might be exposed to similar "scandals" on a regular basis. Second, when you see this kind of behaviour among children in a schoolyard, for example, you usually have equally strong words for all involved. My elementary school teachers would have said something like this: "I don't care who started it. You four were not polite to block little Gordie. He was just trying to be a good whip. And, Ruthie, I saw you moving into the scuffle, laughing, and moving even closer when Justin approached. It's always the same, isn't it? It's all fun and games until somebody gets elbowed in the chest!"

This would be followed by arguments that the good teacher would summarily shut down. "Tom, you're turning red. Go follow Stevie's example and sit quietly in the corner. And, Peter, stop exaggerating and sit down." And finally, "Justin, I accept your apology, but I don't want to see you on this side of the yard ever again! I didn't mind when you came to shake Rona's hand a couple of weeks ago, but this is not acceptable."

Now, let's point out the less obvious and apparently overlooked victims of Elbowgate. It was neither NDP leader Tom Muclair's blood pressure—although we were a tad worried—nor was it Brosseau's crocodile-tear-stained blouse. The real victims were the public, who had a right to be informed of important issues. The House of Commons was debating new legislation on physician-assisted dying (dying with dignity). Many of those concerned by this legislation had a degenerative disease called ALS.

In the end, the brouhaha on Parliament Hill may have favoured an outcome that advocacy groups such as Dying with Dignity Canada were hoping for, as they considered the proposed legislation too narrow and restrictive. Unfortunately, though, we didn't learn much about the actual legislation, as the media were focused on the drama and parliamentary games.

Why did this base media frenzy irk me so? Maybe it's because we're governed by children or because we appeal to the lowest common denominator instead of raise public awareness. Or maybe it's because I had a bad fall the day before. I injured my arm and my head and had a red, black, and blue nose that looked like I really did get elbowed by a 6'2" boxer.

Invisibility and the Cruellest Month

Looking back, it felt like T. S. Eliot was right: April *is* the cruellest month. And that was the reason I hadn't written since March.

First off, I participated in a clinical trial of an experimental drug for ALS. For the first few days, I felt like I was in a Marvel comic, on some powerful medication—a proxy for the original radioactive spider—developed by mad scientists who would turn me into Spider-Man. (A note for all you Marvel enthusiasts out there: I know that it was a radioactive spider and not a drug that turned Peter Parker into Spider-Man, so don't get your stretchy tights into a wad. Just go with me on this!) It made me feel light-headed, dizzy, nauseated, and exhausted. I could also feel the effects on my muscles and the reduced discomfort in my lower back. My overactive imagination pictured me breaking through, casting aside my eyeglasses, and climbing up walls and swinging between skyscrapers. (Hey, I did say my imagination was overactive.) In the end, though, the medication's downsides outnumbered the benefits, so I pulled out after two weeks of exhaustion and sleep deprivation.

Second, between the restless nights, the exhausting days, and the growing restrictions on my mobility, I often felt invisible. This shouldn't come as a surprise, though, since we're all invisible to most people most of the time. With a few notable exceptions—such as small towns, nosey neighbours, and your aunt who just has to comment on your weight every time she sees you—people just don't notice other people. It's not a superpower, nor is it generally positive.

Increasingly, people look at their smartphones more than they do at the people around them. Incidentally, they don't look at the sky much either. They don't take notice of the smell of spring. They see neither the giggling baby in the stroller nor the spirited pug on a leash, but they will "like" countless Facebook posts of dogs and babies shared by virtual friends who are also rushing around with their noses in their smartphones full of the images they could be experiencing in stunning reality right in front of them.

It should be no surprise that I was invisible to such a smartphone-toting urbanite in fashionable heels, a faux-fur collar, and a hat that sat at just the right angle upon her impeccably coiffed head. Her skin was dusted with chemicals to give her the same tone as every other well-heeled smartphone-toting urbanite hurrying to the next destination.

As the winter stubbornly clung to Montreal well into April, refusing to relent to spring, I struggled with the front door of the office building where I was on my way to my April chiropractic appointment. They should have replaced the door years ago, and the sidewalk outside was icy and slick. I transferred my cane to my weaker left hand so I could open the door with my right hand, and I positioned my right foot so I wouldn't slip and fall. I opened the door just wide enough to get through, but I knew it would close too quickly behind me, so when I saw someone approaching, I waited, hoping she would hold the door for me.

But she didn't. Rather, she saw a man holding a door, as men should for impeccably dressed women with places to go and people to meet. "Thank you," she pronounced between texts without even looking up from her tiny screen. She slipped through the doorway past a man who, unbeknownst to her, was hoping she might help him with the door on that inclement day.

Then there were all of those stairs.

I remember my Somali friend Sameer, who grew up on a hill-free landscape, telling me that the mountains in BC made him feel claustrophobic. Similarly, I now see stairs everywhere, and they're like mountains. At the conclusion of a high-level meeting in Ottawa on humanitarian aid, I looked down at the photo session happening with the rest of the group at the bottom of the stairs below. Beside me was another person with physical challenges, one of the representatives of Handicap International. Ironically, just before we emerged from the meeting for the impromptu photo session, the CEO of that very organization had raised the issue of "inclusion," highlighting the importance of ensuring that the humanitarian aid reached those with physical challenges. The minister and everybody in the room agreed emphatically with this assertion before overflowing down the stairs, leaving the disabled behind.

Guru Says: Fail Away

"I have not failed. I've just found ten thousand
ways that won't work."
—Thomas Edison

My inner guru quietly and rationally deconstructed and
put a positive spin on my cruel, cruel month of April. He
told me that last month's challenges were like April showers that bring May flowers. My inner guru urged me to
embrace the setbacks and master the alchemy of transforming "fails" into "wins."

My inner guru should write self-help books.

First, my inner guru re-evaluated the meeting and the
failed photo op. He first reminded me that it would be facile
and inaccurate to imply that the group was somehow hyp-
ocritical by talking about inclusion and then excluding two
of the people in that very meeting. The truth be told, I would
be hard-pressed to find a more considerate, caring, open-
minded group of people anywhere. Let's just call this a lesson learned, he sermonized. Social exclusion is built on
countless barriers whose combined impact is almost invisible to "the included." More important, it had been my
choice not to voice my constraints or make known my challenges, for fear of appearing to seek special treatment. Yet
it was up to me to raise awareness and propose solutions.

Having learned from my mistakes, and once I was off
the experimental meds, my next trip to Ottawa in May was
productive and incident-free, as I made colleagues, meeting organizers, and facilitators aware of my challenges. In
the end, I overcame barriers to my participation and was

overwhelmed by the care and support of those around me.

What about the woman on her smartphone? Again, my guru warned me about blaming someone else for my problems. Besides, I didn't face the same challenge on my next visit. When I returned to that same office building for my May appointment, I faced that stubborn old door again on the way out on yet another rainy day. This time, though, the woman exiting the building with me had no phone in hand and was eager to help. She opened both doors for me as I made my way through the exit. I looked at her and said a heartfelt thank you.

My inner guru also reminded me that my drug trial, however difficult, had taught me an important lesson. It was a sneak preview into a future in which I won't be able to manage on my own. In doing so, it underlined the urgency of better voicing my needs and concerns. It was a wake-up call inciting me to better manage my energy, cut my workload, and prepare for tougher days to come.

Sometimes, though, my inner guru is at a loss for words. I missed a step as I attempted to sit back into my chair at work and fell backward onto the heater, leaving the back of my head looking like it had been in a panini press. I also fell at the train station in Ottawa and during my last yoga class. The fatigue in my voice was an increasing challenge, as were the spasms in my diaphragm and decreased control over my emotions, known as emotional lability. On more than one occasion, my voice failed me during meetings, especially while under pressure and toward the end of each day.

Then, one April morning, I mistakenly took all the day's medication in one absent-minded gulp. I usually also took all of my vitamins that were in another pillbox, but I made a mistake that Saturday. Christine had just bought me a new pill dispenser that looked just like the dispenser for my vitamins except for the colour. With my eyes half closed and my brain half asleep, I grabbed the pill dispenser, opened the compartment for Saturday, and took all the pills at once. Unfortunately, it was too late before I realized I had just swallowed all the pills for the day, including four times the regular dose of muscle relaxants. I spent the rest of the morning spaced out with slightly slurred speech and lethargic limbs.

My inner guru encouraged me to go back to see my physiotherapist, my speech therapist, and my occupational therapist. He reminded me that there's a solution to each problem. So now I was more careful not to keep the whole day's supply of pills on my nightstand, and I made changes to avoid further falls.

Regardless, I fell again in May. I had the face of a boxer who was KO'd, and my head hurt.

Great talk, inner guru. Can you go get me a couple of Extra Strength Tylenols?

My Blog One Year After Starting

More than thirteen months before I wrote this chapter, on April 18, 2015, I clicked on the publish button of my first blog entry. I am from the Western world, so I naturally thought about the future, and in my plan, I told myself I would come to some conclusion after one year of blogging. Luckily, I didn't have a clear conclusion by May 2016.

If I were Jerome (which is a pseudonym), who was diagnosed just two weeks after I was, I would have had a dramatic conclusion to my blog. Jerome's ALS progressed rapidly—meaning Jerome's body degenerated dramatically—since his diagnosis. A year after diagnosis, he no longer worked. He no longer walked, nor was he able to feed or dress himself. He was tired all the time, and his wife was at wit's end.

While I continued to plan for the next step, Jerome slept in a hospital bed in his living room because he couldn't make it upstairs, and there was neither the time nor the money to find a solution.

He had no disability insurance, so he got by on his wife's salary and the anaemic disability benefits from his government-sponsored pension plan. To make ends meet, he contacted his insurance agent to take advantage of accelerated death benefits from his life insurance policy. His agent was happy to inform him that this would be possible but only if he could prove that his condition was terminal and that he had no more than two years left to live. Fortunately (and very unfortunately), his neurologist didn't hesitate to write the letter confirming that Jerome's prognosis was sufficiently grim for him to get the early benefits from his policy. I can't imagine how he felt when he received the written confirmation by his neurologist that he had no more than two years left to live.

Jerome's dire situation illustrated just how fortunate I was to not have such a clear-cut conclusion to share after more than a year of blogging. More than a year and more than fifty thousand words later, I was still able to type. That's not to say that ALS wasn't affecting me every day. There was no denying the degeneration, and I was constantly reminded of what lay ahead. I now had a manual wheelchair. In July, the contractor would install a wheelchair lift on the front of my house.

Shortly after my diagnosis, my former sister-in-law— I'll remind you that her name's Lucy, not Sandy—sent me a book titled *Eric Is Winning!!* by Eric Edney, a Californian who survived eighteen years with ALS. In his book, Eric discusses his strategy, which includes everything from changing his diet to having his dental fillings removed. I even followed some of his advice, including having my own fillings removed.

In fact, I've tried everything, and I've listened to my inner guru. Well, most of the time. I've sometimes just focused on the metaphorical M&Ms stuck in the machine. Instead of writing to the vending machine company, I wrote these lines for others to read. My hope is that you will read them and maybe can relate, because in the end, amid the chaos, the materialism, and the distractions, we need to keep it real and to connect with each other.

Chapter 13

See What Others Can't:
Leap into a Parallel World

Shortly after receiving my worst news, Christine and I sat down to write our bucket lists. A lot of our entries were identical, including an African safari and a trip to Italy. Although I have travelled all of my life, I've often failed to seize opportunities. For instance, we had been planning a trip to Italy for decades but never made it happen. We had planned a Kenyan safari before I was diagnosed, but we had to call it off because our son fell ill.

This was special. Bucket list travel has an unrivalled level of intensity and a heightened sense of carpe diem. And, for me, there was one unexpected discovery: Travelling with a disability is challenging, but it can also be more rewarding. It will open your eyes to a different perspective on the world—a world you hadn't seen before. Join me as I leap into a parallel world, where I saw invisible people and my new needs translated into the opportunity to see the best humankind has to offer.

It was the summer of 2016, and we embarked on yet another bucket list trip that took us to Kenya and then Italy.

A Wildebeest (gnu) dives into the Mara River in Kenya
(July 2016) *Photo by Norman MacIsaac*

First, allow me to pose this question: Why do we travel anymore? You can see remote locations through Google Maps and Google Earth, see the best images in documentaries filmed in stunning HD, and probably learn more than any tourist guide can ever tell you by reading online information at your leisure or watching YouTube videos for free.

Travel isn't about what we see or the photos and information we gather. It's about experience. It's about the unique feeling you get in places. It's about sounds and smells. It's about the way people talk. It's about that veal tortellini that melts in your mouth. The travel experience is about seeing things that catch your eye and that stimulate your imagination rather than the images that documentary filmmakers spoon-feed you, regardless of how amazing they are compared to yours.

In Kenya, when I first entered Masai Mara Natural Reserve, it wasn't a lion or a rhino that triggered something in me but a simple lone acacia tree that stood in defiance, punctuating the crisp line of the horizon where fields of grasslands met the pale blue sky. Umbrella thorn acacia trees are nature's parasols. They create oases of shade in the savannah. Yet the trunk of this one was gnarled. It was as though it had cowered under the blazing sun, leaning to the left before it resolutely spread its branches out to create a light-green canopy and cast its precious shade.

As I grabbed on tight while the van I was riding in dipped and rocked over this bumpy trail, that was my moment with that tree amid tall straw-coloured grass stroked by gentle winds. It was a moment that was mine alone.

The travel experience goes even deeper though. More than the animals I saw, the pasta I devoured, and the sights I visited, my travel experience plunged me into a reality and connected me with people as I would have never imagined before.

Given my new and growing mobility challenges, I faced obstacles and frustrations when visiting over rough terrain and cobblestones. But amid the challenge was a world few have ever entered, so bear with me as I take you along a pathway of determination over disheartenment into the bittersweet reality that you may only perceive if you dare take the time and make the effort to peer into our world. This is not a travel journal of my safari and my trip to Italy; it's about my inner journey and the world of reduced mobility.

❖

Christine was busy carrying the remaining pieces of luggage downstairs, and I stopped to sit down in front of the symbols of my new reality as one who was and still is determined to stay active. I stared at the new rollator/transport chair. A year ago, I didn't even know what a rollator or a transport chair was. Now I was the not-so-proud owner of a hybrid model that combined the two. A rollator is basically a walker with four wheels, and a transport chair is a lightweight wheelchair. This model, the Airgo Fusion, easily converts into a chair for use at airports, museums, or shopping centres, or whenever I'm confronted with long distances that surpass my abilities. A flip and a couple of switches and, voilà, this rollator becomes a chair that my caregiver can push. This new purchase would serve as my travelling wheelchair on this trip.

I used to be the one to carry the suitcases up and down the stairs. No more. There I sat at the bottom, damning the finely designed equipment that screamed out to me and everyone else the extent of my mobility challenges. It used to be just a cane.

I then started using one Canadian crutch (two in icy conditions—with five-pronged ice grips). I gradually learned to use the wheelchair service at airports. I then finally procured my own wheelchair. For nearly a year, I resisted the recommendation of my physiotherapist and occupational therapist to use a rollator, or wheeled walker. I refused to even try one. I must have appeared stubborn to my occupational therapist, but it wasn't stubbornness. It was fear and pride with a healthy dose of sadness and regret.

In the end, though, the multiple falls and the scar on my nose proved me wrong. So, as I planned a trip that included obstacles ranging from uneven, unpaved terrain in parts of Africa to cobblestones in Europe, I finally gave in and purchased a rollator/transport chair. As necessary as all of these mobility aids were, they represented my inevitable decline into a world of limitations. The Canadian crutches were the first adjustment after the cane, but the rollator was the hardest. One might think that the wheelchair would be the biggest hurdle, but, for me, the wheeled walker was the ultimate symbol of advanced old age, used by decrepit old souls as they hunched over and moved so painfully slow that you wished someone would just put them in a wheelchair.

At the young age of fifty-two, I exhaled a breath of total disheartenment in the face of these new mobility aids on which I was growing increasingly dependent. I should have been grateful that I could still travel, still work—albeit at an increasingly slower pace—and still walk short distances with some support. I should have been rejoicing that my breathing was not yet affected and that my voice, that had weakened considerably in June, was actually doing slightly better. But I wasn't.

I instead felt like I was sinking—sinking into a new reality that I silently scorned. *This was not the way I travelled*, I told myself. I was an adventurer. I was spontaneous. I walked swiftly through airports and strolled through new cities with my head held high, admiring the sights, the sounds, and the architecture. But no more. I now had to plan and search for accessible routes. I travelled with mobility aids. It took great concentration for me to walk, so I couldn't look around like I used to. I instead had to focus on navigating sidewalks and carefully making my way down from the curb and back up again on the other side.

I had been forced into this new reality by an ailment that appeared out of nowhere, with no rhyme or reason, and I damned those innovative mobility aids as the guardians of my new reality. I wanted to break them into a million pieces, cancel my trip, and curl up into a ball. I felt cornered, stuck between the rational desire to go ahead with my trip and the resentment and despair over everything I had lost.

Something Gnu

Wildebeest (gnu) dash toward the river (July 2016)

Photo by Marie-Christine Tremblay

A week later, across the Atlantic and just south of the equator, my attention shifted outward to nature's spectacle. Around me, a growing number of gnu (pronounced the same as *new*), or wildebeest, amassed before my eyes, moaning nervously in anticipation of their upcoming challenge.

Hundreds of wildebeest had gathered next to the river while thousands more formed lines, rushing toward the river from multiple directions in the vicinity. Eventually, a couple of the beasts ventured down the dusty path toward the river and then returned, ostensibly having determined that the crossing was too treacherous. Either they had found the path down too steep or they feared the presence of predators nearby—lions, leopards, or hyenas positioned along the riverbank, or crocodiles in the water, lurking patiently in anticipation of an upcoming feast.

The wildebeest kicked up the sand as they returned fearfully from the riverbank, sending a cloud of dust into the air. As the size of the herd grew and increasing numbers congregated near the river, the pressure to cross became palpable.

If you don't know what a wildebeest looks like—and in this case, in the Masai Mara region of southern Kenya, I am referring to the migratory blue wildebeest—it looks like a strange mythical creature a child could have drawn. Technically, it's an antelope, but it looks a lot like a nervous cow with smaller hindquarters compared to their forequarters, a long black face with short horns, a white beard, and the mane and tail of a horse.

They moaned and bleated as the herd swelled near the river. Then a few zebra joined in and headed bravely down the riverbank. We watched this and hoped the wildebeest would follow, but we knew that sometimes they don't cross at all, opting instead to return to grazing. Eventually, though, pressure would grow, as nearly all the grass nearby had been eaten or trampled. They would leave the landscape looking like it was the scene of an epic outdoor rock concert, minus the litter that humans normally leave behind. Fortunately for the Serengeti and the Masai Mara, all the wildebeest leave behind is well-distributed organic fertilizer that will help prepare the land for the next season of the wildebeests' favourite grass.

Mostly, though, this build-up culminates in a massive frenetic crossing, triggered by just a few trailblazing wildebeest, or perhaps by following proactive zebras, who dare take the leap. Since the riverbank is often quite steep and the herd pushes from behind relentlessly, those descending to the river have no choice but to take the plunge.

Finally it happened. As the numbers increased, the wildebeest careered off the embankment into the river below. It was as if the higher and longer the wildebeest jumped into the river, the farther and higher those that followed sprang. The resulting event was of Olympic grandeur, with thousands of five-foot-tall animals weighing up to 270 kilograms hurtling into the river, rustling across, and struggling to make it back up the other side.

This was all part of the annual great migration of the Serengeti and Masai Mara, a natural phenomenon that a panel of six judges in *USA Today* voted as one of the "New Seven Wonders."[4] What impressed me were the group dynamics that could bring a herd of fearful moaning ungulates to leap into crocodile-infested waters, while hungry cats waited nearby, hoping to snatch their latest meal.

---

[4] "New Seven Wonders panel." *USA Today*. October 27, 2006. Retrieved July 31, 2010.

Crossing That River

The wildebeest (gnu) crossing the Mara River in Kenya (2016) *Photo by Norman MacIsaac.*

I sometimes felt like the wildebeest, compelled to make (or coerced into making) those dangerous crossings by the forces of nature. Acquiescing to multiple adaptations, overwhelmed by compound and overlapping challenges, I followed medical advice and gradually found myself living by the prescriptions written for me.

For some time, I found myself resisting the calls of occupational therapists and physiotherapists to do this or that or to prepare for the next inevitable phase. Yet, in the end, the forces of nature proved them right. After multiple falls, a minor concussion, and a lasting scar, I finally gave in and belatedly followed their advice. Despite my pigheadedness, I have been congratulated for my courage and my determination, but I often doubt my merit. I'm just like the wildebeest, I would say to myself, pressured into the inevitable cliff dive that looks brave but really isn't.

Perhaps I'm not giving the wildebeest the credit they deserve. They might appear doltish and damned to follow, but there might just be a method to their madness. For one, the migration has proven its effectiveness for thousands of years, and these so-called "blue wildebeest" are thriving. Second, the strong instinct to stick together protects them from predators, as if their DNA constantly reminds them that united they stand and divided they fall. Third, they somehow manage to communicate and are attentive to warning signs from other animals, such as baboons. Finally, while they might appear to be consummate followers, they can also be seen doubling back across the perilous river to retrieve their offspring that strayed among the frenzy. In short, these are certainly not the most intelligent creatures on the east African plains, but they are survivors that are too easily underestimated by human observers and predators alike.

So there's no shame in being a survivor like the wildebeest, I told myself. But there was more to it because this trip, this metaphorical river crossing, was neither an annual event imprinted in my DNA nor a case of simply doing what needed to be done. I didn't have to travel, just as I didn't have to continue finding ways to keep on working. I wasn't following the herd; I was defying it. I wasn't reacting; I was being proactive.

The very tools that I cursed became my allies in the struggle to overcome my new physical challenges. In the process, rather than staying home and moaning and bleating with the herd, I'd actually increased the challenges I would face. I wasn't travelling with the mainstream herd; rather, I was in another group entirely in the parallel world of mobility challenges.

Before December 2014, I knew nothing of this world. I didn't notice the army of wheelchair warriors pushing the elderly and the disabled through airports around the globe. I hadn't given much thought to how wheelchair-bound passengers got on the plane or down the narrow aisle to their seat. But then I became the one transported separately on and off the plane, often embarking first and deplaning last, taking elevators rather than escalators, and being transported by a special lift from the plane instead of taking the stairs.

With this world came challenges but also unique opportunities for interaction. Christine spent hours researching and planning how to overcome these obstacles, and every day this was combined with countless unexpected hurdles. Together, we defied the limits of what I was supposed to be able to do, knowing full well we would be frequently frustrated but also often equally surprised by the heartwarming acts of kindness along the way.

For instance, I shouldn't have been surprised when a taxi driver in Rome dropped us off—a fifty-four-year-old petite blonde and her physically challenged partner—at a place where a flight of stairs separated us from the Coliseum. By the time we realized this, the taxi was long gone, and we found ourselves staring down at a formidable adversary. Built from centuries-old stones, these stairs were steep, uneven, and narrow, and there was no handrail to hold onto for the last few metres. At this point, we froze like two wildebeest confronted by the steep riverbank leading to crocodile-infested waters. I looked at Christine and then at the stairs, and then I contemplated going back up and around. As we assessed our predicament, a swarm of tourists made their way around us.

It was as though time had stopped and the world was passing us by until a sturdy gentleman appeared and offered to help. His muscular arms were the size of my calves, and his footing was sure. In a soothing voice, he told me to take all the time I needed. My left leg quivered and hesitated as I negotiated each step, but his arm was steady. Propped up by Christine on one hand and this stranger on the other, I made my way downstairs slowly while he coached me on.

As I paused between challenging steps, he told me how he had struggled to walk for three years after his accident. Then, as I resumed and conquered yet another step, he celebrated my victory over each one. "The stairs will not win," he told me. And he was right.

We experienced countless other moments like this one. At the Vatican Museums, we encountered unexpected steps as Christine wheeled me along. Having exerted considerable energy pushing me up to that point and struggling to find the accessible route, she once again just stopped. This time, the reaction was almost instantaneous as a quartet of Vatican visitors reached for the four corners of my transport chair and hoisted me to the next level, scarcely leaving us the time to thank them.

If you observe closely when you travel, you might notice wheelchair lifts, ramps, and other special equipment and services for the physically challenged at airports and museums. What you won't see is whether these services are efficient or even functional. During our trip in Italy, for instance, accessibility was imperfect, inconsistent, and unreliable. The infrastructure we saw was often window dressing, and either it didn't work or nobody knew how to operate it. With the information being either insufficient or imperfect, we were constantly asking questions and preparing for disappointment.

Unlike the wildebeest, humans have developed complex communication systems, technical innovations (i.e., tools, machines, and systems), and norms to overcome the obstacles of the mobility challenged. Yet, in the end, this is not where our humanity shines through. Technology and communication are undependable, and bureaucracy and apathy are often our foes. Despite our so-called superiority, we often end up relying on the same support systems that work in the animal kingdom because when technology and systems fail, all we have to fall back on are our fellow human beings.

Another challenge was my invisibility. At the Coliseum in Rome, a French tourist tripped over my crutches as he scrambled to find his way. As he fell, he was about to swear at the obstacle in his way when he realized it was a man with crutches and a leg brace just trying to remain standing. On several occasions, tourists admiring artwork—their eyes transfixed on the works of Raphael or Michelangelo—almost ended up in my lap as they collided with my transport chair.

At Castel Sant'Angelo, while Christine headed up the stairs to explore the parts of this medieval castle that were inaccessible to me, I sat and looked around. I took the time to enjoy the view of the Passetto di Borgo, an 800-metre walkway linking the Vatican to the castle. It was built by Pope Nicholas III in 1277 and even served as an escape route for popes on two occasions.

As crowds passed by, I looked at the fading frescoes on the ceiling and then at the people around me. Sitting in a wheelchair next to an elderly gentleman was a boy of about ten with his tongue slightly sticking out. Both he and the elderly man beside him looked tired and bored. I sat and observed. This was not the Italy in any guidebook, nor was this a scene that most others would even notice.

Christine took more time than I had expected, so I sat quietly observing harried tourists and enthusiastic travellers as they passed by. Few took notice of me unless my crutches impeded their path. Probably fewer took note of the boy in the wheelchair and the elderly gentleman.

After some time, Christine descended with a camera full of pictures of the sights she had seen, and we gradually made our way to the elevator. Waiting there was the boy in the wheelchair, the elderly man—who I now understood to be the boy's grandfather—and a woman who appeared to be the boy's mother. I explained that we needed to find a staff member with the key to the elevator, and Christine departed on a quest to find him. The boy looked at me as his mother put her camera back into her purse. "I'm also going to wait for my wife's pictures to see what's up there," I told him. His mother smiled in a way that said thank you with her eyes.

Christine and the attendant arrived to unlock the elevator, and the mother then looked at her son and said, "He also had to wait while his wife was visiting, and we'll also look at the photos together." The message was simple: He was not alone. Nobody else seemed to pay any heed to their situation, but we had met in that parallel universe unseen by all others, where we waited to see the pictures of the places beyond our reach.

When we travel, we see all sorts of things. On safari, we were constantly amazed by nature's spectacle all around us. In Italy, we stared in wonder at the ceiling of the Sistine Chapel and were enchanted by the exquisite landscapes of Tuscany. Christine and I took countless pictures, trying to find the angle and frame that represented our unique view and experience.

Beneath this level of observation, though, was a more profound travel experience where we gained new perspectives as well as a few precious moments where we truly connected with others. Mine was that moment with the unnamed boy in the wheelchair and his caregiver. His mother appreciated my comment of solidarity, and I appreciated her need to visit and experience things beyond the physical limitations of her son.

I understood her fatigue and her need to see areas of the castle that were inaccessible to her son because she oughtn't be limited by his constraints. She cherished those precious moments where she lived for herself despite her situation. For her, I'm sure my simple affirmation validated her time alone on the inaccessible level of the castle. For me, it made me reflect on the new club I had involuntarily joined: the club of the physically challenged. It was a beautiful, poignant moment. I connected with another human being who probably would have remained invisible to me had destiny not decided we would share certain challenges.

Despite countless obstacles and limitations, it was an

unforgettable July of new sights and cherished memories, but the one experience I had to share was a world unseen by most: the world of the physically challenged, their caregivers, their friends, and good Samaritans. I encourage you to make an effort to look for it and to seek opportunities to interact with those who live in it. The next time you take the stairs or tread effortlessly up one or two steps to enter your favourite shop or restaurant, ask yourself, "Where are those for whom this is an insurmountable barrier or those who cannot read these signs if they're not in braille?" Then extend this beyond physical limitations to understand those facing depression and other forms of mental illness, the homeless, or any other marginalized people. Let's call it a quest to understand and learn about invisible parallel worlds.

Norman walks along the Kenya coast north of Kilifi
with the aid of Canadian crutches (July 2016)
Photo by Nicholas Trent

Chapter 14

Reaching Out:

*Lessons from India for the
Election-Shocked US and Me*

The 2016 US presidential election and its aftermath dominated the media. You might expect I had bigger fish to fry, but no. I too was sucked into the vortex of this world-changing event. Yet I saw things from a different angle, and I drew parallels to my experiences while living in India as well as to the more recent challenges of living with ALS in Montreal. I explored the delicate balance between the need for empathy and solidarity with like-minded people and the benefits of putting yourself out there. We tend to gravitate naturally to the former but struggle to reach out. But both of these are important ingredients in the quest for the best of the worst news.

Norman's son Alex at the community kitchen of a
gurdwara, a Sikh temple, in India (2002)

Photo by Norman MacIsaac

When people ask me how I liked living in India, I tell
them that, for me, India is like Indian food. It's hot, spicy,
and not like anything you've ever experienced. It will
make you sweat; it might even make you ill. Regardless,
it will titillate you with sensations, sights, and smells you
could never even imagine without setting foot on the Indian subcontinent. It's a land of extremes and contrasts.
It's big. This country of more than 1.3 billion souls adds
close to the population of Canada every two or three years.

India is also a country of massive disparity between
several of the world's wealthiest tycoons, a burgeoning
middle class, and the largest number of poor marginalized
people of any country. It's also a multicultural country
with twenty-three official languages (including Hindi and
English), massive differences between urban and rural life,
and a generation gap that's widening as fast as the econ-

omy expands. It will always be a challenge to understand each other, but in this country of stark contrasts, where one person's India is vastly different from the next, it's particularly difficult to fully appreciate the distinctive reality of one's fellow citizens.

During a stay in Mumbai back in 2004, a Canadian colleague and I took a taxi from the hotel to the site of the World Social Forum. Mumbai is a city where luxury condominiums emerge from the slums, and the two coexist like a patchwork of social disparity. So, on that day, we found ourselves traversing the slums on our way to the meeting. As I usually do, I struck up a conversation with the cab driver. He had expressed a deep criticism of the event we were attending.

He wasn't against the World Social Forum; he just didn't know why they chose India as the venue that year. "There is no poverty in India," he argued in Hindi as we drove between shantytowns and shifted left to avoid a family sitting in the middle of the road. There was a father in rags, a barefoot mother wearing a jute bag as a makeshift dress, and three naked children collecting plastic bottles and cardboard. But the taxi driver saw none of this.

It's difficult to connect with those who experience a completely different reality from us. On that scorching day in Mumbai, I was so fascinated by the extent of such denial that I didn't even challenge the taxi driver's perception of a poverty-free India.

Although these contrasts were particularly striking to me, especially as a foreigner, they are in no way unique to India. On the other side of the globe, on the Island of Montreal, I spent most of the autumn of 2016 in a battle with the city over my rights and needs as a person with mobility challenges. I'm fortunate to live in a country where my rights are guaranteed, as is my ability to vocalize those rights and appeal to elected officials. Nonetheless, there is also bureaucracy and the challenge of communication between people who experience very different realities, so even though I have the freedom to fight for my rights, fight I must.

It started off well enough in 2015, when, at the request of my occupational therapist, the city installed a reserved parking space in front of my house. Given that I have no private driveway to park my car, the city was called upon to make reasonable accommodations to ensure the right to accessibility. So they put up signs in the street so I would have a place to park in front of my residence.

Then, more than a year later, the city began new public works that would challenge my accessibility. In early September 2016, workers in hard hats and orange vests began painting lines and put up a speed bump sign on the same pole where the signs indicated the beginning of the reserved disabled parking space. Days later, they returned to remove the top layer of asphalt eleven feet wide right in the disabled parking space the city had installed for me the previous year.

I called the city at first, only to be told that they were indeed installing a speed bump right in the disabled parking space. I explained that this was problematic because a disabled parking space should be level and free of obstacles to ensure safe access and the ability to deploy a wheelchair ramp. I was summarily informed that my complaint was "not a priority."

And so began my battle with the City of Montreal.

I wrote two long letters to the city and engaged in countless calls, which explains why I didn't write much during that period, opting instead to devote my energy to contacting the councillor and mayor of my borough along with the city's director of public works and a plethora of other municipal decision-makers. I found myself torn between the lack of awareness of the city regarding the rights of the disabled and a deeper feeling that this was perhaps the proverbial straw that could break this camel's back.

Worst of all, it also forced me to project myself into the near future where I would be wheelchair-bound, and that was simply not something I wanted to keep addressing, especially with complete strangers. And isn't that where communication is most challenging? This psychological aspect of the whole incident simply wasn't something I could explain to the bureaucrats of the City of Montreal, but it was slowly grinding away at my peace of mind.

There are definitely limits to how much we, as flawed human beings, can take. On a personal level, nearly two years after my diagnosis with ALS, there were times when I just wanted to pull away and deny the physical side. Instead, my battle with the city was dragging me back to that harsh reality, and I resented it. Meanwhile, my diminishing physical autonomy forced me to choose between remaining ensconced in the comfort of my home turf or confronting my challenges, reaching out and facing the world.

The Divided States of America

"Ab ki Baar Trump Sarkaar."
("This time it will be a Trump government.")
—Donald Trump's message to American East
Indians (borrowing Indian PM Narendra Modi's
slogan and pronounced with the worst Hindi
accent ever)

As strange as it may seem, I saw a parallel with the US presidential election while our neighbours to the south experienced their own communication problems. Rather than reach out to each other, each side became even more entrenched in their respective perceptions of the challenges and solutions for the world's most powerful nation.

Democrats and their supporters commiserated over their unexpected defeat at the hands of such an unorthodox candidate fraught with scandal, the one Hillary Clinton said would be Putin's "puppet." They flooded the streets and social media, decrying that Trump was "Not My President." They vowed to struggle against and resist the Trump presidency. This was to be expected. They needed to fall back on their support network and channel their energy into this new struggle, but was this the best course of action to return to the America they envisaged? Did they also risk becoming entrenched in their own comfortable version of reality whereby the Trump movement had no legitimate basis and was nothing more than a "white-lash" of "uneducated bigots" described by Hillary Clinton as a "basket of deplorables"?

It had been a tough week. The "blues" were blue, and

the disappointment was visible on the faces of those who looked like 11/9 was on par with 9/11. Well, almost.

We could see how little Americans understood each other. Both sides spent most of the campaign pointing fingers rather than elucidating policy and vision. Democrats had an almost perverse obsession with Trump's failings, fabrications, and foibles, while rabid Republicans chanted vitriolic slogans condemning Hillary Clinton as the personification of the cesspool of corruption that is Washington D.C. It wasn't pretty, folks.

The post-election banter wasn't much better. Although both Trump and Clinton made conciliatory statements as Clinton conceded and Trump accepted, their followers demonstrated much less restraint. Meanwhile, nearly half the population had chosen apathy over the candidates, so Trump, the second most popular candidate, would become president, having garnered about a quarter of the support from potential voters, more than two million votes fewer than Clinton did.

After recovering from the initial shock, having vented about their fellow Americans who voted Trump into office, Democrats vowed to keep on fighting. Sadly, few dared to ask if they had missed something. The red-faced and the depressed hardly even stopped to ask why a quarter of the nation opted for "the least qualified person ever to be elected president." You would think they'd be curious to know why one in four Americans voted for this character.

It was a failure to communicate, a withdrawal into Democrats' comfortable notions and media sources. As we expected, the winners gloated while the losers raised their fists into the air. It would have been the same—or perhaps worse—had the complex Electoral College system generated a different outcome. Regardless of who won, though, I wondered: Shouldn't we be asking why these two groups perceive reality so differently? Democrats have hit the streets in protest. Will they also take the time to reflect on these deep divisions?

There's a significant part of the US population that is negatively affected by the downside of globalization and automation. This is masked by the figures and averages that Obama and Clinton have spouted as indicators of their success. Meanwhile, these people see others experiencing the benefits of a strong economy even while jobs leave their towns and the poverty gap widens. Strangely enough, there was a point where Bernie Sanders' criticisms and Trump's call to arms intersected. Although they were coming at it from very different angles, they both appealed to the marginalized people who wanted their jobs back, and they were looking for someone to blame. At the risk of oversimplifying things, we can say that Sanders blamed the oligarchy while Trump blamed D.C.

Divided, each camp stood alone, bitter and bewildered by the actions of their adversaries as they anxiously armed themselves for the next battle. The losers referred to it as the "Brexit effect," lamenting the ignorance of that subgroup. Yet there are trade agreements, such as the Trans-Pacific Partnership (TTP), that people don't understand, criticized by citizens at both ends of the political spectrum. Could it be that their feelings of powerlessness were warranted? Isn't it common sense to fear a 5,600-page agreement, knowing full well that the big print giveth and the small print taketh away? And in a world of growing disparity, is it not common sense to question whether the powers that be really work in favour of the people? And would it not then be logical to be sceptical of a candidate who calmly advocated staying the course?

After scrolling through countless post-election posts criticizing Trump, mocking his incompetence, asking how we explain to our children that sometimes bullies win, hoping for Trump to be imprisoned or impeached, and fretting over the impending implosion or nuclear holocaust, I finally found one article that looked critically at the subtle social exclusion of the working class. It was an article in the *Harvard Business Review* by Joan C. Williams entitled "**What So Many People Don't Get About the U.S. Working Class**," dated November 10, 2016. The article is too multifaceted to summarize here, but it points to the crisis of political polarization that precludes the understanding of the middle-class roots of the Trump phenomenon. The article resonated with me as someone who grew up in a North American industrial town, and it underscored the importance of reaching out beyond the safe spaces and familiar discourse of our respective political camps.

Let's be clear though. I'm not justifying Trump's victory, not by any stretch of the imagination! There was still a part of me that hoped to wake up from this nightmare. I was horrified by what I'd seen in video clips of Trump's rallies, by his despicable behaviour, his lack of respect for women, his bigotry, and his mockery of the disabled. Still, I couldn't help but feel that this nauseating election and the Divided States of America exemplified the human condition. We have trouble understanding those who think differently from us, so we find comfort within the confines of our own camp.

Shock and fear lead us to group together to find solace and comfort among the like-minded. But just as I must struggle to make my needs understood, Americans need to come out of their comfort zone and build bridges with those who think differently. It's probably going to hurt, but as Martin Luther King Jr. so eloquently stated, "Darkness cannot drive out darkness; only light can do that. Hate cannot drive out hate; only love can do that." In short, we have to open up to others if we are to overcome.

Social Isolation

Let's return to India.

There's an image that's stuck in my mind of the time I met two young women shortly before they passed away. In a shelter for survivors of human trafficking just sixty-five kilometres outside of Hyderabad, I met two girls in isolation who were dying of tuberculosis. Thinking back to my encounter with them, I only later realized how painfully alone they must have felt. I didn't think that at the time, but I finally understood what it was like to feel the world go on as I lived out my sentence.

At this shelter for the survivors of sexual slavery, everyone has a story. It goes without saying. This is an oasis for the survivors of the worst form of human rights abuse imaginable, and the majority of the staff there are survivors as well.

Some people there were rebuilding their lives. They had gone through all the painful phases and had suffered setbacks. I met women who had learned skills and obtained jobs. They were now welders, printers, woodworkers, managers, and security guards. Wow, I thought, security guards. These strong young women—whose society had failed to protect them in their youth—were now engaged in the business of ensuring security at schools in the vicinity. They wore their uniforms with pride. To me, they represented the survivors' indomitable spirits and hope for change.

Yet many don't make it. The countless casualties include those two nameless young women, their immune systems weakened by AIDS, who died of tuberculosis two weeks after my visit. Others, like Amina, who was hijacked off the road of normalcy at a young age, will live but will likely never return to anything resembling a "normal life." Kidnapped at the age of four and a half and repeatedly raped for six years, she will probably never manage to chase away her demons. She deserved to return to the age of four to finish her childhood in a safe environment and grow to be a beautiful woman, but it seemed that the best she could hope for was the protection of this shelter. Amina will never leave. She will probably be condemned to a life with the most severe form of PTSD I had ever seen.

I'll never really understand what these women have gone through or the battles they continue to fight. The local organization, **Prajwala,** will help them deal with their trauma, but few can even imagine their harsh reality.

We could hide behind superficial clichés and Internet memes inspired by a few choice words that wrap everything up into one neat formula for living better, but reality is much more complex. These women will find comfort among survivors, but they will also need to confront a world that blames them for their predicament and sees them as lowly individuals. Each one will find her own way as they alternate between bold sorties into a world that belittles them and comforting reunions with loved ones and fellow survivors.

A World of Wounded and Scarred

There's a myth that the wounded are few and that those facing health challenges are the exception. When I think of the millions enslaved in human trafficking or the masses of working Americans who feel cheated as they watch the one percent accumulate unprecedented levels of wealth, I'm reminded of those who face daunting challenges and, amid adversity, want nothing more than to retreat into a world of like-minded compatriots who share similar challenges and aspirations.

Lately, I have felt surrounded by people who are struggling. One friend put the last few months of his life on hold to fight cancer. He mostly slept when he wasn't in chemo or suffering the consequences after chemo. Another friend knows she's next in line to have breast cancer like her mother, a survivor from whom the doctors have been cutting away everything the cancer targets. She battles anxiety with a blog and serial Facebook posts on the subject. Others battle Crohn's disease, cardiac issues, or unemployment. All the while, I wonder when my carefree life morphed into an episode of *The Walking Dead*.

As I approached my third winter since my diagnosis, I increasingly found myself out of sync with the world around me. Everything took longer, from my morning routine to the walk to my car with my crutches or wheeled walker. I found myself at that difficult point where, given the growing weakness in my legs, my sore shoulder, and my tenuous balance, I would be safer and more mobile in a wheelchair.

As I left the Montreal Neurological Institute and Hospital on University Street, I found myself unable to walk with only my cane to my car, which was parked just ten metres down a gentle slope and across the potholed road. Like an old lady looking for a Boy Scout, I asked a stranger to lend me a hand so I could slowly make my way back to my car.

Then, two days later, while in Ottawa on business, I ordered room service at the hotel where I was staying. Only after I had signed the bill and the hotel employee was long gone did I realize that I faced the challenge of opening a tiny bottle of ketchup that I wanted to go with my home-cut French fries sprinkled with enticing sea salt. I struggled and managed to open that tiny bottle, but I paid the price. My hand hurt after that, and it regularly cramped for three straight days.

I could go on and on. Through these struggles, I felt the degeneration long before others noticed it, so I had a clearer idea of what was next than others might have imagined.

I faced not only my physical limitations but also a hollowing sense of vulnerability and an inability to absorb everything at once. There was an upside though. I had grown accustomed to asking for help, and this was more often than not a positive experience. So I could let my mobility challenges and feelings of vulnerability isolate me or I could focus on opportunities to connect with those around me.

The Rewards of Connecting

Despite all the challenges, when we do finally connect, it's a beautiful thing.

Amina would usually wander around in a semi-comatose state, unable to talk and struggling to stay focused, but then she'd smile so genuinely and so wide that she'd forget her demons for a few precious seconds, and those around her would also beam with joy. In such moments, smiles would fill up the entire room.

Likewise, in Mumbai in 2004, an organized visit of a public sanitation scheme in the slums could have been another run-of-the-mill visit. Instead, it turned out to be a unique experience of human interaction.

The visit started rather typically. The more than forty visitors descending from the air-conditioned bus were exposed only momentarily to the sweltering heat of the slums of Mumbai as they entered the newly constructed public sanitation facility. The organizers boasted that the project was an example of self-sustaining social services in action. I accompanied the French-speaking participants from West Africa and some colleagues from India with whom I worked daily far northeast of this metropolis in the nearly created state of Uttaranchal.

The participants inspected the facilities and asked probing questions such as, "Where are the women? I mean, there must be hundreds of thousands in this area, yet we haven't seen a single woman use these services." The organizers argued that it wasn't the busiest time of the day before adding that the facility was new and that a large-scale awareness campaign would soon convince women to pay to use the toilets and showers.

When the time came to get back on the bus, though, our West African friends looked thoroughly bored and urged me to stay back with them and translate for them as they visited "the real Mumbai slums." Since I too was unimpressed by the guided tour and the half-answers to our questions, I dropped the formal tour in favour of a stroll through the slums.

In the narrow alleyways, women and children came out to see the motley group of visitors, which included a slim South Indian with a limp, a bearded Canadian dressed in Indian attire, a young woman from the foothills of the Himalayas, a middle-aged Westerner with long blonde hair, and two Africans wearing traditional clothes and towering above the rest at 6'4".

This was the polar opposite of the traditional project visit. These foreigners had neither funding nor a set agenda—nor did they intend to "save" the people from their squalor. They wanted to listen, not give speeches. The local population was genuinely interested in meeting them. There was no list of questions or any prearranged itinerary.

The discussion emerged spontaneously. People retrieved chairs from their homes while children, giggling and whispering to each other, sat on tin rooftops to watch the curious scene. The people asked why we had come and where we were from. The locals offered us tea as I focused my energy to translate comments and questions from Hindi to French and vice versa.

They laughed out loud at the project providing pay toilets and showers. "No one goes there. We don't have money for such things."

They weren't blind to the hypocrisy of it all. "Why do

they make us pay to use the toilet," one woman asked, "while the rich use the facilities for free as they stroll through air-conditioned shopping malls in the wealthy areas of town? Do they think we don't know what happens in those areas? They keep us here like chickens. We can leave, but we are kept back with sprinklings of feed to peck at."

The conversation covered much more than the project, though, as the locals were anxious to know more about us and especially about the two lanky Africans who responded openly to all of their questions. When the discussion came to a close, they walked us to a nearby area and helped us find two taxis back to our hotel. It was a beautiful, unexpected moment of connecting people from around the globe in the most authentic of contexts, with the sole objective of learning more about people with vastly different backgrounds, cultures, languages, and experiences.

I remind myself of such moments, lest I forget the rewards of reaching out. During these times of political divisiveness and personal struggles, they serve as a reminder to strike a delicate balance. Sure, I sometimes needed to pull back because I have my own limitations. We sometimes need the comfort of those who share our struggles. However, entrenching ourselves in a familiar worldview isn't the answer.

We can choose to play it safe and minimize our excursions into a world that can frustrate and hurt us. We can isolate ourselves and minimize the chances of arduous confrontations and painful disappointments. Or we can remind ourselves that human connections can be far more rewarding than they are difficult. That's a lesson that applies around the globe, from India to the Americas, including the island metropolis I call home.

Chapter 15

Finding Your Zone:
Where the Barbs Shoal

My third year living with ALS was marked by a transition into a new perspective as I investigated the challenges of finding peace and happiness through new activities as my mobility declined.

Christine's "zone" where the barbs shoal
Photo by Marie-Christine Tremblay

"Self-conquest is far better than the conquest of others. Not even a god, an angel, Mara, or Brahma can turn into defeat the victory of a person who is self-subdued and ever restrained in conduct."
—The Dhammapada

Dreadful Dreams

In November 2016, after test-driving wheelchairs in anticipation of my new mode of transportation, I had my first nightmare on six wheels. I dreamed I was alone downtown in a motorized wheelchair, desperately looking for a door near Place Ville Marie, when the battery ran out, leaving me stranded in the dead of night. My subconscious reminded me that this was indeed a *big deal*, despite my stubborn rationalizations and attempts to relativize and banalize this new unwelcome stage of my life.

My disease had progressed. In anything less than ideal conditions, I could hardly make it from my doorstep to my car or from my car to my office with a walker. I planned my movements every day, made accommodations, and decided which risks to take and which to avoid.

By February 2017, I was in my wheelchair again, but it was no longer a dream. The temperature was relatively mild for this time of year in Montreal, and the streets and sidewalks were passable despite the ice and snow, so off I went. My heart was pounding. Every time I had ever walked down the main avenue near my house, it seemed I'd meet someone I knew. Would I now face someone who had never seen me in a motorized wheelchair? How would they react? What would I say?

I was so preoccupied with crossing paths with someone I knew that I wasn't worried enough about the ice and snow. Suddenly, a man in front of me—who was obviously under the influence—stumbled into the way of my chair. I veered to the right to avoid him, but my right front wheel got stuck on jagged ice and my centre-right wheel followed over what appeared to be snow on the sidewalk but was actually snow beyond the curb. I felt the 380-pound wheelchair, combined with my weight, sink quickly on one side, causing the chair to tilt and fall. I grabbed the left armrest, but my right arm was sandwiched between the falling chair and the road where I landed, injuring but not breaking it.

A week later, my right arm still ached. It would take most of the year to heal.

Back at home, I clutched the handrail with two hands as I tenuously made my way downstairs. I strained to focus on moving my left foot down to the next step. Then I repositioned my hands farther down as I moved my feet down, pointed at about a forty-five-degree angle, one careful movement at a time. I tried to imagine how guests to our house might have interpreted this. *Is he afraid or are his muscles too weak? Does it hurt?* Neither, nor, and no. As I descended from the last step, I held the edge of the railing until I was stabilized.

That evening, I began the process of preparing for bed, and I started by removing my shirt. I looked down and reached for the first button, concentrating as I did on the stairs. It sometimes seemed to take forever. I stood there struggling in slow motion to push the tiny plastic cylinders with four holes through each buttonhole on my shirt. This time, Christine arrived just in time to complete the task. Then I felt both relief and defeat.

Socks were the worst, but for that I had an ergonomic aid, the Sock Aid, an assistive device designed for the task. Before going to bed, Christine would place my socks over two plastic half-cylinders with two ropes at one end. I could then place my feet in the plastic under the socks and pull the ropes to bring the socks over my heels and part-way up my ankles.

After preparing my socks, Christine would go on to prepare my pills. Meanwhile, I would stop to rest after completing each stage of preparing for bed. It was as if I could no longer understand how others could do these tasks, perhaps in the same way you watch in awe as Olympians achieve feats that appear impossible—in defiance of all we have learned from personal experience about the limitations of the human body.

This was all like my nightmare again, but this time I was awake. I'd been awake since leaving my home, exiting the front door, and taking the wheelchair lift down to street level to head down my street and around the corner onto the main avenue. I was awake as the wheelchair tipped, as I made my way downstairs with both hands on the handrail, as I struggled to unbutton my shirt, and as I watched Christine put my socks on an assistive device in preparation for my morning routine.

I remembered having dreamed several times in my life that I couldn't move, that I was being chased, but my legs wouldn't react. Now, as I made my way around my familiar environment at home, I clutched furniture and countertops all the way. I walked with a cane on a familiar path.

I expected my feet, especially my left foot, not to obey, so I moved slowly and purposefully. I always planned where I could fall safely because falling now went with walking like eating goes with chewing.

The worst nightmares, I told myself, are those in which you aren't asleep.

Fortunately or unfortunately, depending on your perspective, the limited mobility creeps up on you. It's unfortunate because it would be better it didn't, but it's fortunate because I could adjust slowly. I was especially fortunate because I had more time to adjust than most people living with ALS do. I don't often think of my new life as the conscious enactment of earlier nightmares, but every once in a while, when I get that look from someone who sees me struggle, I get the feeling that I've been suppressing that very thought.

And it's worse than the nightmares I used to have, long before ALS entered my life, way back when I read *Tuesdays with Morrie* and thought of this disease as something that happened to other people, as a freakish rare illness that you only read about in sad stories. It's worse because all the scenes I experienced in my waking nightmares only confirmed the looming spectre of challenges to come, scenes that would undoubtedly exceeded my previous and present-day nightmares not only in terms of terror but also especially because they're real.

Distractions

Maybe the recent events in America were a convenient distraction. Christine and I both shared an obsession with the news feed, with the constant barrage of Trumperies south of the border. Yet while we sat in front of a 3.5-inch screen, time would slip dangerously between our fingers, and consuming this news gave us neither comfort nor a sense of accomplishment.

Arguably, I could turn off distractions, but I couldn't avoid the myriad decisions and adaptations imposed on me by such a tenacious disease. Since December 2, 2014, there'd been no shortage of information to process or decisions to make. By 2017, I was immersed in the long process of procuring an adapted van and the complex issue of converting a two-storey postwar house into a fully adapted residence to accommodate my growing needs. ALS is both relentless and unpredictable, and it seems that every decision is a question of probabilities and guesswork. This is made all the more complicated by alternating waves of optimism, disappointing setbacks, and an overarching aversion to being sucked into the vortex of contemplating the inevitable.

All of this is further complicated by the oft-overlooked reality that life goes on and so do our menial problems. Even the most overshadowing problem won't wipe away those everyday annoyances. In some cases, there will be even more.

The City of Montreal continued to challenge me. The city had granted my occupational therapist's request to put up signage in front of my house for reserved disabled parking. However, I was continually frustrated by cars without disabled parking permits taking my spot. Then, a few months later, the city installed an eleven-foot-wide speed bump in that same disabled parking spot. I eventually won that battle, though, and the city moved the parking signage away from the speed bump. Finally, after a January snowfall, while clearing snow on the other side of the street, snow removal crews dumped a large pile of ice and snow directly in the reserved parking spot.

This time, I tweeted, using the city's hashtag for snow removal status, tagging the borough, the city, and the local media. Just to be thorough, I tweeted in both official languages, tagging both French- and English-language media. The response to my tweets accompanied by photographic proof of the incident was quick, and soon a bright yellow tractor arrived to remove the snow. I posted a Facebook status concluding with a lesson learned about bureaucracy and social media: "When confronted with twits, tweet!"

What annoys me is that I was one of the few with the know-how, the experience, and enough energy left to fight city hall. I know that most people, especially those with as devastating a disease as ALS, just can't manage to put up a fight.

Amid these struggles, I externalized my frustration and disappointment. Then the woman with the aquariums—to whom I'll introduce you below—made me a hamburger (my go-to feel-good food), sat down with me to watch a good film, and erased that feeling that the cosmos were against me. The next day, I woke up to a new day with a fresh cup of coffee on my night table.

So I'll ask again. How can we find peace of mind in a world full of struggle and discord? How can we embrace conflict yet still find inner peace?

Let's recap the lessons I learned so far:

- Come to terms with waking nightmares.
- Take a break from the news and social media, but use them as a weapon in my battles.
- Marry an aquarium enthusiast who'll make me a hamburger and rub my feet (but not at the same time).

Now let's introduce the aquarium enthusiast and her shoaling barbs....

Delightful Shoaling Barbs

Her piercing blue eyes sparkled as she followed the movement in these thirty-three gallons of water. Tiny creases at the edges of her mouth and eyes etched over the years confirmed a propensity to smile rather than frown. Her beaming face reflected a tranquil inner peace as she basked in the simple beauty of the halcyon ecosystem she had crafted. The light from the aquarium added a soft glow to her fair skin surrounded by golden blonde hair that, contrary to her skin, concealed the truth of her advancing years.

Shoaling fish moved gracefully within the confines of their artificial environment like waves in the sea or flocks of birds in the sky. Her eyes followed the flow, then homed in on a specific species and particular social interactions that she observed with unremitting interest.

She monitored even the subtlest changes over time, as fish grew, the snails and other bottom feeders did their job of cleaning the algae off leaves, and another bamboo shrimp moulted, leaving behind a meal that would feed the rest for days to come. She learned about the behaviour of the different fishes, and she scanned the waters and every nook and cranny for the elusive Amano shrimp.

The orange-coloured albino barb was by far the most aggressive. It incessantly harassed the smaller yet more agile pink barb as he asserted his dominance within this 31" x 19" x 13" habitat.

When she heard me nearby, she summoned me to join her. She passionately explained how the black ruby barbs darken when agitated and when competing for food. Her whole body exuded enthusiasm as she reached for the fish food and sprinkled a bit on the water, generating a flurry of activity as the creatures scrambled to get their fair share. Then she sat back down to enjoy the spectacle. She explained to me that barbs don't have stomachs, which is why she has to feed them more often than those in her other aquariums.

Yes, you read that correctly. She had accumulated a total of four aquariums since I was diagnosed (including one just for sick fish, her hospital tank) in addition to a pond outside, which I explain below because it ended even more tragically than she had feared. But in this moment—in the *present*, which is the most important tense—she was calm and focused.

Her serenity in this moment would not have been possible without a lot of hard work. Yet as her gaze shifted from the horned snails perched upon broad-leafed plants to the bottom feeders moving from rocks and plants to the sand that she had gradually added over a three-week period, she felt a deep sense of satisfaction and pride in her achievement. Second-guessing the investment of time and energy took up no space in her consciousness. There was only the beauty of vibrantly coloured aquatic life and the familiar soothing sound of burbling and trickling. Mentally distanced from the everyday stresses and difficult decisions ahead of her, she was at peace.

Inner Battles

There are no easy answers. Even Christine's hobby had turned out to be a source of stress in September 2016. She had invested time, money, and labour into installing something she had always dreamed of having: a small pond in the backyard. Much to her chagrin, though, she didn't attain this source of inner peace, this temple of the beauty of life and nature, without frustration and setbacks.

After she had enjoyed a summer with her new pond, watching her fish and water lilies grow, nearby predators had finally attained their goal. Our neighbour had warned her about those masked mammals, but her fears had faded after a few months. Unfortunately, as though they had been waiting for the fish to grow plump enough, the raccoons attacked the pond one night as we slept. They tipped the filter pump, and it drew all the water out of the pond, allowing them to feast on the exposed all-you-can-eat sushi buffet for raccoons.

Upon discovering her empty pond the next morning, Christine was devastated. She had even bought a large used aquarium to house her pond fish during the cold winter. She had painstakingly scrubbed and cleaned it for hours only to discover that the pump was malfunctioning and had pumped water all over the floor. Only after she had invested hours in this winter residence for her fish did she discover that her aquatic friends concluded their lives as feed for opportunistic nocturnal omnivores.

Zootherapy is nice, but it's not without its trials and

tribulations. Likewise, I couldn't look at her orange fish bullying the smaller pink fish without imagining Trump. I was tempted to give all the fish names like Kellyanne, Keith, Elizabeth, Hillary, and Bernie, so I knew that aquariums couldn't offer me what they offered Christine.

I replaced my work, skating, and cycling, as my physical options for finding my flow became fewer and fewer. Skating had not been an option for years. I held onto cycling as long as I could in 2015. On two wheels, I would feel my body working from my lungs to my legs, like a well-oiled machine. The pavement under my wheels would feel like a movie reel. There's no gait on a bike, just rhythm and rolling. It's soothing, like music. After a long day's work, biking was almost a form of meditation. It cleared my head and replenished my battery after a long stressful day.

In the months following my diagnosis, I had adapted my bike, determined to revisit my zone as long as my body would allow. Then, after cycling had become impossible and my options dwindled, I opted for adapted yoga in my wheelchair.

I had lost a lot of friends to ALS. In the weeks and months before they passed, I had inevitably seen it on their faces. They had zoned out. So I remain determined to continue revisiting my zone.

As the physical ways to find my groove dissolved, I found my zone through writing. I used to think that being in the zone could only be achieved through adrenalin-charged activities. But I learned I could get back into the zone without perspiration through any activity that involved extreme focus. The zone, also referred to as "flow" by Berkley professor Mihaly Csikszentmihalyi in his seminal work *Flow: The Psychology of Optimal Experience*, is certainly attainable without perspiration. I just have to be completely absorbed in an activity, in the "optimal state of intrinsic motivation" as Csikszentmihalyi writes, and end with a feeling of personal achievement.

Canadian winters are challenging, so I focused on writing and on planning upcoming travels much like Christine gazed at her aquariums. During the winter of 2016–2017, I booked us a train trip across Canada. I also took on the necessary task of buying a new adapted vehicle. However, rather than settle on necessity, I decided to throw caution to the wind and splurge, thereby transforming an essential purchase into an exciting new road trip machine—a brand new adapted Toyota Sienna with a sunroof, heated leather seats, and a decent sound system—that would take us on new adventures in the months and years ahead.

There's no set recipe for when your past nightmares are less frightening than the present and an even more terrifying future awaits you. One thing's for sure though: The battle with myself is the most challenging. Even the hardest fought outward battles pale in comparison to the quest for inner peace. That's why finding your zone is so important, but so is facing fears head on. My advice is to brazenly acknowledge your foes and fears before retreating to your sanctuary in space or time, preferably somewhere covered in sand, even if it's just in your mind.

So let it out, avoid distractions that provide no real satisfaction, find out what your zone is, and go there regularly. Find ways to chase away raccoons and care for your sick fish. And between the battles against bureaucracy and physical decline and the cathartic surges to relieve latent pressure and dismay, never forget to treat yourself and your caregiver and to carve out all the time you need to breathe gently and observe the barbs shoal.

Chapter 16

Overcoming Doubt:
The Miasma and the Captain

Maintaining focus on *the best* is not a one-shot deal. It means seeking inspiration from others, and from within, to fight off that noxious cloud of fear and doubt—that miasma—that can reappear at any time.

It was the spring of 2017, and things were looking up. That is, until I saw an interview with a man who was calling for medically assisted dying just a year after his diagnosis with ALS….

Norman and his new adapted van (2017)
Photo by Marie-Christine Tremblay

> "Beyond the place of wrath and tears
> Looms but the Horror of the shade"
> —William Ernest Henley, "Invictus"

Yvon Cournoyer wanted to die on his birthday. Not just any birthday but his birthday that same year, on May 2, 2017. He wanted to die at home in his bedroom with medical assistance, surrounded by his family and friends. He didn't want to wait. "I don't want to finish 2017, that's for sure. I won't see 2018," he said in French during a televised interview on the popular Radio-Canada show *Tout le monde en parle.*

Doctors had told him that his condition was not sufficiently advanced to justify physician-assisted dying. His backup plan was to pay $20,000 to end his life at a facility in Switzerland. He told the show's host, Guy A. Lepage, that his disease was nothing but negative and that physician-assisted dying would be a positive side to this horrible ordeal.

Diagnosed with ALS in April 2016, Cournoyer had made up his mind. His condition was intolerable—psychologically unbearable. Even if they found a cure, he said, he wouldn't take it because he'd lost use of his legs and his motor function and he was too proud. He wanted his friends and family to maintain a positive image of him. He definitely didn't want them to see him emaciated and hunched over.

Miasma

I wished I hadn't checked my social media feedback that day. I wished I hadn't clicked on that link and watched that interview.

Sitting outside on a terrace surrounded by tropical gardens, sipping a margarita as a gentle breeze stroked palm trees under the Caribbean sun, I should have never put down that novel I purchased at the airport in anticipation of a week of pampering and sun-soaked relaxation as a respite from the seemingly never-ending Canadian winter.

I should have kept on reading the book that took me far away to a fictitious family travelling through the night on the Interstate in Pennsylvania to their cottage in Maine. I should have stuck to fictional prose, but instead I put down that novel and—blame it on free Wi-Fi—got caught up in that non-fictional **interview** that had already been uploaded to YouTube.

I never met Yvon Cournoyer, but I won't pretend I didn't know what he was talking about. I felt that same haunting miasma.

I couldn't see it. I couldn't smell it. In my mind's eye, though, it was an obscure, indistinct haze that crept up on me at the most unexpected times. This brumous darkness came from nowhere but appeared to hide inside me, making it impossible to evade. It was an amorphous, odourless, invisible mist lurking gloomily, dragging me down and threatening to disrupt my efforts to remain positive and focused. It was the equivalent of the drone in modern warfare, a stealthy lethal menace. It can either kill swiftly or slowly maim and cripple its victims, attacking frequently and relentlessly, taking bits and pieces until there was nothing left but a man trapped in his body, waiting for his lungs to fail so that he might choke to death or—if he were so fortunate—pass quietly from exhaustion in his sleep.

The miasma would creep up on my legs, starting on the left, spreading to the right, and eventually engulfing my core and my left arm and hand. Then it would reach over to my right hand for one brief yet terrifying moment, twisting it like a schoolyard bully would.

The Bespectacled Little Christ Who Walked on Water

"Out of the night that covers me,
Black as the pit from pole to pole,
I thank whatever gods may be
For my unconquerable soul."
—William Ernest Henley, "Invictus"

I draw strength and inspiration from those close to me who have fought and won.

My father-in-law was a slight man. On the plant floor, where they bottled popular soft drinks, they referred to him as "the little four-eyed son of a bitch," which is a liberal translation for the infinitely more colourful Québécois *le p'tit crisse à lunettes*, literally translated as "the bespectacled little Christ." Despite his disparaging nickname, his three daughters saw him as a loving father, and he was a husband without a mortal match in this world where his lonely wife mourned him still, more than a decade after his passing.

To me, he was a man driven by passion and commitment. He was a master craftsman who embellished the world around him with his hands and his heart. He was as committed to quality and efficiency in the workplace as he was to his family, a priority that seemed to intensify and eventually take over completely as his health faded.

He was born the runt of the litter, and he grew up to be bold, defiant, and determined. So when heart problems plagued him, he proved virtually unstoppable. He underwent not one, not two, but three triple bypass operations and re-emerged time and time again until finally it was cancer, not his faulty heart, that took him from his family.

For me, he was a model of persistence and positivity. On one occasion, after undergoing open-heart surgery, he was told he had a one-in-three chance of survival. So after the second patient in his room had passed away, leaving him alone in recovery, he boldly exclaimed that he had made it. Sure, he understood how probability works and didn't really believe that the misfortune of others guaranteed his survival, but rather than wallow in discouragement, he reverted to his own brand of dark humour. As he shared his tongue-in-cheek proclamation of victory with one eyebrow raised, his smile filled the room. He eased the tension. Through the alchemy of humour, he had converted a sombre moment into a hopeful one.

No doubt, there were moments of sadness, frustration, and even despair. In the final days of his battle with cancer, there were moments when he lashed out as the delirium took over. Those were the moments when the disease took over the man. They remain but only as proof of the depth of the struggle and the unimaginable pain taking away the life but not that scrappy yet focused tenacious fighter who successfully held life-threatening illness at bay for more than three decades.

What's Left?

> "We are all in the gutter, but some of us are
> looking at the stars."
> —Oscar Wilde, *Lady Windermere's Fan*

I've been asked more than once whether I'm truly as positive as my writing suggests. "Are you holding back?" I'm asked.

That's not an easy question to answer, and my reply would vary as the pendulum swings. First, my writing is my therapy, so my conclusions are my medicine. Arriving at conclusions helps me make sense of my changing world and my deteriorating body. Second, just as ALS is characterized by a series of losses and the subsequent mourning, it comes in waves like the ocean. Like the ocean, there is ominous power behind it—regularity and rhythm—but also a destabilizing unpredictability as waves can catch me unawares, toss me around, or pull me below.

When I was first diagnosed, I asked to be referred to someone who would guide me through an approach known as positive psychology. I believed (and still do) in the healing power of the mind and in the importance of stress management under the lingering shadow of the Sword of Damocles in the form of a three-letter abbreviation. Unfortunately, the consultation never materialized. As I discussed in a previous chapter, they first lost my file for several weeks and then called me in for an appointment on the day the clinic was closed. On a cold January morning, I found myself in front of an empty building with a chain and padlock on the front door as if to emphasize the extent of my abandonment.

They never called me back after than debacle, so I decided to take matters into my own hands. I covered the edges of my computer screen with bright yellow Post-it Notes extolling all the positive aspects of my life. Unlike Mr. Cournoyer, and without the slightest bit of judgment of his experience and his perspective, I refused to believe that the only positive thing about ALS was finally benefitting from physician-assisted dying.

I avoided projecting into a dark, locked-in future where I could imagine myself like the main character in the film *The Diving Bell and the Butterfly*, paralyzed and communicating only by blinking—one blink for yes, two for no—and terrified by the image of myself in the mirror—inert and pathetic in my wretched, limp body. But I did watch that movie. And I also watched that seventeen-minute interview with a man in only his first year of ALS who was anxious to check out on his next birthday. I was also familiar with *TransFatty Lives*, *The Theory of Everything*, *Gleason*, and countless other stories of people living with ALS.

The challenge is my increasing dependency on others and the fragility of my positivity. What would I do if Christine were no longer there for me?

I latch onto every positive sign, but I'm often disproportionately disheartened when I face setbacks. As the promise of spring reappeared on the horizon, I was buoyed by something distinctly uncharacteristic of a degenerative disease: progress. With the help of my osteopath and my physiotherapist, my right arm, injured by a fall the previous month, had been slowly healing, and I was once again able to put weight on it.

Meanwhile, the capsulitis in my left shoulder had also been improving at a steady pace, thanks to daily passive stretching with Christine's help. So, one night while on vacation, when she fell into a deep sleep before my nightly routine so crucial to my continued improvement, I was suddenly crestfallen, overwhelmed by the feeling that this one positive element might elude me. Then I sunk further into that state, overwhelmed by a feeling of insecurity at the realization that Christine might not always be there for me. At that moment, I felt truly alone, as if the miasma had seeped into my mind. Maybe that's how Yvon Cournoyer felt on a regular basis.

Personally, I couldn't say if and when the time would come when I just couldn't make it any further. Perhaps I was only a miasma away from turning to medical assistance in dying. I *do* know, however, that the physical, visual memory I leave behind is less important than the message I leave behind about resilience and courage.

On March break, looking up at swaying palm trees under the therapeutic tropical sun, I could have chosen to spend my time lamenting all I'd lost and all I was destined to lose: long walks on the beach, open water diving, and treks through lush jungles. Those thoughts, full of anger and frustration, would sometimes creep up on my consciousness just as physical cramps would clutch my limbs and twist my body. Other times, I would just live in the moment with no signs of that pesky miasma.

Then, as I turned the page and took another sip of a frozen margarita, two lifeguards arrived to help me into the water. They fitted me with a life jacket, picked me up by the arms and legs, and carried me into the ocean. Vacationers strolling down the beach buzzed, trying to make sense of the scene. Was this some sort of prank? As I reached the water, they let me float on my own, riding the waves with my head back, looking at the clear sky above.

Above me was warmth and soothing light blue; below, the water cooled my sundrenched body as the waves rocked me with calming grace and rhythm like they were a gentle giant. I bobbed up and down in salty water bordered by sandy shores and tropical greenery. There were no noisy streets, no crowded sidewalks, no hectic offices. This was the place I associated with connecting with nature, from snorkelling in Oahu's Hanauma Bay to swimming with a giant sea tortoise off the coast of Belize to taking a diving certification course with my twelve-year-old son in Thailand, removing our scuba equipment on the ocean floor and putting it back on again.

The sea commands respect for its power, and breathing becomes the focal point, as it is at the beginning and the end of life, although it is too often taken for granted in between. The ocean is a place of mindfulness and oneness with nature, where, as an amateur scuba diver, I regulated my depth through my breathing as I gently meandered along underwater landscapes replete with canyons and tunnels, surrounded by neon-coloured aquatic life.

Norman accompanied by his wife, Christine, and the lifeguard, Franklin, in the Caribbean Sea off the island of Hispaniola, Dominican Republic (2017)

Occasionally, a strong wave would challenge me, and I'd take in a mouthful of salt water, and the lifeguard, Franklin, would catch me and lift me up. After a few minutes, I removed the vest and swam as much as I could manage. My arms and legs were too weak to swim much at all, and my capsulitis still prevented me from doing a proper front crawl, but the sensation of putting my head underwater and re-emerging to the surface was pure joy, and it must have shown.

I knew the miasma would eventually come back. There would be setbacks. The cramping and fasciculations would twist my body and assault my psyche. My gait would slow until there were no more steps. My hands would ache and curl until I could no longer type these words without new technology. My voice would fade and make me slur like a drunken sailor until my words were no longer intelligible. My muscles would struggle until too few neurons remained and I could move no more.

But I refused to relinquish hope.

That same spring, I returned to spend three successive mornings hooked up to an IV at the Montreal Neurological Institute and Hospital, and I would return month after month for four more months to have NP001 pumped into my veins in the hope that this new experimental drug would quell the inflammation and slow the degeneration of my motor neurons. At the very least, I would have participated in yet another clinical trial to learn more about ALS and perhaps find new treatments or maybe even a cure.

As for that cloud of negativity I refer to as a miasma, I remind myself that it comes from my mind, not from the environment in which I live. Long before we understood the role of germs and mosquitoes in the spread of diseases, the now obsolete miasma theory, which dates back to the Middle Ages, posited that diseases were caused by what some described as "night air." Charles Darwin described it in his journals as **"invisible emanations of infectious substances."**

My miasma is no different in that it doesn't really exist, except in my mind as a manifestation of my suppressed fears. So I model my determination on the dedicated craftsman referred to as the "bespectacled little Christ" and remain mostly positive because the alternative involves surrendering to the miasma and opting for "the definitive trip to Switzerland," i.e., medical assistance in dying. It would mean denying the pure joy I felt during my brief dip in the Caribbean Sea and contravening my conviction that I will leave behind my determination and inner spirit, paying it forward to future generations who will face similar struggles that are an inexorable part of the human condition.

Back in Montreal one frosty spring morning, while I was on the way from my parking space to my office, my neighbour Eric offered once again to lend me a hand. I accepted willingly, as the asphalt was sloped and potholed and there was a heightened risk of falling even with my wheeled walker to guide me. Eric helped me reach the sidewalk and accompanied me all the way to the door of the foundation where I still worked (albeit on an adapted, flexible schedule and working mostly from home).

He asked me about my condition, and I told him it was ALS. He knew of it, referring to it as Lou Gehrig's disease and mentioning some of the disease's more famous victims, including MP Mauril Bélanger and CFL all-star defensive back Tony Proudfoot. I told him that I used to be an avid cyclist, among other sports.

Eric then asked me what I had left to live for. I hesitated just long enough for him to answer his own question: "I guess time with family and friends." I left it at that, but the exchange left me hanging. I hadn't been measuring my life in terms of everything I could no longer do. My baseline had shifted. I loved biking and skating, but I wasn't defined by those activities, and I could still enjoy so much of what I've always loved.

His reference to "what I had left to live for," as if it were hard to define, caught me unprepared. If anything, I thought that my life was too full at the moment. I was still working as I managed symptoms, health appointments, and a constantly evolving list of adaptations. Rather than questioning what was left, I was often overwhelmed by the never-ending stream of adjustments and firsts.

The Captain

"It matters not how strait the gate,
How charged with punishments the scroll,
I am the master of my fate,
I am the captain of my soul."
—William Ernest Henley, "Invictus"

Taking possession of my new van just before Easter was one such milestone.

I've rarely been the first to purchase the latest gadget. I bought my last car used and kept it for nearly ten years, so my new vehicle, an adapted Toyota Sienna with remote-controlled ramp, kneeling suspension, automatic locking mechanism for my motorized wheelchair, and swivel chairs to facilitate my transfers, as well as the latest technology and comfort features, was something extraordinary for me. I was now totally autonomous. I was able to enter and exit the vehicle without assistance while conserving precious energy previously spent struggling to get in and out.

As I wheeled out of the ONroute service centre on the 401, a young boy held the door open for me. His gaze was focused on my motorized chair, which I controlled with a joystick similar to those used in video games. It must have shown that I was enjoying the freedom of coming and going on my own without anyone by my side to prop me up and keep me from falling.

"It's a fun toy," he commented, referring to my wheel-chair.

The adult in me could have easily reacted negatively to his remark. I could have easily retorted that this was no toy at all but rather a necessary mobility aid. I could have said that legs are so much better and that it was anything but *fun* being confined to a wheelchair. I didn't, though, because the boy in me, the one with the chocolate-brown hair, the one whose favourite Christmas gift in the seventies was a wired remote-controlled Corvette Stingray, certainly understood the attraction.

I proceeded to wheel up to my new van, opening the door and activating the ramp by remote control. I then went up the ramp and automatically locked the chair into place, transferred to the driver's seat (which my nephew referred to as "Captain Picard's chair"), and rotated forward. I then pushed a button to turn on the van as a control screen activated, complete with navigation system and backup camera, which is par for the course for many North Americans but whose gadgetry still impressed the ten-year-old in me.

I had managed to do so much despite ALS. I worked two years full-time after my diagnosis, and I was able to replace my fourteen-year-old vehicle with the latest in adapted transportation. I could have chosen to lament that I had already spent tens of thousands of dollars to adapt my house in addition to buying an adapted van instead of, say, buying a sleek white convertible BMW with tan leather interior. The truth be told, though, I wouldn't have bought that convertible in any case. Moreover, having seen close up how the bottom forty percent live, I couldn't help but feel privileged to benefit from universal health-care and to be able to procure the technology I needed to maintain my autonomy.

I decided early on that I would bet on an optimistic outlook. That's why Yvon Cournoyer's decisiveness was so destabilizing. Like the miasma, it made me question my own hopeful perspective. I knew that at some point, while overwhelmed by the helplessness and the indignity, I might regret my optimism and wish I'd opted for door number two. But it's never really been an option because I've never asked myself what's left to live for. Meanwhile, the little boy in me has been recently emboldened by adapted technology, and the man in me remains determined to defy the odds.

Although my decision is vastly different from Yvon Cournoyer's and the decisions of many others, I suspect we can all identify with this unyielding mantra from "Invictus," **Nelson Mandela's favourite poem**: "I am the master of my fate, I am the captain of my soul." Here's wishing us all a bon voyage through troubled waters, regardless of the path of our respective journeys.

Chapter 17

Noise:
The Search for Purpose and Peace of Mind

We live in a noisy world.

Even if you have noise-cancelling headphones, billboards and neon signs will still cry out to you. *Look at me! Buy me! Like me!* All around us, the modern world clamours for attention, spewing an incessant babble of consumerism and self-promotion.

We program noise into our lives. It starts with the morning alarm, and it lasts the whole day long—on the way to work, on the subway, along the highway. Public announcements and intercoms break through it all. Our smartphones buzz, whistle, sing, chirp, and poke us all day, reminding us of meetings, notifying us of text messages, and beckoning us to respond.

I longed for less noise. Less stress. More living.

Finally, after having gradually reduced my office hours and my workload, I stopped working. It was a new beginning, and I approached it with a strange mixture of enthusiasm and trepidation.

With summer just around the corner, I had addressed my last general assembly of the foundation I had managed and led for nearly seven years. I watched the presentation they had prepared to mark my departure. It was funny and moving. Then, for the last time, I addressed the crowd of staff members, board members, volunteers, and partners. It was my chance to speak from the heart, sitting in my wheelchair, harnessing all of my energy to speak as clearly as possible despite those defiant muscles in my tongue resisting the formation of clear Ls and Rs.

With my elbows on the armrests, I held the microphone in front of me with two hands, as if in prayer, and my convictions and emotions flowed. The crowd, which had once been buzzing with the sound of interaction and networking, went silent as my heart emptied into the mic and filled the room. Toward the close of my address, I thanked them for the privilege of working with them. That was it, I told myself. My career had come to an end. They would continue, but I would not.

Few people with ALS could continue working for more than two years, and I considered my case a blessing. I would have liked to continue for years more, but my body begged for rest. When I put the mic down, a crowd of 140 stood and applauded. A few gave me winks of encouragement while André Paul, with a warm smile from ear to ear, gave me an enthusiastic thumbs up. I didn't resist it; I just soaked it up because I knew the following days would be different.

And they were.

The very next day, as I sat there breathing purposefully and deliberately on my deck, I had no big plans but to have no big plans. I'd focus more on my body's needs, on a new exercise program for neurological patients, and on voice banking, recording the hundreds of remaining sentences I needed to be able to synthesize my voice later.

When people had asked me, "What's next?" I told them I first wanted to savour the non-planning, so my first day off was exactly that. There was time to really experience my backyard, to nap in the afternoon, and to top it all off with a massage, as if to cleanse my body of the remaining toxins from decades of relentless planning, haste, and toil.

I thought I'd rekindled that feeling of total mindfulness I had experienced on the rooftop in Kathmandu. I wasn't on my phone, and I wasn't planning my next move. I was listening to my environment again and embarking on a new adventure.

I sat silently in my backyard with the sunrays warming my body, listening to the familiar urban acoustics. For a moment, the sounds emanating from the schoolyard a block away reached a crescendo. Then there was a car horn in the distance and a garbage truck accelerating with a rumble and decelerating with the exhalation of air brakes.

Then there was a hiatus, a relative silence that drew my attention to other senses.

I inhaled deeply.

Gradually, as the wind picked up, the rustling of the leaves and the whooshing of the treetops once again took over the soundscape. Waves of spruce scent filled my nostrils. Meanwhile, the sky cleared, the wind having chased away the clouds.

This was an ordinary scene but not an ordinary day. This was the first day of my "pre-retirement," marking the end of my full-time employment and the beginning of life at a slower pace, where I could focus more on the world around me than on the deadlines that bound me.

But I couldn't keep the noise in abeyance for much longer.

There would be more work crews: carpenters, drywallers, electricians, and plumbers. My to-do lists never grew shorter, and the days were punctuated by phone calls and emails from contractors, suppliers, and healthcare professionals. ALS is a disease that kept me literally off my feet but figuratively on my toes. Home adaptations are almost always complex and time-consuming. Yet, as if to add insult to injury, they were further complicated by two incidents of water damage, the first of which started with faulty plumbing in the master bathroom that literally poured over into the dining room.

I mistook some noises for reassurance and hope. The media screamed about how life would be better. In the spring of 2017, they applauded the FDA approval of a new treatment from Japan that could slow the progression of ALS. By March 2017, the first intrepid Canadians, a Nova Scotian couple, travelled all the way to Japan to get access to this treatment to slow the disease.

It's called edaravone (sold under the brand name Radicava), and it was purported to slow the progress of ALS by thirty percent. A new friend of mine who had ALS spent nearly half her mornings hooked up to an IV. It was costly and complicated. Since the drug wasn't yet approved by Health Canada, she had to travel to Japan and pay for the costly medication without any support from the government or private insurance. And since the Quebec Order of Nurses wouldn't allow its members to administer the medication, she had to find a nurse willing to hook her up to an edaravone IV (at the risk of losing her license) and had to pay for that service out of pocket. In the end, she spent more than $30,000 for one year of treatment.

So along with her and others, we made our own noise.

At the federal and provincial levels, I wrote to Health Canada and the Quebec Order of Nurses about the challenges of accessing new treatments. I worked with ALS societies in Quebec and Canada and met with parliamentarians in Ottawa and Quebec City. It was partly cathartic but equally frustrating. I watched as the eyes of the parliamentarians teared up. They saluted my courage as they pledged their support in the vaguest terms. They passed an empty motion but floundered when it came to implementation and budgeting. It felt like a dance or a charade at which they were so much more adept than I was.

But I told myself they couldn't douse the fire in me, so I forged ahead. I encouraged others to make noise. I knew this noisy chorus, no matter how imperfect or dissonant, was needed to rattle bureaucratic cages and shake politicians out of their complacency. Yet that noise reverberated in my head like the sound of a turbulent battlefield constantly in the background. It broke my concentration and ate away at my introspective time like a scab itching to be picked. It pulled me out of my inner peace as I struggled to find the peace of mind I had found on that clear June day in my backyard.

I tried to convince myself to persevere. Advocacy isn't new to me, I told myself. This is what I've always done; this is who I've always been.

I could still picture myself in 2001, walking from a rickshaw in New Delhi, India, heading on foot up Raisina Hill along the wide empty road known as Rajpath, six lanes wide yet with only a single yellow line in the middle and scarcely half a dozen cars in sight.

Rajpath was and still is flanked by the North Block on the right and the South Block on the left. I walked west from India Gate toward Rashtrapati Bhavan and turned right toward the Home Ministry in the North Block, a structure symmetrical to the South Block building. Both buildings were built of red sandstone on the first floor and had light yellowish sandstone on the upper floors. Commissioned by the British in the early part of the last century, their classical architectural style featured uniquely Mughal and Rajasthani traits and motifs that reminded me of the myriad influences of this great civilization that refused to become a dominion, instead proudly and defiantly declaring independence in 1947.

I remembered feeling more than a bit intimidated as I found my way through the impressive doorway. Then I entered an area where paint was peeling on the wall behind the desk of an expressionless bureaucrat. Among shelves overflowing with stacks of files wrapped in string, dust had gathered where inertia reigned. I realized that behind this majestic façade was an inefficient, overburdened bureaucracy that stood between me and the country office I was setting up in this diverse subcontinent they call India.

The vacant civil servant told me he couldn't help me because I didn't have a file there.

"What does it take to open a file?" I inquired.

He said that he needed a letter from the head of my organization in India. Since I was that person, I returned to my hotel room, typed up the requisite letter with our electronic letterhead, and returned to the North Block the next day to open a file.

"What next?" I asked.

I was told I needed a bank account number to complete the registration process. This was problematic, though, because the bank could open an account only if my organization was first registered. Fortunately, in the end, after countless rickshaw rides and consultations, I found a way around this apparent contradiction by opening an account "in trust" for my organization in order to obtain the necessary account number.

Months (and countless bureaucratic formalities) later, I welcomed the state's top bureaucrat, the chief secretary, to a garden party I was hosting at my home in the state capital, Dehradun. In my mind, it marked the success of a synergistic relationship with the government that resulted in new legislation and the emergence of a new generation of self-reliant cooperatives in this state of lush foothills set beneath a lofty snow-tipped Himalayan background.

Regardless of where I was, it seemed I was often working for policy change. Back in Canada years later, I recalled interacting with a journalist from the *Montreal Gazette* and being interviewed by the CBC regarding market access for Haitian entrepreneurs. This led to a debate in parliament about the overbearing bureaucracy that blocked a Haitian mango exporter whose shipment of produce risked rotting away in storage at the airport in Dorval.

Memories of advocacy also took me back to my youth. As an undergraduate writing for the student newspaper, I wrote about the trees that were being cut down on the university campus. In short, this had always been who I was and what I'd done. I was an advocate, fighting bureaucratic inertia, backing human rights, lobbying for policy change, and writing to raise awareness about the rights of the downtrodden.

This time, however, the difference was that I was fighting for my own rights, my people, and my own cause. In India, I had looked for allies such as Sanjeev Chopra, the deputy secretary of agriculture, with whom my team and I worked in tandem to write and introduce the new Self-Reliant Cooperatives Act in the newly formed state of Uttaranchal. Now, years later, I found myself writing to, speaking on the phone with, and otherwise interacting with Canadian politicians and senior bureaucrats in the hopes of improving the policy environment to increase access to new treatments for ALS.

I volunteered with the ALS Society of Canada and the ALS Society of Quebec. In October 2017, I spoke to provincial parliamentarians at the National Assembly of Quebec, to federal politicians on Parliament Hill, and to senior bureaucrats at the federal department Health Canada. For two solid months, I interacted patiently with someone at Health Canada until I found myself frustrated and discouraged. I wasn't making the progress I'd hoped for. If anything, I thought, we'd moved backward since the government had scrapped the plans to develop the much-needed Orphan Drug Policy.

I found myself writing letters expressing my frustration but to no avail. I doubted I could break through the rigid, impermeable shell of this stubborn bureaucracy. I doubted that the prime minister, the minister of health, or even my local deputy would read my letters. And I started to wonder if I wasn't just writing to vent my exasperation, as it began replacing the time I needed to write and reflect on my personal challenges. I sometimes felt like little more than a prop. Instead of the frustration I felt after lobbying for others, I now felt anger and despair.

At times it was just too much. *Too much noise.* I wished I didn't need this constant struggle that drew me away from the beauty of the present moment, that always had me looking into the future, planning the next step, and battling against the system. I sometimes wished I could think about nothing but now. No planning. No finances. No abstract worries. So I found myself strangely attracted to the way of life of an isolated Amazonian people known as the Hi'aiti'ihi.

I had read about a tribe in the Amazon, a few hundred people living along the Maici River, a tributary of the Amazon, who call themselves "the straight ones," the Hi'aiti'ihi. Their language, Pirahã, is unique. It's comprised of only eight consonants and three vowels, but it's characterized by tones, stresses, and syllable lengths so rich and complex that one can hum or whistle it with neither consonants nor vowels and still be understood. Most interestingly, there is no future tense, no past except that which can be confirmed in the present, and no distinct words for colours other than comparisons or similes, such as *bloodlike* to explain a deep shade of red. As such, these people have no history, no planning, no art, and no story of creation. Mothers don't tell their kids fairy tales because these people don't believe in that which no one has ever seen.

They live in the present and waste no time counting. They have no words for numbers; they don't even count on their fingers. At most, they can refer to few and many. American anthropologist Daniel Everett wrote the first Pirahã grammar and is the only "crooked head" (non-Hi'aiti'ihi) to speak fluent Pirahã. He even tried to teach them numeracy based on Portuguese, but it didn't stick. "In the end, not a single person could count to ten," says Everett in an interview with *Speigel Online* ("Living without Numbers or Time," May 3, 2006). Their language doesn't provide them with the tools to count, he theorizes, because their culture applies no value to it. In other words, he firmly believes they are capable but just see no need for such "crooked" notions. The same applies to the lack of reference to the past and future. "All experience is anchored in the present," he says.

I longed for that peace, for that mindfulness that must exist in a society built around and fiercely protective of the here and now, but I couldn't become a Hi'aiti'ihi. Even if I could learn Pirahã, which only one crooked head has ever done, I couldn't unlearn numeracy, our Western concepts of time, or our obsession with planning. In fact, I didn't want to. I wanted researchers to continue to explore complex concepts, to write papers, and to learn more about ALS. I wanted more research, more data, and more discoveries.

Nor could I deny who I was. Perhaps it goes back to my ancestors whose very survival depended on their ability to plan ahead in order to make it through the harsh Canadian winter. Centuries later, I still winterized my house. I looked to the future, planned incremental adaptations to my home, and fought for change.

I certainly couldn't stop planning ahead to adapt my

home, and I couldn't help but hope for faster approval of new drugs to slow the rate at which I was losing my physical self. There was no utopia where I could get away from the stress of living with ALS.

In fact, forget the very idea of utopia and any romantic notions of the nirvana of the gentle, mindful people of the Amazon. When the Hi'aiti'ihi perceived the foreign "crooked head" Daniel Everett as a threat, they plotted to kill him. You read correctly. They plotted to murder him. Luckily for Dr. Everett, he had overheard their conversation and managed to survive.

We are all human, and where there are humans, there will be noise.

And not all noises come from the outside. For me, there were noises that came from the inside as well. I analyzed every change in my capacities, and my optimism couldn't quell my critical sense. I researched everything from the anti-inflammatory properties of turmeric to stem cell treatments. I knew about pimozide before its big splash in the press, and I waited anxiously for the results of the NP001 trials in which I took part.

I was continually on the lookout for information, so when a new documentary on ALS was released on Netflix, I immediately began watching it. The movie *It's Not Yet Dark* is beautifully done. Narrated by Colin Farrell, it's the story of Irish filmmaker Simon Fitzmaurice, who was diagnosed with ALS shortly after noticing symptoms during a walk through the snow while attending the Sundance Film Festival. I watched as his symptoms followed my pattern, until he quickly declined, leading to full paralysis to the point where his face became twisted, frozen, and expressionless. For weeks after, I would imagine myself in this advanced state and would shudder. Each fasciculation and every cramp reverberated in my body and mind like a noise coming from the inside.

In the movie, Simon Fitzmaurice explains how he tried to walk up and down the hallway each day with his walker. He eventually fell and then walked no more. I saw myself doing the same thing as my stride diminished. By 2017, it had become too tiring and risky to walk outside, but I tried to keep walking inside using mobility aids. Yet, as my steps grew shorter and shakier, I wondered how much longer it would be before I couldn't walk even a single step.

Some might say it was ill advised to watch that documentary, but I disagree. I couldn't deny the facts, nor could I fool myself. I didn't want to be lulled into a false sense of security, to squelch the critical circuits in my brain, as these are often our way of releasing the noises inside. And I certainly didn't want to block out reality only to be hit much harder down the road at some unexpected moment triggered by something beyond my control. I'm certainly not saying it would be healthy to spend the lion's share of my time watching depressing documentaries about how people die of ALS. However, denying that which was to come would only make matters worse in the long run.

I also recognized that I needed to process information and that media accounts would often be misleading. While hunting and gathering information on YouTube, I came across several articles and videos about stem cell treatments for ALS. An Israeli news station related the story of the dramatic cure of Rabbi Shmulevitz, formerly a wheelchair-bound ALS patient who walked again after

BrainStorm's patented NurOwn stem cell treatment. The reports sent adrenalin pumping through my veins. Another video featured a Fox News panel discussion about the breakthrough, a panel that included Muhammad Ali's daughter Rasheda Ali, who talked about her father's ongoing battle with Parkinson's.

But wait. Muhammad Ali died in 2016.... So how old was this video?

It turned out that the story about the rabbi dated back to 2012. The Fox News video was from 2015. Five years after Shmulevitz was ostensibly "cured," this biotech company BrainStorm was still doing clinical trials. Shmulevitz had since died of some undisclosed cause, and NurOwn still had a way to go before it could be approved and available in the US and Canada.

Years after the original hype, eighty percent of ALS sufferers who got their hopes up were already six feet under. Those still around in 2017 would have to wait until 2020 or later to see the results of clinical trials in the US. Eventually, there would be openings for a few Canadians to participate in stem cell treatment clinical trials as early as 2018 (of whom fifty percent would nevertheless receive the placebo). If stem cell treatments continued to show promise without further complications, and if the government managed to expedite approvals as it vaguely and unconvincingly promised to do, stem cells could be an important part of ALS treatments as early as 2021. That was still too late for most people living with Lou Gehrig's disease in 2017.

This doesn't mean that following media reports is a useless endeavour; it just means that the media are sometimes better at making noise than properly informing people. I needed to dig deeper to find the truth. I knew that simply avoiding such reports would only make them swell inside me until they suffocated me. Besides, I needed to be fully aware of any developments if I hoped to be an effective advocate.

But did I want to continue as an advocate? As I increased the intensity of my involvement on that front, and as friends saw me on the news and saw me start a new letter-writing campaign, they asked me whether I was taking on too much.

One such friend came from India like a mythical sage in a fantastical tale. She wore saffron robes and sandals for the entirety of her stay, including the time she was the guest of honour at a black-tie event where men donned tuxedos and women were clad in elegant evening wear. She hadn't worn shoes or jewellery in years, and the hair on her head had only recently grown back into a grey crew cut.

This exceptional woman managed a leper colony in Bihar without accepting a single rupee of salary. She lived simply, accepting both the hot summers and the chilly winter nights and sustaining herself on a simple vegetarian diet. She described herself as a sannyasini, an aspiring ascetic and student of Hinduism.

She told me of her journey, which was marked by encounters with a peculiar "boy" as young as twenty who requested twice to talk with her and conveyed only the simplest message: "The old leaf will shrivel up and fall to the ground, only to be replaced by a new leaf." After meeting him twice and hearing the same allegory, she grew impatient. *What nonsense!* she thought, until one day her father passed and the message finally sank in. So she returned to his village to meet him once again.

She told me the tale of his phenomenal spiritual power. Apparently, "the boy" had travelled back nearly three millennia to meet the Buddha and spoke the ancient but defunct language known as Pali. According to my saffron-clad friend, he had the ability to move through time and into others' bodies.

There I was, on my third day of "pre-retirement," listening to this old friend who used to be a senior political advisor to the prime minister of Nepal sell me on the merits of turning inward through meditation and mindfulness. She was my friend of two decades with whom I'd worked in different countries, so I listened attentively, but she lost me when she spoke of time travel and chatting with the Buddha in his native tongue.

After hours of talking as Christine chauffeured us back to Montreal through Algonquin Park, we all needed a break from this heavy metaphysical discussion. I switched on the radio only to intercept a CBC Radio show that delved into Eastern mysticism, peppered with fusion music inspired by Hindu and Sikh devotional tunes. Geez, I thought, even the airways were conspiring to reinforce the message.

Finally, back in Montreal, my friend gave me a small yet thoughtful gift before returning home. The one-inch-tall brass Krishna sitting cross-legged in a meditative pose was a depiction of one of the principal Hindu deities. She then talked to me again about pranayama yoga and the healing powers of the mind.

I was thrown off—or perhaps even *turned off*—by the talk of her transcendent guru and a time-travelling boy who sermonized through laconic metaphors. Her core message, however, was remarkably simple and practical. She implored me to take care of myself first. "You are a contributor," she told me. "Apply that to your inner development as you face this challenge."

The leaf metaphor applied to me as well. As Nepal had taught me two decades earlier, I am not the centre of the universe. Change can take place through me but seldom—if ever at all—through me alone. Just as each leaf plays a role in the ecosystem, most change will take place over several cycles, and my modest role will likely never be enough to satisfy my Western ego. In the case of edaravone, after having played my modest role, the Quebec Order of Nurse would eventually reverse their decision by the spring of 2018. I had lost my battles, but together we would go on to win that war.

I also won at least one clear battle in 2017. On the municipal level, I used social media. In the fall, I wrote an article and helped my daughter produce a video on accessibility problems for wheelchair users after local contractors failed to respect norms regarding sidewalk curb ramps. In the end, my persistent campaign resulted in media coverage and a follow-up from municipal politicians. Two intersections were subsequently repaved, while another remained to be fixed the following spring. It was a small victory in an isolated battle.

Regardless, the ongoing struggle for accessibility was too much for me. The problem is widespread, and groups that have been lobbying on this issue for decades have had only partial victories. Just a few blocks from my house, they renovated the frontage, the stairs, the ramp, and the landing that lead to half a dozen shops. Their investment was probably more than a hundred grand and resulted in an improved ramp. Unfortunately, rather than build the landing a few inches higher, they made it so there was still a step of several inches to enter each and every doorway, making the entire complex inaccessible to wheelchair users.

However, by then I had come to terms with the need to pick my battles, so I had to drop this one. Instead, I bought a portable ramp to fix my problem rather than address the systemic issue. I struggled with this decision, but I knew I needed to focus my noise on the issues that mattered most to me and where I could make a difference. Like the single leaf among countless others, I had done my job.

Still, I vowed to continue to fight on ALS issues, but that fight was better fought both inside and out. I paced myself and even passed the baton to others who could achieve what I couldn't. Unlike previous advocacy in my life, my new patient-led advocacy involved a whole new range of issues and emotions. The stakes were personal not only in physical terms but also in terms of my new sense of purpose. I needed to limit my actions and often hold back my outer voice so I had the time to reflect and deal with my inner voice. For me, that meant scheduling time to collect my thoughts, to write, and to discuss things with family and friends.

In the end, I vowed to celebrate the various wins. Victories would sometimes be loud and clear—perhaps even as tangible as fresh asphalt. Others would be successes where my contribution was as modest as that of a leaf or as subtle as that gentle moment of inner peace attained amid the delicate ambient noises in my own backyard.

Chapter 18

Fully Alive in the Dead Sea:
Embracing Adaptation

There will continue to be countless times in my physical journey when I have no choice but to accept my limitations. Regardless, I audaciously test the limits. In 2016, I braved the ancient paths in Rome with the aid of Canadian crutches; in 2017, I travelled to the Caribbean and across Canada by train; and to this day I continue to travel.

My destination in March 2018 was Jordan, where my daughter was working. Although it was an unforgettable trip, it was also a challenging destination. It meant being pushed in a manual wheelchair through the streets of Amman, across the beach to the Red Sea, up steep ramps, and over rough terrain that would hardly qualify as "wheelchair accessible."

Travelling through Wadi Rum in Jordan on the back of a
Toyota Hilux (2018)
Photo by Marie-Christine Tremblay

By the end of the trip, my rollator was scuffed and missing a part, and my manual wheelchair looked worn and
dusty with one brake lever bent out of shape and the right

armrest held together precariously with electrical tape I purchased at a local market. Battle scars, I thought.

I chuckle when I think about it. Just minutes before the armrest was shattered, I saw my wheelchair—my proxy legs—perched on top of a horse-drawn buggy just in front of us as we sat in the back of another buggy some sixty metres behind. As the buggy sped off ahead of us, Christine looked at me with worry inscribed on her face. "Don't think about it," I said to her, although I was mostly trying to convince myself. I was worried that the chair would bounce off the roof of the buggy and be unusable for the rest of the trip, but there was nothing I could do and no alternative strategy came to mind. Before I could give it another thought, the horse pulling our buggy departed like a racehorse, and I held on for dear life.

I shouldn't have been surprised. On an accessibility scale of one to ten, Petra is a zero. Nonetheless, I managed to make it all the way to the focal point of all of Petra, Al-Khazneh ("The Treasury"), with its impressive banklike facade carved out of red stone. Reaching that site was our first challenge. We bounced up and down and side to side in a horse-drawn buggy over the rocky path through a narrow pink canyon to the ruins of the ancient Nabatean city of Petra. We had to switch horses after the first few minutes. The first horse bucked ferociously, making a daunting sound as its hooves kicked the top of the sheet metal barrier that separated Christine and me from serious injury and a premature end to our journey.

This was followed by the second challenge. On foot, I was supported on either side by Christine and our driver, Ali, over a sandy road covered with rocks of various dimensions averaging the size of my fist. I overdid it, but my exhaustion was trumped by my elation as I posed for photos in front of the millennia-old Petra Theater built out of the rock face by the ancestors of the Bedouins, the present-day inhabitants of this water-deprived landscape.

I should say that this was *our* challenge, though, not just mine, for when we finally regained the Treasury after the long walk, Christine and Ali each shook out the arm they had been straining to support me. They too were pushed to the limit.

Norman casting a shadow on the challenging terrain of the ancient Greco-Roman city of Gerasa, forty-eight kilometres north of the Jordanian capital, Amman.
Photo by Norman MacIsaac

A few days later, at the site where Jesus of Nazareth was baptized, Ali pushed my chair through unpaved trails, and up and down, within metres of the place where John the Baptist delivered the sacrament to the first-century Jewish preacher and religious leader. Unfortunately, I just couldn't make it down to the river to touch the water. Believers passed by wearing white robes to be submerged in the River Jordan. However, one visitor took the initiative to fill a plastic bottle with the murky water of the Jordan just for me. I thanked her for the kind gesture.

At the Dead Sea, they carried me down the stairs on a chair facing backward toward the hotel. Just minutes earlier, we had been at the top looking down at the beach. Three hotel staff members along with Christine, Émilie (who had joined us for the weekend), and I looked down those daunting stairs without a handrail and took stock of the challenges. While the staff plotted our course in Arabic, I told myself to accept that this might not be possible, that I wouldn't be immersed in those ancient waters where the concentration of salinity is eight times that of any other sea.

Then one of the hotel employees took charge, commanding the others to take action while he propped me up with my arm. My wheelchair remained at the top while they helped me down the stairs. I picked up on the word *kursi* ("chair"), an Arabic word I recognized because it's also used in Urdu. Arun rushed up the convex sandy slope with a solid plastic armchair.

"Sit," he said in a soft, deferential tone as he motioned with a sweeping hand, inviting me to take a seat. "No problem," he then pleaded in response to my expression of doubt. Then he motioned once again, and I acquiesced.

I wanted to reach that destination, and I had grown accustomed, these past two years, to being carried by strong, young, confident men who were eager to help me overcome obstacles to my mobility. This was no different from being carried down the stairs from the plane onto the tarmac at Jomo Kenyatta International Airport in 2016, or from my comfy long chair into the Caribbean Sea by Franklin in the Dominican Republic the following year. I had survived those times, so I sat, took a deep breath, and leaned back as they hoisted me toward the beach.

It wasn't just any beach. This was a beach at 430 metres below sea level. I looked up at a the blue sky delicately adorned by thin wisps of cloud as the front legs of the chair and the soles of my shoes bumped on each step on the way down. I consciously dismissed the thought that one of those legs might catch on one of the stone stairs and send me tumbling backward on my head, bringing my adventure to a bloody tragic end.

Block that thought, I told myself. I closed my eyes for a second and then opened them again.

When we reached the bottom of the stairs, they transferred me to a long chair and used it as an improvised stretcher to carry me the rest of the way. They took me down the sloped sandy beach to the edge of the water, where I removed the clothes I was wearing over my swimsuit.

As a boy, I was impressed by the 1975 film *The Man Who Would Be King*, and today I felt like that "king," the British soldier who was carried and treated like royalty yet was constantly reminded of his own vulnerability.

They put water shoes on my feet and eased me onto a sturdy table, facing the salt water, those ancient waters that had previously existed only in my mind as a feature of biblical tales, a scant fifteen kilometers from the site where Jesus of Nazareth was baptized in the River Jordan. With Arun on one side and Ahmed on the other, my job was to move my feet.

"Slowly," Arun counselled, which was sage advice indeed, but as my left foot tripped on the sandbags that served as a gentle ramp into the water, I was the one who urged them to adjust their cadence so I could have enough time to command my feet to lift.

"Slowly," I echoed.

They paused before resuming at a measured pace. A chill ran up my body as the water reached my swimsuit. Ahmed ordered me to sit. I hesitated. I had heard the tales of the exceptional buoyancy of these waters, but as they eased me back, I was surprised to be cradled so gently, so firmly by what felt like a water mattress—by water so saline I could lie back with my head and chest out of water and with my hands making an enthusiastic two thumbs up. Then, with a gentle movement of my hands, I moved around as if steering a rowboat. I smiled from ear to ear.

Ahmed gently sprinkled water on my chest. There I was, floating on my back as if supported by the hand of God in this sea of biblical proportions, surrounded by the sparsely inhabited hills of the surrounding desert shores of Israel on the west and the settlements and hotels on the Jordanian side. As I floated effortlessly, I pictured myself magically baptized and purified, ready to walk out of the Dead Sea without any help before wending my way back up that beach on my freshly anointed legs as it once was and was destined to be once again.

Why can't I control my overactive imagination?

The sun was approaching the horizon, so the temperature had dropped enough that there was a chill in the air. My legs moved spastically, uncontrollably, starting with the left and followed shortly thereafter by the right. It didn't dampen my spirits though. A broad smile covered my entire face, radiating into the crinkles at the edges of my eyes. Nothing could break the ecstasy of that moment.

As Ahmed and Arun lifted me out of the water, my body lost its weightlessness, and I focused all of my energy on my suddenly heavy legs. After I was out of the water and sitting down again, I mindfully took deep breaths of the oxygen-rich air at this hallowed site, the lowest altitude on the surface of the earth. I closed my eyes and consciously calmed my spastic legs. They stopped jerking, and I opened my eyes again. In front of me, the sun was fast approaching the hills of Israel.

By then, phase two had begun. As Christine and Émilie emerged from the water with smiles as big as mine, Ahmed and Arun began covering me in mud. I felt like I was their arts and crafts project. My wife and daughter laughed joyfully as I was covered in black mud from head to toe. Meanwhile, they began doing the same. This was followed by the requisite photo session, a rinse in the Dead Sea, and a final thick coat of sea salt. It stung a bit as they vigorously scrubbed me with a paste of coarse white salt, but I totally surrendered myself to the process.

As I completed the final rinse, the sun gently embraced the Israeli hills as if to announce closing time. As quickly as we had arrived, I was whisked back up the hill on my improvised stretcher. I was more at ease this time. I was both euphoric and exhausted, so I lay back and watched the sun set while they brought me back up the stairs. Contrary to the descent, my head was higher than my legs this time, and Christine and Émilie looked on against the backdrop of my first dusk over the Dead Sea.

Jordan was both a real challenge and a metaphor for adaptation in the face of natural challenges. The ancestors of the people who inhabit its deserts today, the Nabateans, mastered this harsh environment's most precious resource: water. They maintained their survival and their protection through their ability to thrive where others could barely endure even a few days.

They didn't have armies to ward off enemies. Instead, they devised ingenious technology to conserve water, engineered ceramic aqueducts and storage tanks, and hid water at a series of oases at strategic locations. This technology enabled them to control a vast territory stretching north to Syria and west to the Sinai Peninsula. In doing so, they gained access to trading routes to the east coast of Africa, the Eastern world and North Africa, and Europe via the Mediterranean.

Their descendants, the Bedouins, have maintained this knowledge while adopting new technologies, ranging from Japanese all-terrain vehicles to solar panels and smartphones. Sitting on Persian carpets under a tent covered in sheep's wool and camel hair, they kept a pot of sweet tea on an open fire. I took another sip as I sat there, savouring the unique flavours of cardamom and sage. They wore traditional clothing yet video chatted with family and friends in remote locations across the Middle East and the world. They'd turned this desert landscape into a source of tourist revenue as they learned the languages of their new business partners and perpetuated their tradition of trade. They'd adapted.

And so had I. Years after I began writing about my journey, and near the end of my fourth year since diagnosis, I had accumulated a long list of adaptations. I had an adapted van, a wheelchair lift to the front door of my house, and another lift inside to reach the second floor. I used adapted tools for food preparation and consumption, a bed rail, a partly adapted bathroom, a ramp to the back patio, and a plethora of mobility aids and adapted clothing and grooming items. And those were only a few of the physical adaptations.

I had also adapted my expectations and my self-image. Once the intrepid traveller who walked and cycled everywhere, I was now pushed around on four wheels as far as my caregiver could take me, and I'd watch and wait for the able-bodied to bring back photographs of the sights that were out of my reach. Once a slim fifty-one-year-old, I now had a stomach that protruded, my abdominal muscles having since let go. I struggled to walk indoors, and I hunched over my walker like a senior citizen in his final years.

Like some real-life version of Benjamin Button, all I had gained physically over fifty years was slipping away. It reminded me of that old black and white snapshot of my first tremulous steps at my childhood home in Collingwood. Wearing shorts, a short-sleeved shirt, and a bow tie, I tentatively held onto a bookshelf with one hand. I walked like that once again, making my way around the kitchen by clutching onto the counter, the backs of chairs, and the refrigerator handles as I hobbled around. I'd slide a mug or a plate along the granite, then grab the back of a chair before transferring the dish to the kitchen table slowly and carefully so as not to spill its contents. Just as it took time to master walking, I was destined to gradually lose my ability to totter around the kitchen and to be permanently confined to my chair.

I continuously adapted, but I couldn't feel bitter.

I was repeatedly told to expect my degeneration to be much faster than it had been up to that point. Most people with ALS don't make it more than three years, and most of those who do are much less mobile than I was. Few have the time or resources to adapt as I did. Many just relocate their bedroom downstairs, converting their living room into a hospital room, complete with hospital bed surrounded by equipment and mobility aids, where they end their days.

Those without a natural caregiver or the means to stay at home have no choice but to move to a long-term care facility, cohabiting with cohorts nearly twice their age or with serious cognitive problems. Even in the cases of those who hang on for an exceptionally long time, their caregivers often cannot carry on. I have seen heartbreaking cases where the disease puts so much strain on relationships that couples split up. So I reminded myself that adaptation is a privilege. I was so fortunate. I was the luckiest of the unlucky.

Meanwhile, just north of Jordan, the terrorized masses were fleeing hell on earth. Syrians were dying by the hundreds each day, while thousands embarked daily on the journey to the border. Millions had already left to escape the bombs, the horror. I think of those who were too old or mobility challenged to make the journey to safety as well as those exceptional individuals who managed to make it against all odds. We can and should curse the war, just as we curse ALS. Still, adaptation is a privilege. It's something to be celebrated. It pushes us to the limit. More than anything else, our adaptation in the face of adversity defines us, highlighting the best of our spirit in the face of the most daunting challenges.

In Wadi Rum, the Jordanian red desert valley where they filmed *The Martian* with Matt Damon, my wife invited me to join her in the back of the Toyota Hilux pickup truck we hired for this particular excursion. Some expressed their scepticism, but Christine was optimistic that I could manage and even egged me on. With Ali's help, I made my way to the back of the truck and studied the benches along both sides of the cargo bed surrounded by support bars. With several helping hands as well as Christine to lift my left leg into place, applying the techniques my physiotherapist had taught me to get up after a fall, I made it into the cargo bed and onto the bench.

With a typical Jordanian headdress to protect me from the sun, I sat on that bench across from Christine and took in the awe-inspiring scenery under the warmth of the desert sun with the wind in my face and a profound sense of victory and satisfaction in my core. I made it. Never mind that I couldn't venture into Khazali Canyon on foot to see the millennia-old petroglyphs and Nabatean, Greek, and Talmudic inscriptions on the walls—or run down the dunes, holding Christine's hand. That unforgettable ride through Wadi Rum in the cargo bed of a 4x4 pickup was my Everest, and I had conquered it.

Upon arrival, I assessed the best route back down, and I safely made my way down with help and without incident. As I reached the red sandy ground safely, a round of applause ensued. I looked to Christine and asked, tongue in cheek, "Did they applaud you?"

I too applaud adaptation, and I thank my lucky stars for each and every small victory.

Chapter 19

Test Pilot:

Ups and Downs and Dying with Dignity

A treadmill in a swimming pool.

*A woman on Saint Catherine Street with a wolf pack and
one wet sock.*

*A shiny white crossover parked in a disabled parking
space.*

Four bottles of large red pills on my kitchen counter.

An impassioned letter to Health Canada.

Minor scrapes and bruises on my back and legs.

*An article about a boy in Texas diagnosed with ALS at
age fourteen.*

A test pilot with an eject button.

These are the images of my life with ALS, and they
convey one message: If you understand the ups and the
downs, maybe you can appreciate what dying with dignity
really means to me.

Norman on a treadmill in a swimming pool
(hydrotherapy) *Photo by Marie-Christine Tremblay*

Part I: Pills and Procedures

In late spring 2018, I took an experimental drug and filled out my journal every day. I spent twenty-four hours at the hospital under close observation and went to see the ophthalmologist several times to ensure my optic nerve wasn't affected. I also went to the clinic every week, where they took more blood. I would discretely pass the study coordinator my urine and stool samples from that morning. Each time, I would pity the lab technicians who spent their days analyzing stool in a windowless sterile room.

On each visit, the nurse, Vince, would draw more blood. I would notice his running shoes. He had more than four hundred pairs, and I would try to recall if I'd ever seen him wear the same pair twice. I clearly knew the team at the ALS clinic all too well.

The hospital staff would weigh me and then measure my strength and my motor skills. They would ask the same questions. After participating in several clinical trials, I knew the ALS functional rating scale so well that the research coordinator meekly quibbled that I was answering using the exact wording in the multiple-choice answers below each question. So I mixed it up a bit. At the end of the questionnaire, the study coordinator would ask me the same question she was obligated to pose every time I saw her: "Any suicidal thoughts?" I would chuckle every time. *If you keep asking me this over and over again, I'm eventually going to say yes for no other reason than to avoid being asked that question ever again.*

Then the neurologist would do more tests. She'd tap my elbows and knees with a reflex hammer. She would ask me more questions and scribble illegibly on the form on her desk.

What am I?

A lab rat? Maybe my profile looked a tad rodent-like. But no.

A guinea pig? Definitely not! Way too fluffy for this twenty-first century version of Yul Brynner.

A lab monkey? Closer, since I'm a primate, but it was still a resounding no.

A test subject? I didn't feel like a subject. I chose this experience. It was my body, and I was in control. So, no.

Then, in a tweet quoting an unknown source, I found my answer: *I'm a test pilot. A fearless test pilot. I'm bold and perseverant.*

From mid-May to mid-June, I was greeted each morning by a white pill bottle with an ominous label that screamed: "INVESTIGATIONAL DRUG." Fans of *The Matrix* might read something into the fact that the pills in that bottle were red, not blue. Red means it was the real thing, not some feel-good happy pill. As I took those red capsules, I felt like Neo waking up or perhaps like Alice sliding down the rabbit hole. On the first couple of days, as I downed eight jelly-bean-sized pills once a day, I felt like someone's science project. My mind buzzed with the thought that I was the first and only Canadian taking this molecule that only lesser primates had ingested against their will. *Good monkey!*

Up

Then I started noticing changes: some good, some bad. I had more cramps but also more strength and a noticeably stronger voice. I asked myself if that was good or bad, and I concluded that it was good. This was, after all, the first time I'd felt any discernible improvement during a clinical trial, so I vowed to manage the side effects. Participation in this clinical trial came with the promise of sustained access to the drug with ongoing supervision, so I had a good chance of continuing on this medication.

Down

In the end, after twenty-eight days of pill-popping and rigorous follow-ups, there were no more pills. Yes, I would have access again *eventually*, but I had to wait. So I waited. I waited for some mysterious committee to give the green light. For all I knew, they might have even been waiting for a wizard named Merlin who guarded the bridge to a laboratory in California, where Prius-driving, lab-coat-wearing scientists ran tests to convince Tesla-driving board members that the red pill would make them and their shareholders even wealthier.

After waiting four weeks, I wrote yet another impassioned letter to Health Canada and the hospital. And then I braced for the back and forth.

I had grown accustomed to delays and disappointment. ALS research advances are shooting stars, flashes of excitement, inexorably followed by more endless space. There was much promise, yet my pesky pragmatism reminded me it was probably going to be too little too late for me. Even if they did find a medication to slow or even stop the disease, it still had to make its way through the obstinate bureaucracy. That meant more delays—perhaps more delays than I had time left.

Edaravone, the second drug proven to slow the disease, is a case in point. It was approved in Japan for the treatment of ALS back in 2015. Nearly two years later, in the spring of 2017, it was approved by the FDA in the US under the name Radicava. More than a year later, we were still waiting on Health Canada's "expedited" review, which didn't come until the autumn of 2018, and it was to be followed by more red tape and decision-making at the provincial level, which stretched out into 2019.

The struggle to access the drug started long before Radicava was approved in the US. The year before, a patient with ALS had pushed for the right to import the drug and finally won that battle. It didn't mean the drug was approved though. It just meant that Canadians could bring the drug to Canada at their own expense. There would be more bureaucracy before it could reach patients.

After we, two patients with ALS, argued with the Quebec Order of Nurses, stubborn paper-pushers finally gave the green light to allow its members to administer this intravenous medication to patients who purchased the drug directly from Japan. Patients were finally able to start treatment at one Montreal hospital, yet local health centres stalled the approval of injections.

In the end, some approved injections, some didn't. Unsurprisingly, there were more surprises. My new friend Carole spent thousands to import three months' supply from Japan. She then learned that she also had to fork out extra fees of $50 per injection to mix the medication with a saline solution. Regardless of whether she opted for only ten days of treatment a month at $500 or more, she was already way over budget.

In the case of edaravone, that ship had sailed for me. It's deemed effective during the first two years of the illness. For me, in the second half of my fourth year since my diagnosis and six years since symptom onset, it was already too late to make a difference.

In fact, few doors remained open to me. Nearly all clinical trials, including stem cell treatment, well into its third phase of testing in the US and also slated to be tested in Canada in the near future, were restricted to patients whose symptom onset began in the twenty-four months preceding the trial.

The red pills were the exception to the rule. I figured they were looking for patients so desperate that they'd want to test run a pill before anyone else, even before it was proven safe for humans. That was where I came in. And the jury's still out on the medium- and long-term efficacy. When they finish the paperwork, will I be the patient with front row seats to the latest effective treatment? Or will I just be another Canadian primate who actually chose to work for free for Big Pharma?

I chose my own category instead. I was one of many optimistic patients who were helping prove what did or didn't work. In the end, I might just end up adding the red pills to my list of drugs I've contributed to proving ineffective, just below tirasemtiv and NP001. But those red pills just might be helping. I suddenly felt optimistic, emboldened. I figured I ought to sport a leather jacket and don aviator glasses à la Tom Cruise 'cause I was no laboratory monkey. I was a fearless test pilot in my own story of *Top Pill*.

After the red pills were done, I experienced a brief down as the benefits faded and disappeared. Then, while I waited—and at the risk of sounding like either a drug fiend or a desperate, dying man—I ordered yellow pills, a form of turmeric branded as Theracurmin. This pill combines the ancient wisdom of Ayurvedic medicine with the power of modern science to produce a soluble form of this recognized anti-inflammatory agent that's twenty-seven times more effective than traditional forms. I was back in the cockpit once again.

Fear not though. Not all ups and downs are pill-related.

Part II: Pools and People

I was up…and walking again. My legs moved slowly but surely as I advanced at three kilometres per hour. My hands gripped the handrail of the treadmill as I monitored my progress. It had been five minutes, and I had already covered a quarter kilometre.

I looked forward to this weekly exercise. The justification was to stave off muscular atrophy and control the spasticity in my legs. However, I would have done it regardless of the medical benefits, just to be able to walk again.

Moving on this treadmill specially designed to work in a therapeutic pool, I was freed of the spasticity and clonus that usually plagued my gait. Walking in water felt as miraculous as walking *on* water. The warm water felt soft and comforting on my skin. It held me gently in place and supported my every step.

My weekly stroll on the treadmill was preceded by and followed by plenty of stretching in the pool. Afterward, as

I slowly emerged from the pool one step at a time, with both hands on the rails, my legs felt heavier and heavier as I stepped out of the water, grabbed hold of a walker, and made my way charily to the showers.

I relished hydrotherapy, but I didn't expect it would last forever. I was constantly adapting to new challenges, and I was fully aware of my vulnerability. Life with ALS is a house of cards. If my caregiver could no longer support me, if I fell and broke a hip, or if a cold developed into pneumonia, it would all come crashing down.

Down

Every fall is both physical and psychological, so my falls in July and August of 2018 were no different.

One time, I fell onto a patio of jagged flagstones while I was transferring from a patio chair to my wheelchair. I was prepared though. I was wearing my Lifeline bracelet around my wrist, and I had my cellphone in my pocket. At first, I just lay there. My body hurt in several places, but there was neither a head injury nor blood, only bruises, scrapes, and strained muscles and ligaments.

I didn't call and I didn't move. I just looked up at the trees. No one was anywhere to be seen, so I struggled to pull myself up into a seated position. Using my 380-pound wheelchair as a handle, I lifted myself onto all fours, then onto my knees, with my elbows on the seat of the wheelchair. Then, with both hands gripping the wheelchair, I used my stronger leg to push while I inched my left leg closer and closer until I was able to leverage my injured body into the wheelchair. I was shaking. I was rattled.

When I fell again a few weeks later, I fell from my bed this time. My head collided with my bedside table, cutting me between my eye and my eyebrow. Christine called the paramedics. They confirmed that I didn't have a concussion, only bruises and cuts on my face and an injured knee and back.

Another two weeks later, I found myself sitting with two doctors at the Neuro, discussing options to alleviate the back pain that had plagued me since my falls. They pointed out the fractured vertebrae—surprisingly, not the biggest challenge I faced—and presented me with options. We eventually agreed on a course of action, and I lay down for the epidural. The procedure went well. I returned home and hoped that my back would improve. I was too tired and discouraged to even dream that I'd ever use my cane again.

Then, less than two weeks later, I fell a third time while I was trying to walk just a few short steps between the bathroom and the bedroom.

Three strikes and you're out.

Up

Fortunately, beyond the pools and the plummets, there were quiet moments when I could just enjoy the simple things in life.

Before beginning the red pills, and before my falls and my epidural, the month of May had started off so uneventfully. After the timid spring of 2018, the warm weather finally arrived, and the sun shone with heightened determination. I revelled in the freedom afforded by this long-awaited season of mobility. I drove downtown; parked at a nearby parking lot that had sufficient clearance for my adapted van, automatic doors, and elevators; and headed toward Saint Catherine Street in my motorized wheelchair.

I left my iPhone at the Apple Store for a couple of hours so they could replace my battery. I then proceeded phoneless down Saint Catherine Street.

Kitty-cornered from the Apple Store is a café, so I went in for an overpriced coffee and the right to loiter in a quiet environment. A library would have been cheaper, but this would do just fine. I could use a caffeine boost anyway. I wanted to sit by the window, an ideal spot to read and to take extended pauses to people-watch on the most watchable artery of Montreal's urban landscape.

First, I took on the challenge of opening the restroom door from my wheelchair and circulating in tight spaces as par for the course. "Excuse me. Thank you. Excuse me. Thank you." Then, comfortably ensconced in front of the large plate glass window, and with a frothy soya cappuccino in front of me, I started people-watching before even opening my book.

In front of me on the sidewalk was a homeless woman with three dogs and a sign asking for support for her "wolf pack making their way across Canada." I watched her as she tied her dogs and removed her rucksack. She removed one boot and hung her sock to dry in the midday sun. Then I saw her enter the café, ask for the key to the restroom, and collect water for her dogs on the way back out. She gave the water to her wolf pack, pulled a Sharpie out of her bag, and wrote a new sign on the paper plate the staff at the café had given her.

Her new sign read, "I have a hankering for a cookie," and it had a drawing of a cookie to underscore the request. She smiled and said warm hellos to passers-by, undeterred by the majority who ignored her. A couple gave her a box of sushi, presumably their post-lunch doggy bag. Others gave her change. Then a Japanese woman who looked like she had just descended from the catwalk of some high fashion extravaganza crossed the street just to give her money. She didn't toss it into a Tim Hortons cup though. Instead, she held the money between her two hands, greeted the woman with a smile, bowed respectfully, and gently passed the bill into her hands.

Despite her ragged clothes and crooked glasses, the homeless woman maintained a sense of style, and she smiled broadly and confidently at all who ventured her way. Then, when she'd collected enough change and reached her goal, she went back into the café to get that cookie she'd been craving, along with more water for the wolf pack.

This encapsulates the intensity of human existence, whether alone in a therapeutic pool or in a coffee shop. But there's more. In the end, the woman with the crooked glasses was joined by a bare-chested man with a squeegee, and I returned home to Christine. And that's the best part. We aren't in this alone. We share. We empathize. We give. We receive. Together, we find the missing dimension.

Down

Unfortunately, not all human interaction is pleasant.

On another sunny day in May, years after my first such encounter in the parking lot of the pharmacy near my house, I prepared to confront yet another able-bodied driver parked in a disabled parking spot. Her passenger had quickly darted from the glistening white crossover, leaving her to wait in the parking space reserved for those who needed it.

This time, unlike the incident in 2015 when I walked with a cane, I was in my wheelchair with Christine by my side. I approached the driver with a greeting and segued into my explanation.

"Do you know this is a parking space reserved for the disabled?"

My speech was painfully slow and less than articulate. She winced through a smile as she strained to follow my laboured discourse.

"I know," she said. "I'm just about to leave."

In contradiction to her words, though, the car didn't move.

"Then move," I said. The words emerged so slowly and awkwardly from my mouth that she seemed to focus first and foremost on how I was speaking, not what I was saying.

I raised my eyebrows as if to say, "Then why are you still parked there?" Yet no words accompanied my expression of impatience.

Unlike the driver from my previous confrontation, this driver was neither argumentative nor critical of my tone. Instead, she maintained her smile and listened to what I had to say. Then, in delayed reaction to my comment and gesture, she nodded, put her car in reverse, checked behind her, and began moving.

As I proceeded into the pharmacy, though, I felt not even a hint of triumph. My left leg was shaking uncontrollably, and I placed my left hand on my knee to stop the trembling. I was frustrated by my voice. Clearly, that interjection had brought me nothing but stress and a clear demonstration of my waning capacity to communicate.

Perhaps that driver was confronted by her minor transgression, seeing why the disabled need "special treatment" personified in the feeble voice of the man in the motorized wheelchair. But then I was the one perturbed by that confrontation. I was the one who was struck by my inability to express myself when under stress. I was the one confronted by the fact that others saw me as disabled to the point where I struggled to get even the simplest idea across. I was the one faced with the undeniable fact that my ability to communicate was fading fast.

In a relaxed setting, I'm able to get my point across quite well. Although I speak more slowly, and I sometimes slur or struggle to pronounce certain words, I can manage long, enjoyable exchanges. Add fatigue, cold, or stress to the equation, and suddenly a stranger in a drugstore parking lot was looking at me with a dose of pity, compassionately responding more to my pathetic predicament than her own misdemeanour.

I saw it on Christine's face too. She bore witness but didn't know how to react. Should she have interjected at the risk of infantilizing me? She instead remained silent, wondering all the while if she were doing the right thing. One thing she knows for sure, though. She was witnessing a new stage in my degeneration, another loss that affects what I can do and how others perceive me. In that moment, she felt helpless in her changing role as caregiver.

Up

While I was facing my struggles, I read that Joseph Garza had graduated high school, a remarkable feat for the youngest person in Texas with ALS. I was stuck on the fact that he was diagnosed at age fourteen. Fourteen. I had lived a full life before my diagnosis at age fifty-one, but *fourteen*? *Fourteen!* I was reminded once again how fortunate I was in my misfortune.

I'm grateful for my hydrotherapy sessions, for wheelchair yoga, for every time I swallow without choking, and for every unassisted breath. I'm grateful for that phone-free afternoon with an overpriced coffee, watching the woman with the crooked glasses and her wolf pack. Most of all, I'm grateful for my best friend, who is with me as I face each new hurdle and each new loss.

Unlike books and movies, life doesn't provide a clear plot structure with a gradual increase in tension, a climax, and a denouement whereby the protagonist ultimately overcomes his or her critical flaw to save the day. Instead, ALS is a long haul of countless cycles and ups and downs. Managing those ups and downs is what it means to fight ALS.

In the face of these downs, I need to consistently build a bulwark against negativity and persistently cultivate positivity. That involves avoiding conflicts that bring only stress and taking the time to enjoy the small victories.

I might appear courageous, but I'm not. If anything, I'm

probably more delusional than brave. I secretly plan to beat ALS, and I don't mean just by living my days out fully despite it. I mean stopping the degeneration and miraculously living to old age. I imagine my voice getting stronger thanks to those big red pills as I defy the odds and maintain my autonomy.

Last week, my friend Bala sent me a message of encouragement from Bangalore: "You will recover and come back stronger with your willpower. I know you are a fighter with strong will." I could have reminded him how unlikely that is according to the medical profession. Instead, I thanked him, and part of me believed him.

I think about it this way. Before I developed symptoms, how believable was it that I would have ALS? Not very. In fact, I would have thought it the least likely outcome. I would have dismissed the idea as sheer madness. So I'm going to take my meds, do my exercises, and continue writing for longer than anyone expected.

Does that sound crazy? Like I've gone off the deep end? Fear not. I haven't cracked; I've been this crazy all along. That's why living in a country with access to physician-assisted dying, to dying with dignity, is so important. It gives me the courage to go on through the ups and downs. It gives me the luxury of pushing myself to the next level even if I doubt my ability to go on.

Because I'm a test pilot. I'm a crazy pilot with an eject button that I hope to never use. That's what dying with dignity means to me.

Chapter 20

My Last Steps, My Last Words:
Never Say Never

On the highway between Ottawa and Montreal is a sign announcing that Montreal is seventy-eight kilometres away. Then, more than twelve kilometres down the road, on the other side of the interprovincial border, is another sign informing motorists that Montreal is seventy-six kilometres away. It's a reminder that measurement isn't as easy as it seems. Likewise, it's hard to say how long I'll be able to speak, swallow, or breathe without a machine.

ALS is destabilizing both figuratively and literally. I've fallen coming up the stairs. I've fallen going down the stairs. I've fallen in the living room, the foyer, the kitchen, the bedroom, my home office, and my backyard. I've fallen at the office. I've fallen in the street, on the sidewalk, at the airport, at hotels, and even at the chiropractor's office. I've injured my head, my face, my neck, my shoulders, my hands, my wrists, my knees, my legs, and my back. After I stopped taking the red pills during the second half of my fourth year, I felt closer to all of those abysmal milestones I'd feared since my diagnosis.

After stopping the red pills, I had to repeat myself with greater frequency, and more and more often I found myself just giving up on verbal communication. When I talked to strangers, I'd get that look—the way you look at the infirm and the mentally challenged. They were polite to me but anxious to extricate themselves from an awkward situation. And they didn't expect to be enlightened, amused, or informed. More often than not, I assumed they mistook my slow speech for a slow mind. It makes sense. Why else would someone struggle to say a word or sentence if not because they're slow-witted? So I spoke less. Once the purveyor of witty insight and pithy feedback, I was the one struggling to communicate words such as *spinach*.

"Finished?"

"No, spin—ach."

"Spin it?"

Screw it. I can reach the broccoli, so broccoli it is.

Faced with the rapid return of these challenges and the sense that my condition had plummeted after stopping the red pills, I was ready to reach for the fabled blue pill. On my desk lay an incomplete advance medical directive form intended to formally confirm the medical care I will receive or not receive in the event I'm unable to express my consent. I had already decided to refuse care such as a feeding tube or assisted breathing should I become cognitively impaired. After the third fall and the sudden drop in my vocal capacity, though, I flirted with the idea of severely limiting interventions to keep me alive even if my cognition remained intact.

But why? I could still drive. I passed yet another road test in 2018, so I relished every kilometre behind the wheel, including the twelve-kilometre black hole between Ottawa and Montreal. I was also able to attend my son

Samuel's wedding, something I wondered, after my diagnosis in 2014, if I would have the chance to do. I posed for a couple of pictures standing up with my sons, my expression masking my concerted effort to stay vertical while the photographer captured the moment. I managed to make a speech at the wedding as well. I fought overwhelming emotion and laboured speech, but I succeeded.

These achievements reminded me that, even in a wheelchair and with laboured speech, I had, as Lou Gehrig told the audience at Yankee Stadium in 1939, "an awful lot to live for."

Then, ten days after I started back on the red pills, my voice was stronger again. In the days that followed, my volume and cadence were back to where they were at the end of 2017. My speech was still slow and slurred under pressure, but my voice was stronger than before. I held onto that, and I dreamed that other improvements would follow once my back had healed. I also reminded myself that I had succeeded in managing symptoms and had preserved my quality of life despite the seemingly unstoppable degeneration of my motor neurons.

As my voice improved and my back began to heal, I adopted a more optimist outlook regarding the advance medical directive and recommitted to weathering the storm. In doing so, I was confronted with the cracks in my armour, which, I must admit, is little more than a euphemism for my lack of courage.

In the end, the only thing I was brave about was admitting my weakness. Luckily, I was still able to convince myself that those red pills had a reasonable chance of stopping the demon we call ALS. There was hope. More important, I was reminded to continue focusing on what I could change and all I could do despite it all. Even if my optimism were unwarranted, at least I could enjoy the moment, and if I could string together enough happy moments, I could manage to make the most of the rest of my life. And isn't that all we can ever hope for? In fact, isn't that the very definition of a life well lived?

Chapter 21

Staying Positive in the Age of Social Media

Somewhere in the world, surrounded by the familiar scent of a dank basement with a trace of dirty laundry and Pizza Pops, there's a millennial with matted hair churning out videos on social media. He sits in his dimly lit bedroom staring at the screen. Beside him on the desk are a bag of Cheetos, a bottle of blue Gatorade, empty pop cans, wrappers, a mess of cables, and a stack of old video games on DVD-ROM.

After his mother yells at him to go to bed, he turns off the light and stuffs a towel under the door. Now he finalizes his latest YouTube video. "Bill Maher DESTROYS Trump," he types, and clicks enter like an artist dabbing the finishing touch on his masterpiece. He leans back, reaches for a handful of Cheetos, and finishes off his favourite blue beverage. Within minutes, he's smiling as the "thumbs up" counter tallies the first two positive reactions.

But Trump wasn't destroyed at all, nor was the "leftist feminist" reporter "annihilated" by Jordan Peterson, as he asserted in the title of another of his videos. In fact, she kept her job and had developed quite the following—ostensibly, a motley crew of rabid leftist feminists, he imagined. Sheep, he thought. Sheep.

He never attended university despite the eighteen years of registered education savings his parents had amassed in the hope that one day he'd make them proud. But he wasn't one to fall into the trap set for him and other middle-class millennials by an elite that ruled the world and controlled everyone's thoughts. No, he considered himself way too clever to be brainwashed by overeducated professors in sweater vests who had lost the capacity to think for themselves—except perhaps for Dr. Peterson, the Canadian psychologist who "annihilated" a British feminist.

Like his hero—the one he failed to recognize as the father figure he longed for—he too thrashed and crushed. Peterson did it with ideas, controversial insights, and sharp comebacks, while he did it with the swift twitch of the joystick and a double-click, his signature move that had won him quasi-celebrity status in his own finite gaming entourage. Yet his mother still did his laundry and paid for snow removal, as he had more important things to do and critical targets to annihilate. Yet Trump and that "leftist feminist" remained despite his claims that they had been respectively destroyed.

Meanwhile, I also sit at my computer, reading Facebook posts and tweets that range from comical to angry, and hopeful to crestfallen. I turn to social media in a quest for information, for insight, and perhaps for connection. Indeed, I have found some of that, but I have also found a representative cross-section of the ALS community and a clear example of the good, the bad, and the ugly of social media in general.

I connect with people living with ALS, caregivers, researchers, and organizations around the world. I tweet at Canadian MPs, several of whom I have met on Parliament Hill, calling for action eighteen months after Motion 105 had passed unanimously, committing to funding research and developing a strategy for ALS. I still haven't managed to "annihilate" anyone or persuade the government to make good on its promises.

I'm now a member of half a dozen ALS Facebook groups, each with their own particular slant on ALS, all created by people with ALS or their caregivers. It started with a Facebook group of people living with ALS in Quebec, many of whom I had met at the bimonthly get-together in Lorraine, a sleepy residential town just north of Montreal. We kick off each meeting by announcing the members who'd passed away since the last gathering. Following the obituaries and other announcements, we break into groups of caregivers and people with ALS. The former inevitably end up crying, and the latter almost always ending up laughing. Between get-togethers, some of us also share things on Facebook. Like the meetings in person, our virtual exchanges similarly include obituaries, laughing, and crying.

I subsequently joined ALS groups on social media from the rest of Canada, the US, and the UK (where ALS is referred to as MND). Most were established as places to share information on advancements in research and mostly just to commiserate with or seek advice from other "persons living with ALS," affectionately referred to as PALS.

Some groups are thematic. Before they approved my application for membership, I'd had high hopes for the Laughing in the Face of ALS group. In the end, though, it was little more than a page to share jokes, especially politically incorrect ones. It had little to do with ALS, but I stayed on and enjoyed reading a new joke every day. It then revealed a political side, ripping to shreds the likes of the former 49ers quarterback Colin Kaepernick for apparently disrespecting the American flag and the nation by kneeling during the national anthem. Fear not, though, as Kaepernick survived his "annihilation" to become the poster child of Nike's latest ad campaign.

I did, however, have a humorous anecdote to share on another Facebook page. While looking up the definition of a rollator (a wheeled walker) in the French version of Wikipedia, Christine happened upon the most hilarious definition, which described a rollator (*déambulateur*) as "a paramedical apparatus [...] referred to as a walker in Canada [...] that allows those who are near death [...] to walk like zombies." The English definition was accurate but, much to my dismay, infinitely less entertaining than the French version, which I assume was written by fans of *Shaun of the Dead* or *Pride and Prejudice and Zombies*. (The former film is *to die for*, but I digress....)

All the groups feature occasional outbursts of anger and frustration that are then met with comments to console or to validate such upsurges. That's because you've inexorably been there, probably more than once, if you have ALS or care for someone who does. Facebook groups also often feature inordinate optimism following announcements of scientific discoveries, stories that will rip out your heart, and obituaries of both group members and celebrities—including Stephen Hillenburg, the creator of the animated television series *SpongeBob SquarePants*.

Hillenburg was diagnosed in March 2017 and died in November 2018.

The upsides of these groups include the camaraderie, information, and helpful advice. I can't imagine what it was like for PALS before the advent of social media. The manifestations of ALS vary so much from person to person that sometimes a PALS just wants to know if others experience the same difficulties and what tactics others employ to deal with the symptoms. Other times, PALS and their caregivers just want to vent. In doing so, they benefit from a kind of virtual "group therapy" and gain insights into how to deal with their predicament. Social media also come with the added advantage that you can post or comment at any time that suits you.

Sometimes you just want to get a patient's perspective on your doctor's recommendations or to ask others to weigh in on a policy pertaining to ALS or a novel treatment. People learn differently and pick up snippets of information that beg to be complemented with the knowledge and perspectives of others. Most of all, it means you're not alone, which is especially important to those with a disease that hits hard and fast and renders you less mobile.

Nonetheless, there are also downsides. For instance, just as social media can provide varied perspectives and complementary information from different sources, it can also spread misinformation or reinforce misconceptions. I find it hard to bear virtual witness as people with ALS pursue diets that cause their weight to drop dramatically or opt for treatments that are bound to hasten their demise.

Social media users are often like schooling fish.

Schooling provides protection, but it can also be a smorgasbord for predators. I discovered another Facebook group, ALS Naturally, that is intended as a safe space for those who seek alternative treatments and find solace in their Christian faith. They share information on everything from the ketogenic diet to scripture. The group has been plagued with infiltrations by peddlers of natural herbal remedies posing as caregivers. Their sales pitch is always the same, starting with a miraculous story of a dear family member cured of ALS thanks to a patented (and costly) herbal treatment. Their garden is fertile with scams that prey upon a vulnerable group desperate for any hope of slaying a merciless disease that kidnaps, tortures, and kills.

Of course, the holy grail is a cure, and the closest thing to that are "ALS reversals," i.e., cases where people have allegedly stopped or even reversed the degeneration caused by an otherwise incurable and terminal condition. Dr. Richard Bedlack at Duke ALS Clinic in North Carolina has documented approximately forty cases of supposed ALS reversals. He also created the website ALS Untangled to assess alternative treatments deemed by PALS to be effective in slowing the degeneration. The treatments range from donkey milk, hyperimmune goat serum, and fecal transplants—no, you didn't misread that last one—to cannabis, acupuncture, and coconut oil.

The advantages of Dr. Bedlack's initiatives are twofold. First, by documenting ALS reversals, he hopes to pinpoint the common factors of success. Second, by evaluating even the most bizarre-sounding alternative treatments, his site provides guidance regarding

a. which ones to avoid based on an analysis of the po-
    tential working mechanism, efficacy, risks, and cost;
b. the potentially beneficial treatments that can be tried
    with low risk; and
c. those treatments that merit further study.

Contrary to much of the information and potential misinformation on the Internet, ALS Untangled offers a credible assessment that is reviewed and finalized by a panel
of experts. This is particularly relevant for a disease so
ruthless and deadly that patients are often ready to take a
chance on any treatment that offers them even an iota of
hope, regardless of the risks. The Internet is full of Chee-
tos-eating basement dwellers who are ill informed and believe in simple fixes. I often find myself referring
information from ALS Untangled to PALS considering a
given treatment.

Those who purport to have succeeded in keeping ALS
at bay or even reversing the symptoms often share (and
sometimes sell) their protocols, including long lists of sup-
plements, treatments, and exercise regimens. Some have
set up websites. Eric Edney, an eighteen-year ALS survivor, even wrote a book titled *Eric Is Winning!!: Beating
a Terminal Illness with Nutrition, Avoiding Toxins and
Common Sense*. As I mentioned in a previous chapter, my
former sister-in-law sent me a copy when she learned I
had ALS.

These protocols, including Edney's, are all different.
They cite everything from diets and stem cell treatments
to having your fillings removed. There are some good
ideas that warrant running them by a neurologist and ALS

Untangled, but I'll pass on the electroshock therapy and the transfusion of a young person's blood.

All of them have one recommendation in common though: a positive mindset. That's where we all agree. If I formalized my own protocol, it would include adapted yoga, hydrotherapy, meditation, ashwagandha (an Ayurvedic herb), riluzole, and more, and it would end with that same recommendation as the others: staying positive. My protocol would also include travelling to five continents, unlimited crying and laughing, friendship, and love. The unique benefit of my protocol is that, even if it doesn't cure you, you'll make the most of the precious months or years that remain. And you can do it all with or without kale.

While I certainly don't have any miracle cure, I'm pleased to say that I'm doing considerably better than I ever imagined I would back in 2014. I'm in my fifth year since I was diagnosed. That milestone was something to celebrate. And I did it without donkey milk, a gluten-free diet, or blood transfusions from young virgins. (Okay, I admit it; I added the "virgins" to the last treatment for artistic flair.)

If I had a YouTube channel like the fictional basement dweller at the start of this chapter, I could post a video titled "MacIsaac DESTROYED ALS!!" But I wouldn't. Instead, I'd keep up to date on research and alternative treatments, and I'd try the most promising ones only after vetting them through professionals and reliable sources. Most of all, I'd prescribe enjoying life. As I commenced my fifth year after diagnosis, I was breathing on my own, enjoying red wine and fine food (as long as someone was there to cut it), and experiencing some of the best things in life, including travelling to Scotland with my eldest son in the autumn of 2018 and to Alaska with Christine in 2019. My number one treatment is staying positive and focused. I'll focus on my peace of mind and leave the destruction to others.

Chapter 22

Dealing with the Worst:
The Warning Label

On August 11, 2014, Robin Williams was found lifeless, hanging from a belt on a closet door. The beloved Oscar-winning actor was known for his high-octane comedy, whether in live-action films, in his voice work for animated features, or in his legendary stand-up routines. Few could have imagined that behind this lovable, extraordinary, bubbly personality was a man on the brink. His millions of fans had had no clue, no warning signs whatsoever.

His untimely passing highlighted the invisible struggles that plague those around us and on the screen in front of us. The case of Robin Williams isn't unique. We would be well advised to remember that under a cheery exterior is a friend, a family member, a colleague, or an acquaintance who's living under the stress of ALS, grief, or any number of major life challenges. Unfortunately, we often fail to acknowledge this reality until it's too late.

A woman living with ALS in Maine writes that her family refuses to even acknowledge her disease, let alone provide her the emotional support she needs. A man from Tennessee learns he has ALS while living independently in Indonesia. He's stuck in Jakarta without proper healthcare, bereft of the resources he needs to return to his family in his home country. Meanwhile, on yet another continent, a British man sits simmering in his makeshift bedroom on the ground floor while his children play outside and his wife struggles to juggle laundry, childcare, her life as a caregiver, and preparing dinner. She doesn't remember the last time she even had time to think other than to curse the disease the Brits call motor neuron disease (MND). The one thing I've seen on social media and all around me is that an alarming number of patients and caregivers lack the support they need.

I was alone when I learned my worst news nearly five years ago, but that didn't last long. Within hours, I was surrounded by love and support. I even called ALS a team effort. "If there's anything we can do, just ask," family and friends had affirmed back when it all began.

But the world doesn't stop turning because of my ALS, nor do humans stop being humans, which includes entering into conflict with each other. And it got worse as some people got used to my condition and forgot how challenging it really is. While I was echoing Lou Gehrig's heartfelt yet defiant statement about being the "luckiest man on the face of the earth" and focusing on the "awful lot" there is to live for, the very people who were in shock years ago got wrapped up in their own issues and interests and forgot what I was facing. A part of me wanted that, but it has its downside when you need support and compassion.

That's why I might just need a warning label. I'm not alone on this. In fact, anybody who tells you that their struggle has helped them achieve full-blown Zen is, to put it bluntly, full of it. Either that or they're heavily sedated, delusional, or a Vulcan. And people who think that of me do so at their own risk and peril.

Do you ever feel that way? Perhaps you're too good at focusing on the positive, but you also know how much you're keeping under wraps. You're already pushed to the limit, but you don't want to be a person who loses their cool. Maybe it's not apparent that you've made a conscious decision to seize every moment despite it all. Perhaps you're too good at hiding the fact that there'll be no safety, no filter, no pulling back, no control if you're pushed or cornered.

I know I'm not the only one with that feeling, even in my own house. As we kicked off our fifth year living with this disease, the one person I depend on most said to me, "I'm doing well, but I wouldn't be able to take a single more surprise." It's to be expected. Christine's caregiver to two people: yours truly and her mother, who suffers from dementia. It was and still is an untenable situation. And I felt exactly the same way. I mean, life's good, but underneath the heartfelt laughter and good cheer, we're nonetheless operating at peak capacity.

Then came the next surprise. Conflict. Suffice it to say that she wasn't the only one under undue strain, and those who had vowed to support her ended up doing the exact opposite, adding to her pressure.

I thought that sharing about my unending barrage of challenges would be enough for those around us to appreciate that—despite broad smiles, sparkling eyes, and the baffling absence of moaning and groaning—we are nevertheless juggling so many challenges that one more might send us over the edge.

First, the medical challenges never stop. The last time I slipped, I didn't even notice the bruises on my chest until Christine told me about them. She would also frown when I choked at every meal in February and March 2019 and as I battled a chronic cough for two solid months. Behind her eyes, I could read the worry about what was to come. She feared that our meals together would very soon become a thing of the past or, worse, that I'd choke to death. And that fear lingered like crocodiles along the banks of the Mara River, waiting for the young wildebeest to stray or for the elderly to stumble and falter.

Add to that the administrative problems and the constant repairs to the mobility aids on which I depend—devices ranging from the ramp on the van to my wheelchair. At the start of my fourth year with ALS, for example, the contractor who was supposed to install the elevator dropped us in favour of a more lucrative contract in Westmount.

Meanwhile, as Christine persisted in her impossible mission of caring for two people with neurodegenerative conditions, I'd like to think that friends and family were there to help, and they had been most of the time. It's just that in 2019 some had inadvertently made matters more complicated, causing me to fantasize about moving to an isolated cottage in the woods at the end of a private lane on a tranquil lake where loons outnumber people.

And as if all of that wasn't enough, I kicked off the New Year with the devastating news that my friend Eddy—my buddy and the personification of hope—had passed. Eddy Lefrançois had turned a five-year prognosis into more than a quarter century of defiance. He was my pen pal and my partner in advocacy. We fought side by side, advocating for the government to make good on its promise to fund ALS research and make it easier to access innovative treatments.

But it was more than that. Eddy was the only one with whom I could share my frustrations concerning the daily emotional battle of this godforsaken disease. He was my living, breathing beacon of the potential to do more than survive—to savour life despite it all. Eddy used to say he could do anything other people could do, just differently. And he wasn't easily discouraged. For instance, he fractured both of his arms while indoor skydiving in the spring of 2017. By the fall of that same year, he was back at it, crossing yet another item off his bucket list: deer hunting on Manitoulin Island. He was relentless and determined, convinced that we would find a cure for ALS. In 2018, he tweeted, "I was diagnosed twenty-five years ago. I now finally see and feel hope for the future."

Eddy understood what I wrote in ways that no one else could. Last year, he told me he looked up to me. Frankly, I was embarrassed by the compliment. He was the one who'd come this far—further than I could imagine having the fortitude to survive. He was the one who raised more money for ALS in 2018 than I had since my diagnosis. He was the one who gave me hope that I could go on, that I could beat the odds, that I could continue to enjoy life even after I could no longer move or talk. He was the one who beat the path that I would aspire to follow.

But more than anything, he was my friend—a friend with whom I had a unique bond, a series of secrets that were out there for all to see but were for us to understand like some sort of coded language summoning us to the battlefield that we shared and from which few emerge after two to five years on the frontline.

In the end, this exceptional twenty-six-year ALS survivor took his last breath as the rest of us were optimistically kicking off 2019. His executioner was the flu (aka ALS kryptonite). Weakened by ALS, he was unable to battle the infection. It ended his protracted standoff with a disease that was committed to taking him within five years. He had made it wait more than two decades longer. He was my mentor and, most important, the one person who understood my aspirations, vexations, and defiance. He alone seemed to understand that you can be angry, grateful, and hopeful all at once. And I wished I could have written to him about what happened next.

It was to be a belated holiday time breaking of the bread, a time to share. Instead, it turned out to be a threat to my health, as the visitors carried the very kryptonite that killed the brave Eddy. They crossed the threshold into my home, not only coughing and sneezing but also bragging about the flu that everyone had caught at the office. They said that it had deteriorated into pneumonia in several cases. Pneumonia—the very thing that had brought down the once seemingly indomitable man—was in my home, suspended in the air, and clinging to door handles.

My first reaction was to flee the scene. The longer I stayed with them to explain the situation, the more I would have exposed myself to that risk. So, as the virus entered, I swiftly exited, retreating to my room far away from the menace to my survival. Yet, rather than celebrate my stealthy escape, I stewed. It was emotional acid reflux, burning my throat as it rose. The voices of joy and cele-bration—that under normal circumstances might have been as infectious as the virus I saw as my nemesis (but in a good way)—wafted into my room like a foul odour. I could hear the sneezing. I pictured it coating the living room, dining room, and kitchen with the very threat that killed my buddy. I spiralled downward into a deep funk populated with increasingly irrational negative thoughts.

Then, as I sat forlorn at my desk, picking away at my dinner in solitude, desperately trying to focus on a movie or a book instead of my real-life predicament, the walls closed in. When dessert arrived, I felt like a prisoner being punished with solitary confinement. Then, to add insult to injury, when I pushed my dinner plate away to make room for dessert, my computer monitor fell on my meal, dam-aging the screen. As I narrowly escaped another fall my-self, off balance with one hand holding the screen and the other barely able to keep me from tipping, I boiled over.

Why was I the one in solitary confinement? I asked my-self. Why was I the disposable one in this scenario? Why did I have to retreat into a corner of my own house while my guests celebrated?

You might ask whether these sentiments were too ex-treme. Certainly. Without a doubt. Did this warrant my fit of indignation? Not logically. But logic is hampered by fear and anger. It might also be overrated, at least within the realm of human interaction and emotions. Pushed to extremes, logic is the antithesis of our humanity, encour-aging us to act like robots rather than passionate social be-ings. Being excluded from a meal in my own home and being placed—albeit voluntarily—under house arrest under the pretence of protective custody undercut my primal need to feel included and protected.

In retrospect, though, this was all too irrational. It didn't jibe with my otherwise balanced reasoning. I wished the whole evening had transpired differently and that I had been able to reach deep down inside myself and see that this was simply an oversight without any malice whatsoever.

Then, three months later, Christine had her meltdown. I wish people would better understand those who attempt the impossible task of caring for not one but two relatives at odds with neurodegeneration. But that's not real life. Perhaps it's more like the lives on the Hallmark Channel. Again, there was an absence of malice and a misunderstanding that should have been resolved with a little insight into the strain on a caregiver who was already stretched to the limit. Maybe she too should have opted for a warning label—perhaps a MedicAlert bracelet or a warning of possible side effects of adding more pressure to a woman who was already on the edge.

Perhaps this is the downside of positivity, I pondered. Maybe in my insistence on focusing on the positive, suffering quietly through the cramps that lasted up to twenty minutes, and defying this disease, I had created an illusion of invincibility. I wondered if that led others to believe that I might also face the flu as fearlessly. Perhaps I shouldn't have misled them into thinking I, or my caregiver, were ever that strong. The next time someone asks us how we're doing, I mused, I should tell them we're ticking time bombs to be treated with the utmost care.

That fateful evening and Christine's conflict both challenged our wishful thinking that those around us not only cared but also understood. Yet it's wrong to assume that people could ever fully understand what we—or anyone else—are going through. My guests that evening didn't know that Eddy had passed, which means they didn't know about the cause or what it all meant to me. Also, not everyone has the same awareness of or attitude toward colds and the flu, and few understand the particular danger the flu poses to people living with ALS.

Yet even in our darkest moments, there's a positive side. We learned a lot from these conflicts. My exclusion from our dinner party, for instance, taught us the importance of not only setting limits but also communicating and enforcing them in unison. So we laid out a clear policy banning infectious diseases from our home and future gatherings.

By the way, I didn't catch the flu. Also, my friends and family have been amazingly supportive. And that man with ALS stuck in Jakarta? He made it home to Tennessee, where he lived out his final days. Focusing on the best often requires dealing with the worst, and clearly communicating one's personal limits and vulnerabilities is key. Thinking of it as a "warning label."

Chapter 23

My Caregiver, My Muse,
My Strength, My Achilles Heel

Photo by Line Fortin

The caregiver is the unsung hero of ALS. It's often (but not exclusively) a role taken by a close family member, and it's a tremendously demanding job. The emotional strength of the caregiver is a determining factor in the patient's outlook.

I find it hard to imagine the prospect of living out my days alone in a long-term care facility. Fortunately, I'm poised to continue living in our home with my life partner. That's why I left it to my final chapter to focus on the most important person, the one who is my strongest ally in my quest to make the best of the worst news.

As I mentioned in an earlier chapter, those who meet someone with ALS might surmise from the slurred or laboured speech that their mental capacity has been affected. But that would be a mistake. We need only cite the case of the late Stephen Hawking to convince the casual observer that within the feeble body and behind the twisted voice of the ALS sufferer resides a healthy mind and a fully functioning intellect. There are, however, many (including myself) who suffer from what neurologists call the pseudobulbar affect (PSA), which messes with our ability to control the physical expressions of our emotions. It's also my convenient excuse for the following dewy-eyed ode to my caregiver, my muse, and my best friend.

I began seeing signs of PSA soon after my diagnosis. In my case, this simply means I laugh and cry more readily and with greater intensity. I perhaps also write more romantically than I did before I developed ALS. I doubt my neurologist would agree that PSA affects my writing, but that's the best excuse I could come up with for this chapter, so I'm sticking to it.

I started my adulthood somewhat shorthanded on the emotional front—let's call it being *crying impaired*. I'd follow my heart and pour everything I had into any challenge at hand. I'd laugh a lot, but I wouldn't cry. I would also keep certain feelings in check, holding onto the feelings I chose not to reveal and carefully demonstrating my fears and sadness only in measured doses.

I've always been the strong one, or so I imagined. If there were an equivalent of the Homeland Security Advisory System for the risk that I might cry, then my modus operandi would have been a consistent code green, or "low: low risk of crying."

But that's all changed. Before 2014, I could recall crying on only two occasions in my adult life. The first was when my father died, and the second was when my mother died. I certainly didn't cry at movies. I didn't cry tears; I'd dry tears. Christine was the emotional one, and I was the shoulder she'd cry on. Recently, though, I cry more in a month than in all the previous years of my adult life. I began with a code yellow (or "elevated: significant risk of crying") and progressed from there.

Now I feel teary-eyed seventeen minutes and twenty-five seconds into the movie *If I Stay*, a tearjerker teenage romance where Chloë Moretz's character spends the entire film in an out-of-body experience reminiscing about her young romance and her witty, loving family, who die while her ghost runs around pouting and crying. (Code orange, or "high: high risk of crying.")

I'm told it's a symptom of ALS. It could be worse. I could be developing a really bad taste in movies (but not actresses, like the "kick-ass" Chloë Moretz). I fear the day

I might start crying at movies based on the books—or should I say versions of the same book?—by that best-selling author whose books turn up time and time again on the silver screen.

Take your pick because they're all the same story of learning how to love again, set on some scenic waterfront property so the main character can look pensively at the water as they resist that romantic interest on which the plot has been carefully constructed. In the end, the main character comes to terms with his or her damaged soul, climaxing with the requisite kiss in the rain. So if even the nth version of that romantic drivel can make me cry one day, I will truly be a code red (or "severe: severe risk of crying").

That said, you're entitled to denounce what follows as so much worse than that. You can call it my own failed foray into trash romance, or what Gordon Lightfoot calls a "paperback novel, the kind the drugstore sells" in the song "If You Could Read My Mind." But I don't care. Christine loves trash romance—and I have gone from only drying tears to frequently and awkwardly shedding some—so this is our romantic story.

It started off with blind attraction. The first time I met her, I didn't think she was the most beautiful girl in the room. I thought she was the only girl in the room.

Thinking back on that time, it was as if there was a cut-off point where an unassuming girl in tight black jeans and an incongruently frilly white blouse occupied the entirety of my consciousness. For my friends who looked on—and I assure you that, to this very day, I can't say with certainty who was there with me—I was just a tipsy, overconfident young lad enchanted by just another pretty face. But that wasn't it. It was the only face.

She looked at me calmly but with wonder. Who was this zealous guy with long dark hair, sparkling eyes, and—oh, God forbid—a moustache?

I saw gentle features, soft blonde hair, and eyes that glittered, and I smiled at her. She smiled back. I lay down on the table in front of her and extended my hand to introduce myself.

We talked. We danced. I looked at her, and she looked at me. Then, after a long party, we returned to my place with two other friends to look at my pictures from Somalia. After that evening, I searched for her, but it would be months before we saw each other again. I looked for her in the halls of our small regional university and at the student café where we had met. But she was nowhere to be found.

Finally, I ran into Angie, the girl who had introduced us. I asked her, "Do you think she'd be interested?"

Angie was standoffish and replied nonchalantly, "I don't know. You ask her. I don't know."

I later learned that Christine had specifically asked about me and instructed her friend to let me know that she indeed was interested. Apparently, Angie took those instructions as a broad guideline rather than a rule. She chose instead to improvise a response in what she considered to be her friend's best interests. Not that she had anything against me. Angie was my friend too.

Still, it didn't dampen my hopes. I soldiered on, and on a Thursday evening in January, Christine and I kissed in the deep powdery snow under a star-filled sky.

We were together from that kiss onward. My damaged soul would never be the same after that first romantic kiss worthy of a Hollywood romance—provided it were filmed north of the 49th parallel…in the depths of winter…and not on a waterfront property.

Norman and Christine at the Université du Québec à Chicoutimi in the "Kingdom of the Saguenay" (1986)

But our story had only begun there. More than three decades later, we began a new chapter in our lives. I would like to point out one thing in this latest chapter that has changed and another thing that has stayed the same.

Our roles changed. I used to be the handyman. Christine could rely on me. I was always the one who was supposed to be there for her. I was the strong, confident one. That was my role. But then, seemingly overnight, I was told to prepare to be the one who needs support. At the garden centre, Christine is now the one who loads and unloads bags of sheep manure and garden supplies into the back of our vehicle. In the kitchen, I'm the one now asking her to open the jar of pickles for me.

If our relationship were based solely on our roles as we saw them before that fateful diagnosis, we'd be up the proverbial creek without a paddle. Yet we know that there's so much more to our relationship than my role as the fearless provider and protector. Christine may have signed on "for better or worse," but I don't suspect she ever imagined her role as future caregiver.

After three decades of sharing chores and meal preparation, she now prides herself in preparing healthy, hearty meals, especially since my neurologist emphasized the importance of maintaining my weight. It hit me one evening when she put out candles to accompany Chinese dumplings and curried vegetables. She sat down beside me and reached out to touch my hand. After years as my caregiver, her hands were rougher than ever from doing all the manual labour that used to be my domain, ranging from shovelling snow to home repairs and renovations. Mine, in contrast, had grown softer. My callouses were gone, leaving my hands softer than they'd ever been in my adult life.

I vowed to myself to take note of all of Christine's challenges and efforts. I wanted to take nothing for granted. Through the stories I have written over the past few years, Christine was there, living the flip side of every tale. As I struggled, so did she. Long before we were challenged by ALS, more than twenty-nine years ago, while I sneaked quietly into a waiting room with our newborn son who looked up at me with his big eyes, she was recuperating from a long, painful labour. Years later, she was the one corralling the children in a chaotic environment as I gathered our luggage at Tribhuvan International Airport in Kathmandu. More recently, in 2016, I cursed the mobility aids just before our trip to Kenya, but she was the one who carried the luggage, helped me down stairs, and pushed my transport chair.

She experiences much of the same emotions I do. She too grieves the loss of a future we had planned together. She too mourns the loss of long walks on the beach and plans to retire early to volunteer and do one or two more treks in the serene beauty of the Himalayas. In fact, most of the times I've written in the first-person singular, I could have just as well written *we*.

She appears sweet to most people, but few know the lioness I married. She gets angry at the discourse in the ALS community of *hope* and *dying with dignity*. She's far too grounded to accept the lines people feed her. She gets irritated when she hears about physician-assisted dying as if it were the answer we were looking for, as if this safety valve were enough to appease the ailing masses who know full well they're dying of a disease because it's underfunded.

She's too practical to blindly rejoice at all the research and "hope," since access to that hope is the real issue. She and I both know that the government can buy votes through the legalization of pot while ignoring those most in need of systemic change in public health. She knows what she wants, and she's not partaking in the opium of the people that is physician-assisted dying. She just won't.

She has taken on all the additional work without question, just as she left for Nepal without even knowing if she'd have a refrigerator in her home. But she won't tolerate false aid, a lack of consideration, or those who would take advantage of us because they know we're vulnerable and our energy is more finite than ever before. Those who mistake the lioness for a pussycat do so at their own risk.

I remember, long before our worst news, how she would lose patience when our children weren't there to help her bring in the groceries or when they'd leave their shoes lying around. Now she's alone in bringing in the groceries and running errands. She manages my medications and is constantly on the lookout for ergonomic aids to make my life easier. When there's water damage, she's the one going up and down stairs with buckets and devising the most ingenious system to gather water, using little more than a dustpan and an oversized Tupperware container.

Lines form on her forehead whenever I choke or cough. She worries that it's becoming more frequent and questions my reassurances that "It's okay…it's okay." She watches as I struggle to do countless things we used to take for granted. After repeated falls, she encouraged me to use my walker. Then, whenever I made my way around the house, leaning on my wheeled walker, she'd be there watching, analyzing. She's taped down rugs and moved furniture to clear paths for me. Whenever she allows herself to relax, she feels guilty if I falter or if I tell her about a new challenge before she realizes it herself, as though she ought to be able to prevent every fall and cramp and foresee every new hurdle even before I do.

She observes without judgment when I laugh or cry in uncontrollable bursts as I watch an elated Olympic athlete on television celebrating her gold medal or a sentimental commercial about a father who introduces his disabled son to adapted hockey. Admittedly, I wasted a lifetime of opportunity to practice. I treated my tear ducts like levees. Now those levees have weakened, and they burst at the slightest emotion with unruly surges so ungainly it's difficult to distinguish laughter from sobs. I sometimes even laugh at my own feeble attempts to cry, making for indiscernible sobs, sputters, and outbursts that can only be understood in context. She knows how to deal with it though. Her father was the same way after his heart surgery. So she accepts it. She accepts the new awkwardly oversensitive *code red* me.

Christine also accepts that her house has been modified and adapted, defiling the charm that attracted her to this house in the first place. But the house was never as important to her as I am. That I knew for certain because she allowed me to lowball my bid for it amid a seller's market. She was convinced we would never get the house unless I submitted a bid above the asking price. Despite everything, she left me to my own devices with the certainty in her own mind that we would miss this opportunity. In the end, though, I closed the deal at a much lower price than she imagined possible. But that's not the issue here. The most important thing was that she backed me despite what she saw as insurmountable odds against us. And that's just one illustration of the clarity of her priorities. So when it came time to make the necessary modifications, she had already made up her mind.

She finds it difficult to constantly adapt, but she does it because there's no other way. She soldiers on. We sometimes push ourselves too far, but we're there to help each other through. After the last big snowstorm in 2017, she came back inside frustrated after nearly three hours outside clearing the snow off and around our cars. She was frustrated by a neighbour who had pushed snow in front of my adapted van. She was also frustrated by our snow removal service that just wasn't doing the job we needed done. So we hired a new crew to remove the snow, paying nearly double for the remainder of the season what I would have paid for the entire season with the previous service provider.

While I do my stretching in front of the television while watching a movie, she prepares dinner. After years of discussions over sharing housework, it's hard not to feel guilty. Instead, she thanks *me* for taking care of myself because it helps *us*. But I still feel guilty. The life of a caregiver is demanding, and it can be a thankless role. People express their support to me and often overlook the one who shoulders the burden. Caregivers often work in the shadows, only to be noticed and severely judged if they're no longer able to continue their saintly efforts.

I perceive Christine as my greatest strength but also the Achilles heel of my perseverance because I can't imagine this struggle without her. She is my harshest critic, my number one fan, my muse. She's my soul mate in the truest form of the word. We face challenges together. We support each other. Once, at an adapted yoga class, I glanced over at the only one who wasn't in a wheelchair. I was glad she was there, although I missed regular yoga, where I could admire her warrior pose: focused, determined, and ready for battle. She's the audacious hero in my story. After reading these lines, she also tells me that she couldn't be strong without me. Back atcha, Christine.

It goes both ways.

We knew what my diagnosis meant from the outset. This journey could have been a short, rapid descent. We really couldn't say, and we've oscillated between denial and preparing for the worst. Luckily, one thing hasn't changed in our relationship. Whether we're living in the moment or facing challenging hurdles, we're there to catch each other. For me, she's still the only girl in the room.

Conclusion

I pulled into the restaurant parking lot ten minutes early for our noon lunch date. By the time the wheelchair ramp was deployed and I began my descent from the van to the asphalt, a man roughly my age approached to greet me. I probably wouldn't have recognized him had we crossed paths unexpectedly in a crowded shopping mall, but this was our meeting place, so I knew it was him before I could fully process what he looked like forty years after we'd last spoken. Then, as he shook my hand, I instantly recognized the way his mouth moved when he spoke.

By the time we were seated in the restaurant, I was transported back to our youth. I recognized the way he listened and responded as we interacted. It took me back to one precise moment, sitting by the record player in his house where we listened to Bachman–Turner Overdrive (BTO) belting out "Takin' care of business" and first heard George Carlin's iconic monologue "Seven Words You Can Never Say on Television."

We reminisced about the pranks we used to play, particularly the wallet trick. We would hide inside the school bus parked in his driveway with one hand on a string we'd attached to the wallet that served as bait for passers-by. Then, as soon as an unsuspecting pedestrian leaned over to grab it, we'd pull it away a few inches. When they took another step to catch the wallet, we'd yank it again, observing their reactions as the elusive wallet slipped away. Some would give up after the second try, but some would follow the wallet nearly under the bus. Others would stomp with frustration or just go on, quite aware they were being toyed with.

I probably wouldn't have reconnected with my childhood friend Len if it hadn't been for ALS. I probably would have been too busy to track him down online, which wasn't easy because Len wasn't on social media. He's also not the kind of person you read about in the media, except perhaps in the obituary section, which is exactly where I'd found him. An obituary mentioned how Len Jr. mourned his late father, Len Sr.

Émilie probably would have taken that contract in the Middle East starting in September instead of delaying her start date for two months in order to spend time with family. And I wouldn't have ventured off to reconnect with family and friends had it not been for Émilie's call for a road trip. Life is busy. Who has time to talk to people who were once part of our lives but who have probably developed completely different interests and priorities?

I did. Paradoxically, I found the time because I felt I had less time left.

That lunch date with Len felt playful. In addition to the nostalgia, we shared our respective journeys. Although our paths were indeed vastly different, I found it comforting to know that the person who was my best friend in primary school was still the same positive, grounded soul and that he had a close-knit family and a marriage that was still going strong. It reassured me to know that the important things I remembered about my best friend of yesteryear remained the same despite all of his trials and tribulations. So I delighted in that smile, that genuine interest, and that down-to-earth perspective on the world, the way a kid savours an ice cream cone on a hot day.

I've had countless such reunions over the years since my diagnosis as both my timeline and my stride grew shorter. And I know that I probably wouldn't be here and that neither I nor my old friends would have likely reached out had it not been for that pesky ticking clock.

So reconnect I did, with more old friends. Christine and I sometimes made the detour, such as working in a stop in Edmonton along our cross-country journey by train. Sometimes they made the journey or offered their hospitality. Friends such as Véronique and Bilal in Maryland opened their home to us, and Jo-Anne made a 560-kilometre detour on her way back to Calgary.

I grew closer to my brother, Brian, as well. This is the brother who left home before I was sixteen, the one with whom I fought incessantly as a child, the one with whom I shared a room, and I just couldn't wait for him to leave. And the feeling was mutual.

I knew him so well in many ways, but I actually knew very little about him overall. Over the years, we got to know each other but from a distance.

Still, there is something there: a link, something that only *we* share. It manifests itself in humour—a humour we understand and appreciate as we build upon each other's jokes in a way that only *we* could do. It reveals a shared past and a rare synergy that only grew stronger in recent years. Brian was the first person outside of my immediate family whom I informed of my diagnosis, and his support ever since has been unwavering. That belongs squarely in the category of the best of the worst news.

A few friends were suspiciously absent for some time before showing up and subsequently admitting that they'd feared seeing me "in this condition." One such person was Frank, a friend from a neighbourhood where I grew up in Southwestern Ontario and with whom I'd remained in contact for four decades. Finally, though, after several meetings since my diagnosis, he'd grown accustomed to my new reality and exhibited his unique way of coming to terms with "my condition." Frank and I have been friends since prepubescence—long enough to know that pity has no place in our relationship. So, as if to make a point of *not* walking on eggshells, he sometimes goes completely the other way, intentionally acting ill-mannered.

On one evening together, when Frank came to visit, we went to a comedy club in Montreal. After the show, I asked him to help me with the door to the washroom, and he was quick to help but not without setting limits up front in language and tone that were reminiscent of the mischievous, often unsavoury banter of our youth.

"I'm not doing any paperwork, though," he barked. "I mean, I'm not wiping your ass!"

I think he purposely said it loudly enough so that strangers within earshot might take notice. One of these days, I thought, he might end up in a wheelchair beside me if his jokes are mistaken for abuse. Apart from such risky behaviour, though, the best of the worst news includes finding time to be with friends old and new, without foregoing the opportunity to laugh, even at the worst news.

Regrettably, though, some people find it easier to identify with the negative aspects than with the positive. Stuck in our Western paradigm of good and evil, we fail to see the yin and the yang. In fact, it's taboo to recognize the positive in an overwhelmingly negative situation. I have a different perspective. Take the loss of self-reliance and mobility for example. Being vulnerable can be a curse, but it can also be blessing. I've replaced my proud self-reliance with an appreciation for the kindness of others. These days, when discouraging news abounds, it's popular to post videos with the description "faith in humanity restored." When you need more help like I do, such faith is restored on a regular basis even though they're most often small gestures.

On one occasion, as I rolled toward the restroom at the local movie theatre, a man with a young boy opened the door for me. When I went to exit the restroom a few minutes later, I saw that the father had placed the trash bin next to the door to keep it open so I could easily get out. I left the theatre feeling thankful for that kind gesture and optimistic for the next generation, as there is a good chance his son will emulate such consideration for others. Do I dare recognize that this is a benefit of being mobility challenged? I do.

I also did what a lot of people in my situation do. I sat down—in my case, with my wife—and wrote out a bucket list. We then crossed Canada by train, travelled to Alaska, made that trip to Italy we'd first hoped to do thirty-three years ago, and went on a safari in Africa, another adventure we'd been planning for years. In doing so, I discovered not only the elation of living out my bucket list but also a new perspective on the world as I struggled to overcome barriers and crossed paths with others who refused to live on the margins of a world designed for the physically able.

I also finally committed myself to writing. Before my worst news, with the exception of professional writing, I wrote only sporadically. I started a novel that I never finished and occasionally wrote and published articles for the sheer pleasure of it, but I invested myself fully in writing only after my diagnosis.

My worst news had called me to task. It was my last chance; it was time to lay it on the line and hold nothing back. So I wrote like I was bleeding. It was gratifying to write and terrifying to share.

Although I need more help than ever, I also have more time to spend with and help friends and family. People often say to me, "You have bigger worries." I'm no Alfred E. Neuman, but I can't imagine a better way to spend my time than listening to and helping friends despite my challenges. This is especially true because now, more than ever, I understand the importance of just being there.

We all know our time is limited, but our worst news accentuates how precious that time is. I now invest more time in reflecting on what's important, which is something we too often neglect. I value life for the sake of life, not according to the priorities imposed by society. We often reserve this for vacationing. Then, and only then, do we put aside our mundane distractions and focus on those finite "days off," those precious days of relaxation with loved ones. We take walks on the beach because we can in that moment, and we know all too well we'll soon be back home living by a to-do list rather than a bucket list.

Instead of focusing on the losses, I savour every aspect of my physical being before I lose it. I imagine a sudden departure without the chance to say goodbye, and I'm thankful every day for all that I have. Not every moment and every day is like that, but it's certainly more intense, as I'm constantly reminded of the limits ahead. You might find me wasting time or seemingly not appreciating things, being disagreeable, petty, or coy, but it will soon break as I'm cast back into reality. I imagine myself as the Buddhist monk caught between the long sharp blades of the thieves above and the razor-sharp teeth of the tigers below, and I turn to the bright purple blossom in front of me and smile.

The worst news slows down time. Time sometimes stops. The value of time skyrockets. It's now a precious commodity not to be wasted. If time were water, my time before my diagnosis would be akin to a canoe ride through the endless lakes and rivers of Northern Ontario. Since my diagnosis, though, it's become like a desert crossing. Time has become a precious commodity to be cherished and savoured.

Meanwhile, with one final test, one fateful diagnosis, *The End*, formerly something to be avoided indefinitely, became visible on the horizon, prompting the question I'd been avoiding for half a century: What will I do when I get there?

There was a time when I thought dying quietly and painlessly in your sleep was the best way to go. Everyone wants to live a long, full life, and everyone would prefer a painless death to a slow, agonizing one. However, once death had announced that I'd been chosen for preboarding, and after the initial shock had passed, my focus shifted to dying well. Michel—my friend who was diagnosed with terminal cancer and who openly shared his experience of "dying well"—was my mentor in this regard. He cherished every moment and every extra day as an opportunity for the best goodbye.

Still, embracing the best of the worst is riddled with challenges. From the frustrations of bureaucracy to the constant threat of choking and the painful recovery after falls, at times it felt like the world was conspiring against me. I had to devise strategies to focus on the best. First and foremost, I didn't waste time asking, "Why me?" Instead, I answered with my own question: "Why not me?" As I wrote in Chapter 6, if this were a choice between losing one of my children and living and dying with ALS, I'd definitely choose the latter.

Second, I learned through trial and error that battling bureaucracy and the drug approval process is a double-edged sword. On occasion, my advocacy skills have served me well. They have, for instance, improved my access to services, righted wrongs, and resulted in tangible improvements for me and others. At times, it has been cathartic. And perhaps I have made a modest contribution, just as a sole leaf contributes to nature. On the whole, though, the bureaucratic battles and advocacy have caused me plenty of frustration and have eaten away at my peace of mind. My journey to focus on the best of the worst news has often been derailed by my ongoing battles against the bureaucracy, the inertia, and a drug approval system that is ill-adapted to such an incurable terminal disease. As I reread what I have written over my years with ALS, I realized that this is where I have faltered most in my quest to embrace the best of the worst news. This is where I needed to re-evaluate my approach. That doesn't necessarily mean I'll stop getting involved; I will continue to face the bureaucracy as it affects me directly. I will, however, have to better focus my energy and remain constructive.

The overarching lesson learned, however, is that talking and writing about these issues are what led me to this realization. This is one of the many benefits of daring to share my life with ALS. It's what I call my keyboard therapy.

Michel demonstrated to me the importance of sharing the journey with others. For me, that meant devising my own strategy to share my worst news with others in order to facilitate my own acceptance and to get the support I needed from others. And as time went by and friends got caught up in their own challenges, I was reminded time and time again to keep the lines of communication open and ensure that my network—starting with my family and closest friends—could understand my growing list of needs and constraints.

I learned the importance of replacing the joy of skating and biking with other ways of finding "my zone" and drawing energy from it. That zone might be found in the time spent in front of an aquarium or a keyboard. It might involve model trains, fantasy baseball, meditation, or something else, even if it means more than one zone.

Just don't expect it to be easy. Yvon Cournoyer's plea for physician-assisted dying sent me into a tailspin in March 2017. Diagnosed with ALS in April 2016, he was already looking for a way out. Like his father did, he wanted to die on his birthday. He definitely didn't want to extend his life into 2018. Despite a prognosis of two to three years to live, he was unwilling to face what he described as "psychological suffering."

When I wrote about this in March 2017, a friend who'd already been living with ALS for fifteen years told me that this was a stage that most people with Lou Gehrig's disease experience in the first year after diagnosis. Reading back on my own reflections from the first year, I realized that it's a critical period. Shortly after my diagnosis, I wrote mostly because I had to make sense of the diagnosis. As the disease progressed, I came to terms with my new reality. The feelings of sadness don't diminish though. In fact, the miasma—that sinister cloud of self-doubt and fear that lingers and sneaks up at the most inopportune moments—seems darker and more haunting, and I often struggle to block the noise and find my zone.

I have already faced more challenges than I could write about in a single book. I sometimes saw them coming. They sometimes emerged without warning, without time to prepare. The key for me has been to deny the inevitability of my condition. I continue to remind myself that there are always exceptions to the rule and that a positive mind is a powerful thing. I remind myself that the placebo effect is very real and is as scientifically sound as any medication I might be offered. So I soldier on against this invisible enemy. I have learned to manage symptoms and to not lose hope when some doctor or some website insists that ALS is an unavoidable downward spiral into total paralysis and premature death.

Not abandoning hope has served me well. After a series of bad falls in my fourth year with ALS, I felt like my condition had worsened more in a matter of weeks than it had in months. The vulnerability I felt had suddenly slapped me in the face. I would struggle to shuffle down the hall to my bedroom. I barely had the strength to stay vertical as I leaned heavily and tenuously on the walker. I felt myself spiralling downward, and I saw it in Christine's eyes. It was a look of terror and sadness as I slipped into the next step—a step we had convinced ourselves was months, perhaps years, away.

I had been more hopeful than ever, buoyed by the hope that an experimental drug appeared to be working. Then, once the first trial was over, as I waited and waited to start the extended trial, I fell again and again, and then I began to wonder if it would be too late. Maybe this would be just like edaravone, a new hope entangled in the web of a heartless bureaucracy as I suffered repeated losses until my armour was weakened beyond the point of no return. ALS is often a deep, dark downward spiral, and at those times I struggle to remain positive. My approach has been to write it down so I can understand it better and seek out the support I need from others.

I also reminded myself that the flip side is equally intense. I focused on savouring each moment, and every time I overcame that fear, the miasma retreated and my resilience grew. Each inner battle I won, every time I got back up and refused to accept that there's nowhere to go but down, I grew more emboldened. And then, within less than two months, I was back on that experimental medication, and my voice suddenly got stronger again. I held onto that hope and soldiered on.

The first time I drove on the highway at the age of sixteen, I learned the importance of focusing on the horizon. I knew that looking over the hood of the car at the lines on either side would be exhausting and would cause me to wobble and sway. Likewise with ALS, I set my sights on the horizon. I seek inspiration from the most exceptional ALS survivors.

ALS's premier outlier, Dr. Stephen Hawking, saw a silver lining adorning the cloud of this debilitating condition. As Professor Brian Cox told *The Independent*, "if you spoke to Stephen himself, he would say that he considered himself a fairly average scientist whose condition provided an opportunity to focus on his work. One thing he told me was that he spends a great amount of time theorizing as he gets in and out of the bath, simply because it takes so long." That's not to say I would ever aspire to Dr. Hawking's impressive contribution to this world. I'm not going to revolutionize the field of astrophysics or advance the study of quantum mechanics, but I might just be able to find my personal best while living through my worst news.

Eddy Lefrançois, a twenty-six-year ALS veteran, had tattooed on his arm a bar code with his five-year expiry date, April 14, 1997, as an act of defiance against the foregone conclusion of his diagnosis. "Since April 1997," he told me, "five years after my diagnosis, I stopped asking myself, *'Why me?'* Life has been better since." When I asked him what prompted the shift, he said that surpassing the five-year milestone had transformed him. "Over the years," he added, "I also learned that for me, personally, it was easier to smile than to be ticked off at my fate, that tomorrow will be a new day…a fresh new day, and I decided how I would live my day." I will miss Eddy, that seasoned ALS warrior who inspired so many. He is a friend who remains with me even after he left the body that couldn't keep up with his unwavering spirit.

The ALS outlier I see most often is Ginette, a fifteen-year survivor whom I've never seen frowning or complaining. She thanks her lucky stars for her friends, and she expresses it without reserve. She is grateful for the option to die with dignity but celebrates the experience of beating the odds. "I can tell you, after fifteen years living with ALS," she said to me, "the majority who are diagnosed, including me, at the beginning, we have almost the same reaction as Mr. Cournoyer. Then, slowly but surely, we adapt to the various changes we must face. We develop experience, and, often in spite of ourselves, we become models of resilience and courage. What a pity it is to abandon ship before learning to navigate." Well said, Ginette. Although, if you ask me, Ginette doesn't have to say a word to communicate her optimistic perspective on life. Her infectious smile says it all.

Ginette, Eddy, and Dr. Hawking have inspired me, even though only Ginette remains in the flesh. They have been my horizon and just one more reason I haven't considered physician-assisted dying. In fact, although I've been living with ALS for only a fraction of the time they lived with this disease, I've already stopped viewing it as a terminal condition despite the frightening mortality rate. We all die, and I will too, but today I live.

That's not to pass judgment on anyone else. I'm just one of the luckier unlucky people to be diagnosed with ALS. I've seen so many people struck down so quickly by this horrible disease. I know that most often ALS advances too quickly for patients to ever have a fighting chance. Conceivably, though, from what I have seen from the likes of Ginette and Eddy, a positive outlook is a fierce weapon against this merciless opponent. I can't say when the Grim Reaper will come for me, but regardless of whether it will be sooner or later, I can't find a rational argument in favour of fixating on the gloom and doom. That's why I've decided not to waste my time on negativity.

But positivity ought not be equated with denial. Over the years, I have proactively adapted my office, my home, and my mode of transportation. I know that I suffer setbacks whenever I fall and that a severe fall causing something such as a broken hip could put an end to what limited self-reliance I've maintained. So I do everything I can to avoid accidents. I learned to use a walker and then a wheelchair, and I installed an elevator in my home before it was too late, knowing full well that every time I ventured downstairs, I risked giving myself another concussion.

I also remind myself that we never know when death will come a-knocking or when we'll evade it. I had booked seats for the whole family for a trip to Ko Phi Phi, Thailand, for a Christmas vacation in 2004. I had to cancel it at the last minute. Instead, I watched in horror from our home in India as the deadliest tsunami in history ravaged that tropical Southeast Asian island, washing away hundreds of tourists amid the holiday season.

Shortly after I started writing about my journey with ALS in 2015, Martha and Anthony, two friends we'd made in Nepal, stopped by our house in Montreal on their way to Nova Scotia, where they planned to live out their retirement together. They were devastated by our news. Then, in the spring of 2017, Martha posted a couple of comments on my page. Regarding the piece on "Shoaling Barbs," she wrote:

> Anthony sent me your last two blogs this morning. Early May in Nova Scotia and bulbs finally poking up to acknowledge spring. And I rejoice. I'm still here. Your blogs make my day. Love this from February. My choir is my fishpond serenity. Hugs to you and Christine.

I wondered why Anthony had to send her my blogs, but I didn't comment. I took "I'm still here" as reinforcement of the message of my blog: that we all need to celebrate what we have in the here and now.

Then, regarding "The Miasma and the Captain," she wrote:

> Norm, so powerful raw reflective. Invictus.
> Great photo of Mighty Car!
> The leaves on the tree outside my window have opened, so now I can see tiny green buds. It's enough.

Her last sentence was so reflective of a profound pensive state that it marked me. "It's enough." Little did I know it was to be her last spring, her last buds. Only a month later did I belatedly learn of her diagnosis with incurable brain cancer. Unfortunately, the message that had been sent to inform me of her worst news had been misdirected. The news had escaped me.

Then, more than a year after her passing, I watched in admiration as Anthony mourned with wisdom and grace, hiking with loved ones and posting the most beautiful memories of the love of his life who graced this earth in her own gentle, unique way. Martha's passing was a powerful reminder that we know not when death will swoop down and steal the lives we cherish. The friends who were so concerned about my incurable condition ended up being the first to go and the first to mourn.

It was a powerful reminder of the ephemerality of life, a reminder that we all die, sometimes prematurely, and often without warning. Since my diagnosis, I have watched friends and family struggle with cancer. Some, like Martha, who I was sure would survive me, had gone prematurely. I can't even count the victims of mass shootings in the US or the thousands of migrants who've perished in pursuit of a better life. Almost all of them would have expected to live so much longer than the man diagnosed with an incurable disease in 2014. And, sadly, few of them had had time to prepare for the end.

Few were able to *die well* as Michel did, but each individual's idea of dying well is probably different. Yvon Cournoyer advocated fiercely and effectively for his right to control his endgame, a struggle that was marked by love and caring. His quest for physician-assisted dying wasn't a scornful suicide but a choice to live and die with dignity in accordance with his personal worldview.

In an interview by Marianne Bergeron, posted to YouTube on June 14, 2017, he talked about his struggle for physician-assisted dying as his new purpose. He spoke to members of provincial parliament about his struggle, and he managed to obtain a ruling in his favour. It wasn't on his birthday as he had hoped, but it was before the end of the year. In the meantime, he spent the remainder of his life on his own terms, and he even managed to go skydiving during his final weeks.

Finding one's purpose is an important element in embracing the best of the worst news. It's about finding a reason to go on. In Mr. Cournoyer's case, it was about controlling the terms of his departure. By November 2017, the government had granted his wish. On a quiet Saturday, surrounded by his closest friends and family, he died with dignity as he had wanted. Between March and November, he had led a very public battle for dying with dignity, and he made the most of the last months of his life. He lived and died on his own terms, living with purpose and dying with dignity, enwreathed with caring and warmth.

As I go through my own process of grieving the manifold losses of ALS, the different ways that others deal with this disease encourage me to reflect on my choices and my battles. That was, after all, my goal when I began to write about this challenge years ago. So, what have I learned about the "grieving process" of ALS?

First, I learned that the "stages of grief" aren't stages at all. There's no set order. Rather, the Kübler-Ross model teaches us first and foremost that it's okay to feel a whole range of emotions. In fact, it's par for the course. What I discovered is that those feelings can come over and over again. Over a period of nearly five years, I also noticed that the need to make sense of my worst news was most intense at the outset. It then morphed into a struggle to redefine my purpose while dealing with the noise and fighting off a tenacious miasma.

Meanwhile, I grew accustomed to dealing with the feelings. I also bore witness to and accepted that each individual's life is a work of art to be lived on that person's own terms. In other words, the best of the worst news for me is not the same best of the worst news for Michel or Yvon. And that's the way it should be.

That's why this isn't a self-help book. I'm just grappling with the inevitable ups and downs. Of course, I'm prone to excess and errors. As I've highlighted throughout, I can't do it alone. Nonetheless, if my stories and reflections encourage you to find your own path, then I'm pleased. But please don't follow me because my approach will inevitably differ from yours. The best I can do is share the lessons I've learned from my own experiences and identify the commonalities with the experiences of others.

For instance, I have noticed that those who live their last moments best are those who share that experience with others. It might be one person or millions, but that sharing is a gift to others, and it often bears more than we can otherwise give.

After writing about ups and downs, I fell once again. But I also received the good news that the open-label extension study had finally been given the green light. I started again on the one experimental drug that showed promise. There was hope again.

I avoid the word *still* as much as possible and remind myself of all I have. When I need to, I surround my computer screen with Post-it Notes of all the positive aspects of my life, such as:

- I enjoy quality time with family.
- I laugh every day.
- I cry when I'm sad (and that's a good thing).
- I'm planning yet another great trip.
- I spend more time loving and being loved.
- I enjoy researching and writing.
- I was there to attend my eldest son's wedding, to guide my daughter through the start of her career, and to watch my youngest son graduate, start his master's degree, and kick off his career.

The key is to change your baseline. I celebrate all that I can do that I was told would be out of reach as I live out my fifth year since my diagnosis. If that sounds delusional, answer this: Why would previous expectations be the only valid baseline? Before ALS, did I lament that my stride was lagging compared to Usain Bolt or that my swimming was pathetic compared to Michael Phelps? Of course not. I choose my baseline as we all do.

I've also learned that the supposed stages of grief often come in waves. Like waves, those feelings are powerful, but they can't (and shouldn't) be resisted. I have always loved the ocean. I have never slept so well as those times when I drifted off to sleep to the sound of waves gently caressing the shores just outside my window. Nature and life both travel in waves. Like the emotions that come with grieving, I sometimes venture in just up to my ankles, I sometimes dive right in, and I sometimes instead sit by and watch nature's spectacle. But I can't stop the waves.

I've always considered waves cleansing and rejuvenating. When I struggle, waves remind me of the consistency of opportunity, that nothing is final, that we can get back up again and be certain there will always be another wave. There will be low tide and there will be high tide. Like the waves, to make the best of the worst news, you need to face the issues and let in the pain, the hurt, and the frustration.

If you're facing your own worst news, focusing on the best of things is the optimal way to live out the remainder of your time, be it brief or uncharacteristically long. Diagnosed with a disease with such a devastating prognosis, what a pity it would have been for me to spend my last years dying instead of living. As I reread each chapter in this book, I realize that this is as much a celebration of my life as it is mourning the loss of future opportunities. Do I have any regrets? No, because my past, both positive and negative, is the foundation on which I live the present. And that applies to everyone.

It is also clear that my family and friends are the most important to me. They are my life. They are also my purpose, my support network, and my happiness. They are the key to my embracing the best of the worst news.

What a pity it would be to spend your remaining days and years—whether many or few—stuck in a job you don't enjoy, counting the years to retirement and waiting until your mortgage is paid off so you can finally be free. What a pity it would be to deny yourself friendship and peace of mind by holding onto petty grudges.

For most readers, the best of my worst news is that it's not your news. So run, dance, ski, and skate—skate like you've found a river you could skate away on. You've read my experiences and perspectives. Now dare to ask yourself what you would do if you were diagnosed with

Lou Gehrig's disease. Take the opportunity to step back and examine your life. Put Post-it Notes around your computer screen *now*. Make your bucket list *now*. Hug your family and friends *now*. Tell them you love them, and do it *now*.

Maybe the real challenge is to make the best of life long before it's beleaguered by the worst news. But this doesn't mean it's too late once the worst news strikes. Rather, it's a reminder that every time you postpone experiencing the best that life has to offer is a missed opportunity. It means that the time for the best is *now*.

CPSIA information can be obtained
at www.ICGtesting.com
Printed in the USA
BVHW030518250520
580234BV00004B/586

9 781554 832392